Atrium buildings

Development and design

āt'rĭum, n. (pl.-a, ums) Central court of
Roman house; covered portico, especially
before church door. (L) O.E.D.

Covered courtyard space within or between
buildings, usually on several levels, and
acting as arrival and circulation focus. RGS

1 **The original atrium**
a roman house

Atrium buildings

Development and design

Richard Saxon

VNR **VAN NOSTRAND REINHOLD COMPANY**

NEW YORK   CINCINNATI   TORONTO   LONDON   MELBOURNE

Printed in Great Britain

First published in 1983 by
The Architectural Press Ltd, London

Published by Van Nostrand Reinhold
Company Inc.
135 West 50th Street
New York, New York 10020

16 15 14 13 12 11 10 9 8 7 6 5 4 3 2 1

**Library of Congress Cataloging in
Publication Data**
Saxon, Richard.
   Atrium buildings.

   Bibliography: p.
   Includes index.
   1. Atrium buildings.   2. Atriums.   I. Title.
NA4160.S28 1983   720   83–10424
ISBN 0–442–28045–9

Designed by Rod Morris FSIAD and
John Green MSIAD, MSTD

Printed in Great Britain by BAS Printers Limited
Over Wallop, Hampshire

For Anne

Contents

**Part two
Constructing
the atrium**

Notes on contributors

The creation of the technical chapters of the book (9 to 14) has been made possible by the contribution of experts in several fields.

The chapter on fire safety (9) was jointly written with E G Butcher BSc (hons), M Inst P, FI Fire Eng, and Alan C Parnell FRIBA, FSIAD, FI Fire Eng, DipTP. They are the directors of Fire Check Consultants, London, and are internationally recognized authorities on fire safety in building design. They are the authors of Smoke Control in Fire Safety Design, E F and N Spon, 1979 and of the projected Designing for Fire Safety, Wiley, 1983.

Acknowledgements

In addition to my co-authors there are many others whom I must thank for their contribution to this book. The concept developed from an article commissioned by Sherban Cantacuzino, then executive editor of the Architectural Review and now secretary of the Royal Fine Arts Commission.

The crystallizing of ideas was immeasurably helped by the efforts of John R Street, senior associate of John Portman of Atlanta, Georgia. He took time and trouble to bring together the experience of John Portman and Associates. John C Portman himself, Irving Wiener and Gayla Wingate of JPA all gave of their time.

Helmut Jahn and Carter Manny of Murphy/Jahn, Chicago, assembled their many ideas and provided stimulus. Dean Hawkes, director of the Martin Centre, University of Cambridge, gave valuable advice and encouragement.

Special thanks go to the members of the Technical Advisory Service of Pilkingtons, the British glass makers. Ken Jackson, Ray Jennings, J D McCann and Peter Owen who also translated Swedish source material.

Substantial information on the use of elevators in atria was provided by Otis Elevators, and also by Hammond and Champness (Dover).

Author's note

This book is written for designers throughout the world, but principally for those in Europe and North America. English is supposedly our shared language but certain conventions have had to be adopted to limit confusion. Spelling is English, but American technical terms are often used. This occurs whenever the British term would be unfamiliar to

'The living atrium', chapter 13, was written with considerable help from Janet Jack, AADip, RIBA, ALI. She is a landscape architect, a director of BDP Landscape, London, and an expert on the use of plants indoors. She is the author of the projected book Gardens in Buildings.

Chapter 14, 'The Economics of Atria', was compiled with the assistance of Peter N Snape RICS. Peter Snape is a construction cost consultant and quantity surveyor and is involved in several atrium building projects. He is a partner with the author in Building Design Partnership.

Cost comparison information was released to me by Ray Stainback of Thompson, Ventullet and Stainback of Atlanta, and by Maurice Philips of Stevens Associates and his client, Granada Motorway Services.

I must thank a large number of people within Building Design Partnership: my partners for giving me some valuable time; Bev Fenby, Ian Duncan, Tony Sluce, John Troughear, Mike Hargreaves, John Ellis and Bill Wilson for ideas on and calculations of environmental engineering aspects; Greville Griffiths, Sheridan Besford, Eileen Kenny, Jan Siddons and Jackie Lawler for their advice and help; Steve Gardiner, Paul Taylor, Muriel Sharp and John Davey for their help in the production of this book.

Special credit must go to Ruth Berry, for painstaking typing of the manuscript, and to Rod Morris and John Green for the design of the book. Line diagrams were drawn by Howard Irving.

Many other individuals, publishers and practices helped with illustrations and are credited in the illustration source list.

Finally I must thank my publishers, Architectural Press. The book has improved markedly with the advice of Maritz Vandenberg, Margaret Crowther and Esther Eisenthal, and with the production skills of Keith Kneebone and Lorraine Abraham.

Americans; the British are usually familiar with American usage. 'Elevator' is therefore used, for example, in preference to 'lift'. Measurements are given in the units used in the country of the example quoted. Conversion factors are provided in Appendix 7 on page **175**.

Sources of illustrations

Endpapers John Portman and Associates;
1 Architectural Association; **2** John Portman and Associates; **4** Terry Farrell and Partners/ Crispin Boyle (photographer); **5** Wim Jansen, Centraal Beheer/Foto Starke (photographers); **6** John Portman and Associates; **7** Greater London Council; **8** redrawn from Space Design 13; **9** Architectural Review; **11** Brown Palace Hotel; **12a** Architectural Review; **12b** Johnson Wax Company; **12c** Frank Lloyd Wright Foundation; **13** Architectural Review; **14** Ranulph Glanville/ Architectural Association; **15** Gruen Associates/Warren Reynolds, infinity inc (photographer); **16** Gruen Associates; **17** John Portman and Associates; **18** redrawn from Reyner Banham's Megastructures; **19** Richard Einzig; **20** John Portman and Associates; **21** Architectural Review; **23a** redrawn from Titus Burkhardt's The Art of Islam; **23b** Iraj-Naimir/Architectural Association; **24** Rhode Island Tourist Promotion Division/Gilbane Building Co; **25** Mark Girouard/Oxford University Press; **26** National Trust; **27** after J C Loudon; **28** Illustrated London News; **30a/b** John Hix; **31** Ehrenkranz Group/Northern Solar Energy Center; **32** Tim Street Porter/Architectural Review; **33a** Terry Farrell Partnership/Jo Reid and John Peck (photographers); **33b** Architectural Review; **34** Ron Thom/ Architectural Review; **35, 36** Roche and Dinkeloo; **37** Trustees of Sir John Soane's Museum; **39** Archigram/Architectural Review; **40, 41** Architectural Review; **42** Paulo Soleri/ MIT Press; **43** David Barnes; **44a/b** Building Design Partnership; **45** Foster Associates; **46** Architectural Review; **47** Harvey G Oppmann; **49** Frederick Gibberd and Partners/David Atkins (photographer); **50** Architectural Review; **51** Peter Shuttleworth/ Building Design Partnership/Sidney W Newbery (photographer); **52** Murphy/Jahn; **53b** Progressive Architecture; **55** Roche and Dinkeloo; **56** Murphy/Jahn; **57** Architects Journal/Philip Sayer (photographer); **59** Rob Krier; **60** EPAD; **62** after National Geographic Society; **63** James A Sugar; **64** John Portman and Associates; **65** redrawn from John Halpern's Downtown USA; **66** Architectural Review; **67** Hugh Stubbins and Associates/ Norman McGrath (photographer); **69a** Architectural Press; **69b/c** author/Architectural Review/Space Design; **70** Manfred Sack/ Klaus J Kallabis; **71** Richard MacCormac/ Architectural Press; **72** Cesar Pelli/Norman McGrath; **73** Architectural Review; **74** redrawn from Ralph Erskine in Architectural Design; **75** Terry Farrell and Partners/Crispin Boyle (photographer); **76** Arup Associates; **77** Harbeson, Hough, Livingston, Larsen/ Robert Harris (photographer); **79** Architectural Review; **78** Diamond/Myers/Reyner Banham; **80** Progressive Architecture; **81** RIBA Journal; **82** Tennessee Valley Authority/K D Lawson; **84** Foster Associates; **85** Mike Davies/Chrysalis Architects; **86, 87** Foster Associates; **88** Gruppe M/John Hix; **89** Camera Solaris; **90** John Portman and Associates; **94** BP; **96** Building Design Partnership; **97** Murphy/Jahn; **100** Architectural Review; **101** Pilkingtons; **105a/b, 106** redrawn from Architectural Record; **108** Progressive Architecture; **115** Building Design Partnership; **116c-f** redrawn from Progressive Architecture; **118** author/Fire Check Consultants; **119** John Portman and Associates/Paul de Cicco; **120** Fire Journal; **121–127** author/Fire Check Consultants; **128** based on De Cicco and Cressi; **129–132** author/Fire Check Consultants; **133** Fire Journal; **136a** Skidmore Owings and Merrill/HNK Photography; **136b** Skidmore Owings and Merrill; **138** Arthur Erikson/Architectural Review; **139** John Portman and Associates; **140** Douglas Stephen and Partners/Martin Charles (photographer); **141** McGraw Hill; **142** Pilkingtons; **143** Architects Journal/ CyRo/Everlite; **144** Architects Journal; **146** Doulton Industries; **147** Kalwall Corporation; **148, 149** Owens Corning Fibreglass Corp; **152** Murphy/Jahn; **153** Foster Associates/Architectural Review; **154** Architectural Review; **155b** Architectural Press; **155c** McOG; **155d** Skidmore Owings and Merrill; **155e** John Portman and Associates; **155f** Murphy/Jahn; **156** Otis Elevator Company; **157** Dover Corporation; **158–60** Otis Elevator Company; **162** Thompson, Ventulett, Stainback and Ford, Powell and Carson; **163** John Portman and Associates; **164** Murphy/Jahn; **165** Roche and Dinkeloo/ Architectural Review; **166a** Janet Jack; **166b** Hugh Stubbins; **166c** John Portman and Associates; **167a** Janet Jack; **167b** Architectural Review; **168a** Janet Jack; **169, 170, 172–3** Steven Scrivens; **176** Simon Engineering; **177** John Portman and Associates/author; **182** New Yorker. All other illustrations are by the author.

Introduction

The phenomenon of the modern atrium is also known in other forms as a galleria, an arcade or a wintergarden. The most precise distinction is that 'atria' are static, arrival spaces, with if anything, a vertical emphasis; and 'galleria' are linear routeways, passing through a building. A 'linear atrium' is not a contradiction in terms: it may look like a galleria, but it is an arrival point and not a through route. The term 'arcade' when used to describe a glass-roofed street is synonymous with a galleria. A 'wintergarden' is a habitable greenhouse, usually related to a building—a form of atrium with a long history.

The atrium is a very old idea. It has a 2,000-year history as a grand entrance space, focal courtyard and sheltered semi-public area. Within the limits of masonry and timber technology it developed over centuries into the central concept of mediterranean and middle-eastern architecture. Since the industrial revolution the western world has added the great covered court and arcade to its repertoire, using glass and iron technology: splendid but never common sights. Now, suddenly in the period since the late 1960s, there are hundreds of 'atrium buildings'. Not since the skyscraper, 100 years ago, has a building form spread with such speed and success.

The skyscraper was the result of a technological breakthrough—the safe elevator. No such simple technical trigger can be found for the rise of the modern atrium building: a larger number of influences came into play. These influences are of a strength that promises to make the atrium building one of the generic building forms of the late twentieth century.

It is in this belief that 'Atrium buildings' is written. In 15 years rapid development of the atrium concept has been successfully applied in a wide variety of contexts. A range of technical innovations has been created to handle the new demands of the idea. This book aims to equip the designer to use the concept creatively.

Part 1 covers the history of the modern atrium and its potential as a design concept. The interlaced strands of thought set down provide a rich source for further originality.

Part 2 looks in detail at the major technical challenges involved in atrium building. It sets out to equip designers to be able to develop their ideas in informed discussion with specialist consultants.

This is a first attempt to pull together the forces, cultural and technological, which can act upon a designer considering an atrium

building. More could certainly be written about the interior design of such spaces: their finishes, their acoustics, their use of art, some of which can be spectacular. At this stage I leave these aspect to be developed and interpreted by the individual. I have tried to put down the big questions and to show the concept as a creative tool.

Apart from general encouragement to exploit the concept of atrium buildings, I stress the key ideas elaborated in this book

Think urbanistically Let the city's fabric and the site context suggest the desirable outer envelope of the building. It may already exist of course. Wherever possible let the atrium be a public space.

Think climatically Devise the arrangement of envelope and inner fabric to modity the site climate passively and leave the least load to be picked up by purchased energy.

Think kinetically Allow people to move into and through the building as a sensuous experience. Give users natural orientation as they move.

Think in terms of safety Build in safe escape and fire-control concepts: do not try to bolt them onto preconceived plans.

Think socially Give the building a heart and a focus. Let people appropriate it and come together.

Let green plants into the space, as the most acceptable bridge between the technological objectivity of any building and the subjective nature of people.

Be open to the cultural and technological influences which can animate the concept. There is a new architecture of the great interior emerging.

Do not be too tasteful There are sterile atria, produced by designers who did not realize the essentially playful, festive essence of the concept.

Do not be afraid of the economics Use them in support of your ideas to get the most cost-effective design.

The next generation of buildings must be much more worthwhile and publicly acceptable than most of those built since the Second World War. The use of the atrium concept is one way in which this can be achieved.

Richard Saxon

Part one

The rise of the modern atrium

1

Why atria?

The case for a new building concept

Four functions

What are the virtues of the atrium concept? At first sight it looks like a luxury, an attention-gaining gimmick, that can be afforded only in high-value development. The fact that it first appeared in spectacular hotels reinforces the image. The truth is that the atrium concept has wide-ranging advantages over conventional modern building forms.

Bill Hillier[1] devised a most useful way to look at the purpose of buildings. He thought buildings exist for four reasons which he called the four functions of architecture—a modernized version of Sir Henry Wotton's Commoditie, Firmenes, and Delight.[2]

Cultural function: to modify culture
We build to make statements about ourselves and our culture, by making an impact on the senses.

Economic function: to modify resources
We build to employ resources and we employ resources to build: money, time, manpower, energy, materials. A return is expected.

Shelter function: to modify climate
We build in order to have shelter from the elements and from each other. We seek comfort.

Accommodation function: to modify the earth's surface
We build in order to create 'shaped space' or extra space that the natural or existing man-made world does not give us.

Cultural function
Atria appeal to the mind and the senses. They put people at the centre of things in a way lost in recent architecture. They encourage play: people-watching and promenading, movement through space, enjoyment of nature and social life. They provide a visual antidote to the oppressive interiors and the formless external spaces of today.

Atrium buildings are far from being retreats from the city, but contribute to it by restoring its character: the street-line, fragmented by modern development, can be regained; the plaza, usually an uncomfortable desert, can be made welcoming. Culturally therefore, an

2 **The atrium as an economic machine**
John Portman's Peachtree Plaza Hotel, Atlanta, Georgia

3 **The atrium as cultural symbol**
Crystal Court, Minneapolis, by Johnson/Burgee, has become the symbolic focus of the city

3

atrium building speaks of a more welcoming, popular city and a less puritanical architecture, attuned to the post-industrial age. We will in future come to town to enjoy ourselves. The absolute need to come to work or shop is declining as telecommunication advances. The atrium building also speaks perhaps of a culture more open to introspection, to eastern thought, than before.

Economic function

Many atrium buildings appear expensive compared to conventional forms of development. Whether or not this is so they are successful because of their extra attraction and earning power. Atrium hotels rarely have empty rooms. Shops and offices built around atria let quickly for premium rents. As Louis B Cushman III, Texan realtor, stated *'Atriums have sex appeal'*[3] Their people-pulling power pays for them.

Atrium buildings offer larger, more efficient floors than their tower equivalents. They are also capable of providing 'shallow' space for perimeter offices rather than the deep spaces of a tower or low-rise, block-covering building.

This is premium space: more attractive to higher status occupants, and able to be sub-divided more easily. And there is an economic factor which is also a cultural one: atrium design can allow more successful recycling of existing buildings, with consequent saving of investment. Old courtyard buildings can be converted into atrium buildings. Overdeep space can be hollowed out to more useful depths.

There is sound evidence that atrium buildings can be built and run for less than conventional buildings. They have 'extras' like courtyard roofs, fire safety systems, possibly special transport systems and landscaping but they save on height and surface area. They are quicker to build than their taller equivalents. In operation the buildings can use less energy. Daylighting is simpler, heat loss and gain reduced. Solar energy can be harnessed in the right circumstances.

The economic picture is thus of costs which can be lower, for capital and in use, and earning power which is usually higher.

Shelter function

The question of shelter is central to atrium buildings. The sheltered central court is a great amenity in itself, creating a type of space not otherwise available in most cities—an all-weather public gathering space.

It is in the interaction between the court and the space around it that the more subtle sheltering goes on. The atrium can bring light but keep wind, rain, solar gain and extreme temperatures away from overlooking space, reducing costs and increasing comfort. It is a form of giant double-glazing. The shelter effect is most marked when the atrium is not serviced to reach full-comfort conditions itself, but acts as a buffer space, a transitional area from outside to inside.

Accommodation function

The need for accommodation is usually the force which triggers the building process. It is usually the space around the atrium which is directly required, and the atrium space is a bonus. However, the two interact. The atrium itself can provide useful space. Apart from constituting a lobby and circulation space with access to all parts of the building, its floor can be a restaurant, lounge, exhibition or performance space, or a market area. The vistas and accessibility it creates can enable upper levels to work as extension of the 'ground' level. In Richard Rogers' Lloyds insurance building in London, the 'room', where all underwriting activity is centralized, can spread over six floors without losing its sense of unity. At Herman Hertzberger's Centraal Beheer offices in Apeldoorn, Holland, four levels of offices feel like a single floor as miniature atria link them together. Shopping on eight levels, as at Water Tower Place, Chicago, is unimaginable without the lure of the atrium. Stores on all levels are given maximum visibility and accessibility.

On all four interlinked counts the atrium concept deserves to be taken very seriously. It is not a panacea for all building needs, but suggests a better solution for many needs than any others in the repertoire of modern building forms.

1   See Bill Hillier and Adrian Leaman A New Approach to Architectural Research, RIBA Journal, December 1972, p 577 et seq

2   Henry Wotton, The Elements of Architecture, originally published 1624

3   Louis B Cushman III, quoted by Andy Leon Harney in Those Proliferating Atria, AIA Journal, July 1979, p 50-59

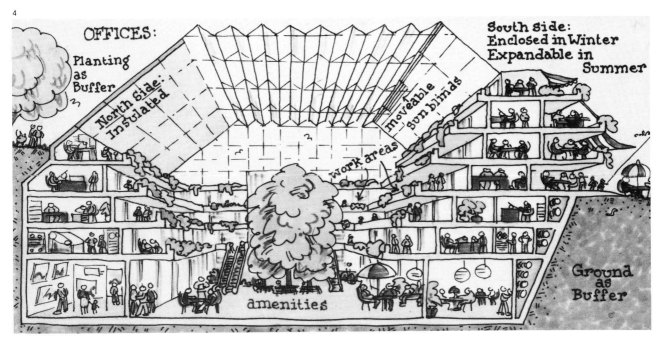

4 **The sheltering atrium**
from Terry Farrell and Ralph Lebens'
thesis, 'Buffer thinking'

5 **The accommodating atrium**
Centraal Beheer offices, Apeldoorn,
Holland
Herman Hertzberger

2

Milestones and influences

The broad pattern of development

6 **'An idea whose time had come'**
Regency Hyatt Hotel, Atlanta, 1967
John Portman

7 **One of the first true atria**
the glass-roofed cortile of the Reform
Club, London
Sir Charles Barry, 1837

When John Portman unveiled his Regency Hyatt Hotel in Atlanta, Georgia, in 1967, the Architectural Review called it 'an idea whose time has come'. This acknowledged not only that the idea was a good one, but that for many reasons it would be used again. The concept seemed so right for the times because it satisfied so many desires. It appeared at once to combine the excitement of the city of the future with the enjoyment of the city of the past. It raised the 'symbolic content' of modern architecture to a point where it became truly communicative and popular. Compared to the aloof stance of high modern architecture, at the time it smacked of the fairground, and was all the better for that. The great boredom and disenchantment which mainstream modern architecture was beginning to generate amongst public and practitioners badly needed alternatives.

Portman did not invent the atrium so much as revive it and sell it. Koestler's 'Act of Creation' defines creativity as the original combination of existing ideas, and John Portman brought what had been several small streams of ideas together into the mainstream.

Milestones

1800–1900
The Roman and Islamic architects worked within the limits of masonry-, wood- and cloth-technology to produce their atrium courts. Seldom were they really enclosed, but they worked in the Mediterranean climate. It was not until the industrial revolution brought iron and glass that anything new could happen.

Greenhouses appeared very early in the nineteenth century, utilizing the strange phenomenon of solar heat passing through glass but not passing back out again so easily, so that, in spite of the insubstantial nature of the enclosure, significant climatic change could be achieved. Central heating enabled glasshouses to work all year round at a price, and they began to attach themselves to conventional buildings as conservatories.

Public building in the nineteenth century aspired to the grandeur associated with royalty, but did so with the more modest means available. The creation of monumental interior spaces is extremely costly, especially if they must be layered on valuable sites. Consequently the useful spaces of most buildings became gradually smaller in scale and more regular and economical in structure. The arrival of framed building only continued a trend.

Innovative architects adopted iron and glass very early as a way of creating grand, well-lit interiors economically. John Nash used the new technology to roof the picture gallery at Attingham Park, Shropshire, in 1806 (see **26**).

Within 10 years of J C Loudon setting down the principles of greenhouse construction, the first inhabited glass-roofed spaces appeared.

In 1828 Warren and Bucklin designed the Arcade, a three-level shopping galleria in Providence, Rhode Island. Charles Barry roofed the 'cortile' (courtyard) of his splendid palazzo, the Reform Club, Pall Mall, in 1837. In 1847 J B Bunnings built the Coal Exchange in London where four storeys of offices are accessed off iron galleries around a circular glass-domed exchange floor—an amazingly modern design except in its decoration. The Sailors' Home in Liverpool, built in 1849 to the

7

8 | Plan

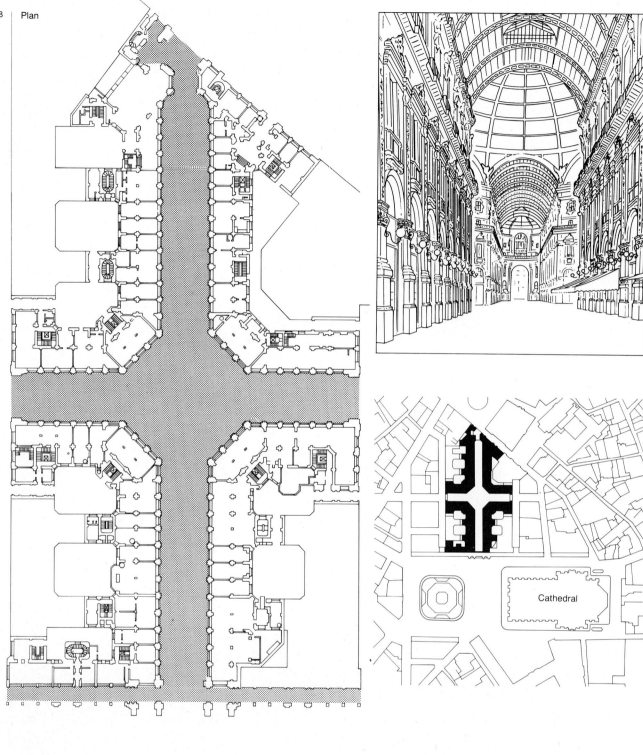

Section

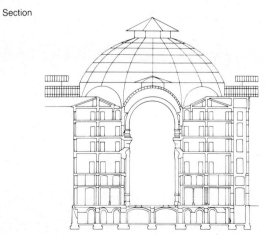

Cathedral

8 **The Galleria, Milan, 1867**
  by Mengoni. Site plan, ground plan, section and typical view of the masterpiece of the genre

designs of John Cunningham, placed sailors' cabins off iron galleries in a ship-like manner, but wrapped around a five-storey glass-roofed court—it was in every sense an 'atrium hotel'. The even grander spaces created by gardeners and railway engineers as the middle of the century approached, stimulated architects to wrap conventional buildings around them.

By 1867 Mengoni's Galleria in Milan had shown that whole streets could be roofed in a version of an Islamic bazaar on the scale of a Great Exhibition building. Arcades blossomed everywhere. In 1871, in the high-Victorian city of Manchester (England), Corbett, Raby and Sawyer's Barton Arcade combined the

concepts of the Galleria and Coal Exchange in a classic example: shops at ground level, three storeys of gallery-accessed offices above, and a fantasy of iron and glass, are contained within a masonry outer shell (see **29**).

The Rookery Building in Chicago, 1885, absorbed Barry's 'cortile' into the evolving office-building form. John Root, who had seen what could be done with iron and glass during his stay in Liverpool in the 1860s, roofed the court of his framed 11-storey office building at the third level. Thus he gained a grand lobby space, with shops at two levels, without sacrificing anything of the economy of the framed tower. The circulation stairs are here treated in a flamboyant manner to give memorable views and viewpoints.

9 **The lobby of the Rookery Building**
  Chicago, 1885, by John Root, roofing two floors of its courtyard

9

A full-height atrium court appeared in the 13-storey Chamber of Commerce Building in Chicago in 1889.[1] Baumann and Heuhl used iron galleries to access offices, though with conventional elevators outside the court. Only four years later George Wyman's Bradbury Building in Los Angeles brought the circulation into dramatic prominence. Open iron elevator cages and stair-towers, as well as large palm trees and ferns, stand in the central glazed court of this four-level structure.

Another strand of development, the western hotel,[2] culminated in Frank E Edbrooke's Brown Palace Hotel, Denver, Colorado, in 1893. The typical saloon, with a central bar space and gallery access to bedrooms, served as a simple security system: all movements passed the bar-keeper's eye.

The Brown Palace keeps the principle but inflates it to eight storeys to create the social focus of the State.

10 **The Bradbury Building**
  Los Angeles, George Wyman, 1893. Wyman based the design on science fiction stories about buildings of the year 2000, and the building was featured in the 1982 science fiction film Blade Runner.

11 **The heart of Denver**
  The Brown Palace Hotel
  Frank Edbrooke, 1893

10

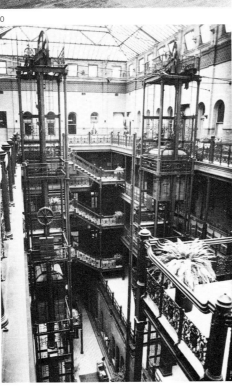

11

The rise of the modern atrium

12a **The Wright Connection**
  Frank Lloyd Wright bridges the gap
  between the first and second atrium
  periods.
  The Larkin Building, Buffalo, NY,
  1903, is of the first period

12b **The Johnson Wax Headquarters**
  Racine, Wisconsin, is from 1936
  when he was almost alone in using
  the concept

1900–1960

At the start of the new century two great
architects were using the concept in a more
restrained way. Berlage was designing the
Amsterdam Stock Exchange, the Beurs, for
all the world like a railway-station shed with
galleried offices overlooking the trading floor.
It is Bunning's cross-section built in masonry
up to the springing of great arched roof-
trusses. Also in progress was Frank Lloyd
Wright's Larkin Building in Buffalo, New
York (1903). On a site with no outlook, and a
pollution problem—a coalyard—Wright
arranged the office space on four open-sided
levels around a sky-lit court and fed filtered air
into it. The whole building had a single interior
volume.

By the time of the First World War this steady
development of the covered courtyard had
stopped. Skyscrapers in North America, and
modern architecture in Europe, took over.
The zoning regulations in New York, and the
huge floor-space permitted on small blocks,
removed the scope for courtyards. In Europe
courtyards were condemned as sordid relics
of the past. Light and air were to be sought via
glass towers and dispersed development.
The only European examples of note in the 50
years between 1914 and 1964 are Owen
Williams' Boots factory (1932) in Nottingham
(England), and Alvar Aalto's Steel Federation
(Rautatalo) Building in Helsinki, completed in
1953. The unique Boots building delivers
daylight to five levels of working space

12b

12a

12c **The Guggenheim Museum,** New
  York City, 1959, was a direct
  inspiration to Portman and others
  who began the second period

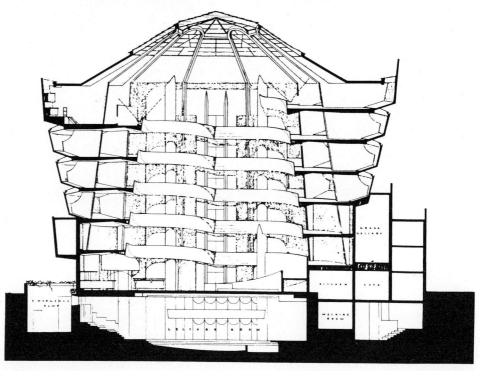

13 **Berlage's Amsterdam Stock Exchange, the Beurs, 1903**, an early twentieth-century European atrium

14 **Alvar Aalto's Rautatalo building** Helsinki, 1953

15 **Victor Gruen,** seeker of urbanity, created the covered shopping centre, out of town and in town. Southdale Mall, Minneapolis, was opened in 1952

16 Gruen's Midtown Plaza. Rochester, New York was completed between 1956 and 1962

arranged in several courts beneath a glass-concrete roof. Aalto's Rautatalo Building has a three-level, roof-lit court with gallery access to offices and a coffee bar on the atrium floor. The Aalto building later inspired the Cambridge University 'courtyard school' of architects, Colin St John Wilson and Richard MacCormac amongst them.

Frank Lloyd Wright is the living link between the first modern atrium period and the second. He remained interested in the flow of space from level to level. The Johnson Wax headquarters in Racine, Wisconsin (1936) has top-lit space generally, with two or three levels of galleries around the entrance lobby and main office space. The circular 'gilded cage' observation elevators, bridges and rounded balcony forms are clear ancestors of Portman's forms. The V C Morris store in San Francisco (1949), and the Guggenheim Museum in New York (1959) are both top-lit, spiral-ramp buildings with focal central spaces, which Portman acknowledges as inspirations. Wright's Marin County Civic Centre, finished in the early 1960s, returns to gallery-accessed offices along top-lit malls.

Another major strand in the development of the modern atrium is the enclosed shopping mall. Shopping arcades proliferated to the benefit of almost every nineteenth-century city, and A N Pomeransev's GUM store, Moscow of 1889–93 was its apotheosis. As with other building types the enclosure idea strangely vanished after the First World War and did not return until the regional shopping centre movement began in America in the 1950s. The first suburban centres had open-air malls and canopies. When Southdale Mall in the extreme climate of Minneapolis was designed in 1952, it was seen as essential to have complete weather protection. To save cost on the climate-controlled spaces they were made compact, and the shops were set on two or more levels. The result was an urban atmosphere: The Architectural Forum of March 1953 acknowledged that 'for tangible climate and intangible atmosphere the like has never been seen in a northern city'.

Victor Gruen was the architect responsible, a man dedicated to urbanity. He introduced the benefits of the enclosed mall to the city centre in the pioneering Midtown Plaza project at Rochester, New York, in 1956–62. By roofing a former street between old and new stores, and incorporating parking, buses, offices and an hotel, Gruen created a vibrant element in a decaying city core. The social focus and public-event space created is valued and used intensively.

The development of integrated new-town and district centres in Scandinavia proceeded simultaneously. The separate, grouped buildings of the 1950s were followed in the mid-1960s by centres with covered malls and squares. Redovre and Lyngby centres, both near Copenhagen, have multi-level focal covered squares with a mixture of uses on terraces around them.

17 **Antoine Graves houses,** Atlanta, Georgia, 1965
Covering the court brought an air of luxury to basic accommodation

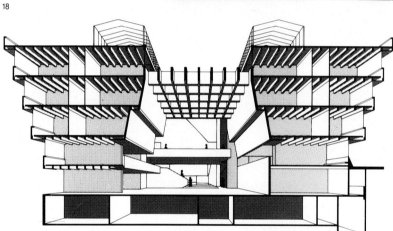

18 **Section of the Commons building**
Scarboro College, Ontario
John Andrews, 1965

19 **History Library,** University of Cambridge, England
James Stirling, 1968. An unprecedented form

20 **The Regency Hyatt,** Atlanta, Georgia, 1967
Plan and section of the hotel whose covered central court was first called an atrium

21 **Project for Liverpool Civic Centre**
Colin St John Wilson, 1965

1960–1967

In 1962–3 John Portman was commissioned by the Atlanta Public Housing Authority to design a 210-unit development for elderly individuals and couples, the Antoine Graves houses. The site was too small for the conventional three-storey terraces, and the Washington administrator in charge, Dorothy McGuire, encouraged Portman to do something more interesting. Seeking to provide a socially stimulating environment, Portman arranged very simple apartments like motel units around two gallery-access courts. By putting a sun and rain canopy over the courts whilst still allowing natural ventilation, he created a place to sit and talk and watch neighbours come and go. A resident summed up reaction: 'I would like to meet the guy who designed this; he had a head on his shoulders'. Dorothy McGuire thought the design too grand to be executed on budget, although it had been, and considered it a more suitable idea for a luxury hotel. In 1965 Portman had the Atlanta hotel which was to be sold to the Hyatt corporation on his drawing-board.

Portman's motives for including such socializing spaces stemmed from his desire to attract and please people rather than from conscious architectural aims. Retailing experience in his youth had given him insight into what pleased people and what was lacking in the cities of the United States—public space without noise and fumes, with greenery and water, where people can watch each other and mix informally.

It would be unfair to credit John Portman alone with this new idea. In Liverpool, Colin St John Wilson was commissioned in the mid-1960s to design a civic centre. His design consisted of four seven-level office wings, converging in a pin-wheel pattern to leave a central well. The court was glass-roofed and the galleries around it served as public counters to city departments. Escalators and glass-enclosed elevators and stairs reached up to the galleries. The project stalled, but the model shows that it would have had most of the ingredients of the modern atrium.

John Andrews, the Australian who made his name in Canada, used similar thinking in his Scarborough College, Ontario, in 1966: the first-phase buildings are slashed open in section; corridors in the spine block become galleries and culminate in an internal courtyard 'meeting place'. With this indoor public square Andrews was realizing an idea he had first proposed for Toronto City Hall in a student project which reached the final stage of the 1958 international competition. In Montreal, a shopping complex called Alexis Nihon Plaza, by Harold Ship, was part of the rush of significant development in building for Expo '67: it provides five galleried levels of offices and shops overlooking a covered square, all connected to a Metro station.

In New York, Kevin Roche and John Dinkeloo completed the Ford Foundation headquarters in 1967 (see **35**). This most unusual building arranges most of its space in an L-shape of

20

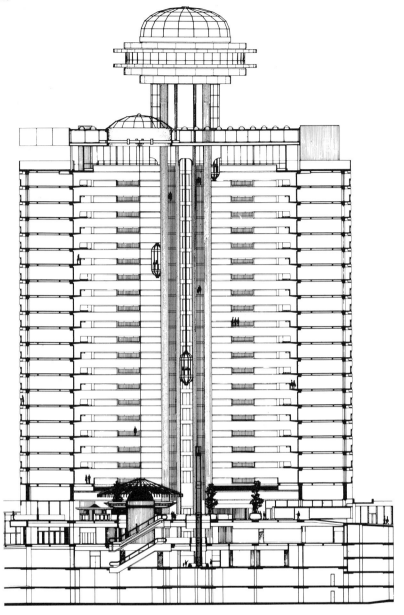

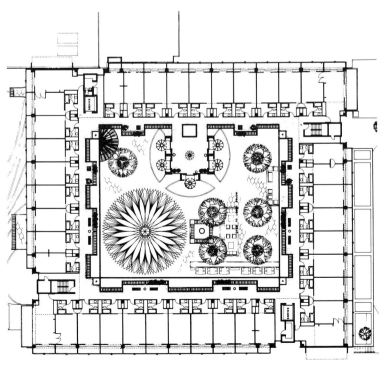

12 storeys of inward-looking offices. A square is completed by a stair-tower and two glass walls to enclose an enormous garden. Two top floors actually go right round the square, and leave a top-light. The splendid entrance garden and the introversion of the office space are hallmarks of the atrium as it has developed.

Finally in England in 1968 James Stirling completed the History Library at Cambridge University. As in the Ford Foundation, two multi-storey wings form an L-shape. But the space embraced is then roofed by a sloping glass tent to form the reading-room. This can be called an atrium as it is so focal to the building. Corridors to the rooms in the 'L' overlook the reading-room, with overhanging conversation balconies glazed in for quietness.

Of all these pioneers it is, however, to John Portman that the credit must go for giving the concept momentum. It was his flair for popularization, and the commercial success that followed it, which ensured that there would be many more. It was his showmanship that led him to adopt the wall-climber elevator devised by Otis for fairground observation towers, and which concealed the existence of the spectacular space until the visitor was confronted with it: a low doorway off the street suddenly opens into the 220-feet tall space. Marks on the floor show the place where guests drop their bags and exclaim—it is called 'profanity corner'.

The Hyatt Corporation's public relations team came up with the term 'atrium' for the Regency Hotel, crystallizing the luxury image which gave it an immediate 'cachet'. The occupancy rates for the hotel made the owners and their competitors sit up, and the movement was on its way.

21

22 **The network of influence** acting on the atrium concept

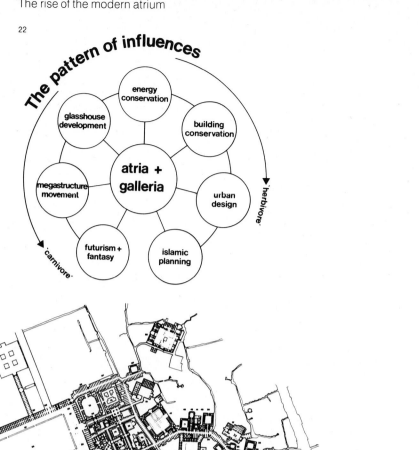

23a

23a **A city of interiors,** Isafahan, Iran. All buildings are courtyard-form, and abut each other. The major street, the bazaar, is enclosed

23b **Kashan, Iran,** the covered bazaar

24 One of the first multi-level 'galleria'
the Arcade, Providence, Rhode Island, 1828, by Russell Warren and James Bucklin, restored by Irving Haynes, 1980. The Arcade follows nine years after the classic single level Burlington Arcade, London, by Samuel Ware. Both are western interpretations of the arabian bazaar, made fashionable by contemporary travellers

Influences

The influences at work in the historic and current development of the atrium building have been and are many and varied. Some have been alluded to in this brief history. It is the richness of the ideas in the background which reveal how far the concept could be developed.

There are two quite different types of thinking. There is the optimistic, progress-oriented, high-technology futurist way of thinking: the so called 'carnivorous' approach. And there is the 'herbivorous' way of thinking: conservation of energy and of old buildings, sensitivity in urban design, historical and cross-cultural awareness, love of growing things. The use of new technology as it becomes available is a 'carnivorous' enthusiasm. The Crystal Palace and wall-climber elevators are from the same school. The use of ideas and motifs from science-fiction literature and films to heighten the sense of 'progress' is also plainly seen in many recent atrium buildings. They are saying *'this is the shape of things to come'.*

The herbivorous motivation is almost equally strong however. Energy-conscious designers use atria carefully as passive solar climate-controllers. The building conservation movement uses atria to revive old buildings, either those with existing courts or covered halls, or those too deep-planned to be used without hollowing out. Urban designers use atria to provide more sympathetic building masses and good pedestrian routeways in cities. The emergence of the ideas of shopping street and public square in their covered forms as galleria and atria is one of the intriguing design developments of the 1970s. That this should coincide with the rise of interest in Islamic culture is not surprising.

The Middle-Eastern pattern of city development, courtyard planning with totally introverted buildings, continued from the Roman tradition. In cities such as Isfahan one can see no 'outsides' of buildings in the western sense at all. The main public route is the bazaar, a prototype galleria. Off it lie the courts of caravanserai, colleges, mosques and houses. All are essentially courts with their backs to party walls and alleys for secondary access. The result is a city of 'interiors' although open to the sky generally.

As interest in eastern thought grows in the West, so the emphasis on building interiors compared to exteriors grows with it. With the Islamic states controlling western prosperity and commissioning most leading western architects to build in the Islamic tradition, it is not surprising that the 'public interior' architecture of Islam should be influential. The Arabian states have built many magnificent atrium buildings in the last decade, as a product of this cultural convergence.

1 See also the Guaranty Loan Building (later the New York Metropolitan Life Building), Minneapolis, 1890 by E Townsend Mix. This 12-storey atrium has cast glass floors to the access galleries. Illustrated in Whiffen and Koeper, American Architecture 1607-1976, Routledge & Kegan Paul, 1981

2 See Courtyard Hotels of the Wild West by Professor John D Hoag, Architectural Review, April 1969, p 259. Hoag illustrates the 1875 Palace Hotel, San Francisco, which was destroyed in 1906. Its seven-storey atrium housed the hotel carriage drive as well as a restaurant

24

3 The greenhouse effect

This chapter is not about the phenomenon of solar heat retention behind glass but about the contribution of glasshouse development to the story of atrium building. It is valuable to our study to look at the emergence and development of greenhouses. Their technology was long in advance of that for conventional buildings, and current usage may yet have lessons. The symbolism of the use of glass enclosures in building is suggestive of the way in which the tradition may be used and extended.

Symbolism

The symbolism of the greenhouse, glasshouse, conservatory or winter-garden, encompasses the ambivalent relationship between man and nature, between town and country, and between indoors and out.[1] Two streams of building development interacted in the early nineteenth century, the horticultural forcing house and the gallery spaces of great houses. Galleries were the indoor spaces provided for private promenading in inclement weather. In Tudor times these were long, narrow spaces, side-windowed with extensive

26 **The first modern atrium,** the gallery at Attingham Park, Shropshire John Nash, 1806

26

vistas over parkland, and were retreats from the bustle of the house. By the eighteenth century the galleries had become the respository of art collections, and a courtyard form was more popular, deliberately reminiscent of the Roman garden court or atrium. The garden association persisted as a symbol of freedom from care but the top-light then favoured was for sky-light, not view. The new glazing techniques developed for horticulture made these skylights easier to construct, and more generously proportioned.

Public buildings soon began to use the new techniques and changed the gallery/garden from a private retreat to a place of public promenading and therapeutic contact with 'nature'. Highly fashionable, the glass building was seen as both gallery/garden and room at once. Diverse functions were accommodated—markets, museums, shopping—with the combined function of healthful promenading and the inevitable reference to the garden, by actual planting or by decoration.

The concept returned to the home in altered forms. The bourgeoisie in England, living in suburbs, expanded their houses with attached glass conservatories and verandas. Their European equivalent, still compacted into defensible cities, used the stair-halls of their apartment buildings as glasshouses. The conservatory entered deeply into the character of the age. Passing through the door from the dining-room one was suddenly able to escape into the distant countryside, or even into the jungle. Victorian public dining-places often followed the same theme: the guests were really in a garden, far from care—glazed laylight ceiling, trellised, ornamented walls and giant plants were constant reminders. As a fantasy world of exotic plants it became a retreat for the romantic mind, and featured in countless novels and plays: one of Disraeli's characters observes *'it is impossible to live without a conservatory'*.[2]

The year-round indoor garden retains its evocative power: to induce relaxation, imagined escape to the natural world, and to give inner privacy in a public place. These images of arcadia, secrecy, retreat and dreams inform the most successful modern examples also.

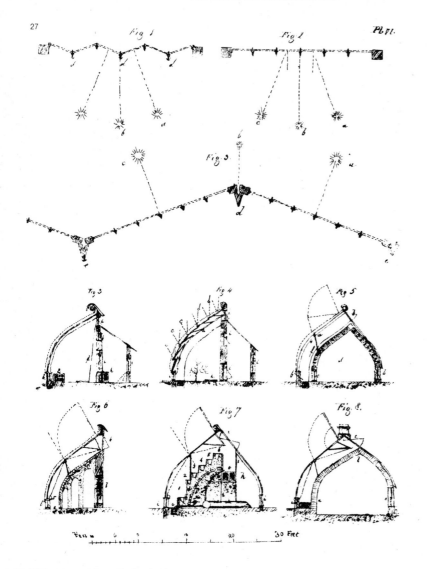

27

Technology

The technological development of the glasshouse is the story of the industrialization of construction, and the mastery of artificial climate control. Both passed to conventional building from the work of the horticulturalists. Eighteenth-century Dutch forcing-frames had developed basic passive solar storage techniques, shading and insulation shutters and blinds, and auxiliary heating systems. By the turn of the century, the gentry of Britain had become intensely interested in the possibilities of growing under glass the exotic species discovered in the colonies. They also had the wealth to experiment: in lively debate empirical thinkers tackled the idea of large glass enclosures.

One of these empirical thinkers was John Claudius Loudon to whom must go the credit for systematizing the new technology. First as experimenter and inventor, then as author, he advanced construction considerably. He advocated sloping rather than flat glass, to drain the inevitable condensation. He proposed ridge and furrow glazing which also drained condensate, but was intended more to improve solar penetration. The transmission loss through glass is minimized by angling the panes towards the late morning and early afternoon sun, thus receiving a continuous, strong solar flow for three hours around mid-day. He incorporated his ideas in the development of a drawn iron sash-bar to carry glass in curved, and therefore stiff, segments.

Loudon's 1817 designs set down alternatives for the necessary top and bottom ventilation of glasshouses, the use of canvas heat-retaining blinds, and the back-wall heat store which also incorporated a furnace. Techniques of central heating and of automatic control of heat and ventilation were invented progressively to ensure the survival of exotic plants. Such precision, available for the comfort of plants, was not incorporated into conventional buildings until 1914 onwards, the time of Willis Carrier, the inventor of air conditioning.

The first great conservatory utilizing these principles was completed in 1827 at Bretton Hall, Yorkshire, by the Bailey brothers, to whom Loudon sold his design rights when he turned to writing. Exploitation of the idea was rapid for horticulture, but also in other building contexts: only seven years later D and E Bailey's large conservatory was open on Oxford Street, London, at the Pantheon Bazaar. It was the 'glass of fashion' and provided a place to meet and promenade such as had never been seen in town before.

Iron and glass technology was grafted onto conventional building almost as soon as it was available. John Nash had access to the secrets of iron-making through his freemason connections with the Shropshire iron-founders. Commissioned in 1805 by Noel Hill, First Lord Berwick, to add a picture gallery to Attingham Park, he used iron ribs to support a flat ceiling and a unique cove of

27 **J C Loudon set down the basis of greenhouse design,** the overall form and the idea of angled glazing to catch more sun (1817)

28 **Industrialized greenhouse construction,** Paxton's Crystal Palace going up in 1850

29 **Arcade buildings from the catalogue**
Barton Arcade, Manchester, England, built in 1871 by Corbett, Raby and Sawyer using standard assemblies from McFarlane's casting book

29a

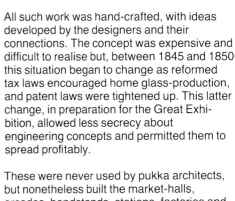

29b

skylights above the Roman atrium-style room. That the garden court, so popular in the architecture of the time, could become an indoor saloon by means of the new technology, was not lost on original architects like Sir Charles Barry who employed the same principle at the Reform Club (1837).

The Crystal Palace devised for the 1851 Exhibition can be fairly credited as marking the start of industrialized building. Paxton's genius was to refine the design into a few, mass-produced components erected by rapid methods. The techniques he created laid the basis for a considerable industry. The iron-casters were able to create a strong export and home market for complete buildings assembled from kits of components.

All such work was hand-crafted, with ideas developed by the designers and their connections. The concept was expensive and difficult to realise but, between 1845 and 1850 this situation began to change as reformed tax laws encouraged home glass-production, and patent laws were tightened up. This latter change, in preparation for the Great Exhibition, allowed less secrecy about engineering concepts and permitted them to spread profitably.

These were never used by pukka architects, but nonetheless built the market-halls, arcades, bandstands, stations, factories and small bridges in Britain and the Empire. MacFarlane's Casting Book, from one of the major Glasgow casting-houses, was the source of some splendid arcades, notably Manchester's Barton Arcade. Similar industries covered America in glass and iron. The simplicity of their component systems is an object lesson for designers today who have retreated from industrialization rather than advanced with it: Konrad Wachsmann and Buckminster Fuller were Paxton's heirs, visionaries never in the mainstream.

The greatest enclosures produced by the Victorian glasshouse technology were railway stations and exhibition buildings, often encompassing several acres under a single span. The railway sheds were permanent, and accommodated the uncontrolled climate of the train hall. Ancillary accommodation—restaurants, offices, hotels—received conventional buildings at the end or side of the shed. The relationship between the two is often arbitrary, with the curve of the shed slicing across the façade of the conventional building: the architect and engineer did not interact adequately in the design of St Pancras Station, for example. The results, with occupied spaces often looking out into the train hall, are close forerunners of some of the atria of today.

30a **The maximum space house,**
Cambridge, England, 1969
A research project led by John Hix.
The house is built within a
commercial greenhouse structure.

30 a

30b Axonometric of the maximum space
house

30 b

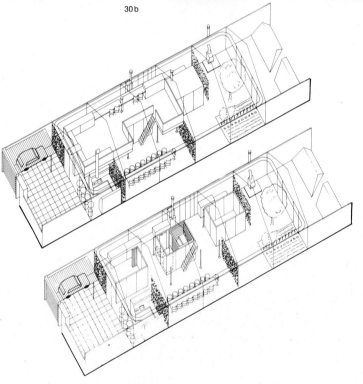

31 **The urban rooftop solar
greenhouse**
an illustration from a study by the
Ehrenkrantz Group, 1980, which
looked at the viability of adding food
producing greenhouses to New York
rooftops. The greenhouse buffers the
building below and pays for its own
heat

31

32

Glasshouse as building

The modern horticultural glasshouse uses lightweight aluminium frames and patent glazing systems that have been perfected over a century of development. It provides very low cost enclosure about one-third of the price of conventional envelopes. This fact encouraged John Hix and his students at the University of Cambridge to see if a glasshouse could constitute a competitive and workable house. Their prototype Maximum Space House (MSH) of 1969, and similar office structures, showed the possibilities. The MSH mixes occupied space and garden area freely within a generous envelope. A spacious, arcadian environment results for a single home and for potential communities of glasshouse-dwellers.

Plastic enclosures for horticulture, inflated by air adjusted to the exact temperature, humidity and CO_2 concentration needed, pioneered air-supported and fabric structures. They are now becoming practical for more permanent structures. A small greenhouse on a site near Paddington station, West London, attracted considerable attention in 1980. It was designed by the Terry Farrell Partnership for Clifton Nurseries, as part of a garden centre. Farrell's team were using a new, insulating, double-skinned polycarbonate sheet which was stiff when curved. The curvatious form was memorable and the summer climate-control device, a solar chimney, of interest. What caused greater interest, however, was the simultaneous proposal by Farrell and Ralph Lebens for the use of conservatories to keep conventional buildings warm. The 'buffer thinking' thesis (see p. 57 ff), is an excellent example of the interaction between the greenhouse ethos, its technology and conventional architecture.

33a

32 **Glasshouse as building**
Crystal Cathedral, Garden Grove, California, by Johnson/Burgee, 1980. It even uses natural ventilation

33a **Clifton Nurseries, London, 1980**
Terry Farrell Partnership: a prototype for wider use as a buffer space to occupied buildings

33b Section through Clifton Nurseries building
See illustration 145 for construction detail

33 b

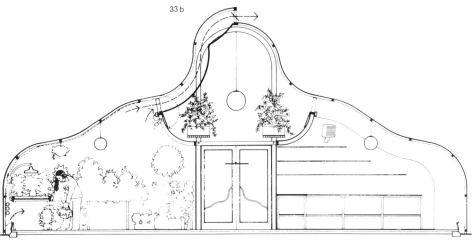

34 **Atria North, Toronto,** by Ron Thom. Central court in a low-rise office building; visitors and workers enter the building through this garden from the parking garage below

35 **The Ford Foundation headquarters,** New York City, 1967. Roche and Dinkeloo: one of the founding buildings of the modern atrium period.
See illustration 166 for plans and sections

34

35

Glasshouse as atrium

Whilst complete buildings as glasshouse are still rare, the glasshouse influence on the atrium concept has been pronounced. It is often the architects who are also landscape designers who make most imaginative atrium builders: Sir Frederick Gibberd, the British pioneer of atrium building, is a distinguished landscape architect as well as a building designer.

Particular designers have shown strong interest and skill both in the use of greenhouse technology and in ways of planting indoors. Most notable is the work of Kevin Roche and the late John Dinkeloo. Since they succeeded Eero Saarinen in 1963 their work has been preponderantly under glass, and brilliantly planted by Dan Kiley. The Ford Foundation building, New York, was completed in that annus mirabilis of the atrium building, 1967: in that year both the Regency Hyatt and the Cambridge History Library were also completed. Roche and Dinkeloo's reorganisation and extension of the Metropolitan Museum, New York, produced a series of glazed pavilions, pyramids and landscaped courts, exploring many atrium design ideas. The little Irwin Bank extension, in Columbus, Indiana (1973), is a model conservatory atrium, and operates as a public promenade between two buildings. Their contemporary proposals for a National Aquarium in Washington DC used a huge wedge-shaped glasshouse to encompass several shoreline climates. Their triumph has been the second phase office building for the John Deere Company in Moline, Illinois, 1978, known as Deere West. The garden atrium there is lyrically designed, and maintained at exhibition pitch.

The Ford Foundation (see **35** and **166**) was a proving ground for the introduction of large-scale planting in atria. A 12-storey L-shaped office building turns away from an uninspiring view of 42nd Street and a power plant to wrap itself round two sides of a garden court. On a steeply sloping site, a storey change of level is retained in the garden, and must be crossed on a stairway path to reach the elevators. Dense planting, as in a palm house, forms a private world overlooked by half the offices.

At Deere West a spreading two-storey office building floats just above undulating natural ground level. A third storey is slotted in at lower garden level to provide staff amenities including a restaurant. The large, long garden court is under 'gambrel' arched glass roofs, reminiscent of the shape of barns belonging to the farmers served by the company. All accommodation is open to the garden, which is large enough for a lunchtime stroll, and provides comfortable access to nature in the height of torrid summers and the depth of snowy winters (see **36, 165** and **168**).

Successful planting is very often the key to a visually successful atrium. The bright light needed and the colour and texture produced can transform a possibly dull void into the

36 **The garden at Deere West,** John Deere Company Headquarters, Moline, Illinois, by Roche and Dinkeloo: the apotheosis of the indoor garden.
See illustration 166 for plan and section

living heart of the building and a magnet to its users. Canadian architects are notably successful at using the greenhouse aesthetic. Arthur Erickson has been involved in a series of splendid planted atria, notably the Law Courts in Vancouver and the Bank of Canada, Ottawa. Barton Myers lives in an atrium house, the court roofed in standard 12-metre Glass Reinforced Polyester resin (GRP) greenhouse construction. He was responsible for the Alberta University HUB project, providing lines of student housing flanking covered streets across the campus. Here too he used greenhouse roofs. Another good scheme is at Atria North in Don Mills, Toronto. Architect Ron Thom has provided copious sky-light through a greenhouse roof in the heart of a deep-plan office building, then paved and planted a spiral path down to the basement garaging through which most staff and visitors arrive (see **34** and **167**).

The empathy between people and plants, in buildings especially, is a considerable modern phenomenon. In a period when we have no accepted rationale for decorating our artefacts, the presence of live plants seems to act as a connector between people and the built environment. This presence raises morale, according to surveys, and combats the supposedly debilitating effects of positively ionized urban air. Apart from the keeping of small plants at the work-station, an atrium offers the chance of bringing nature into the building on a large scale. The greenhouse effect—philosophical, symbolic and technical—is a force to be understood and respected.

1 See Victorian Glass by Judi Loach, RIBA Journal, February 1981

2 'It is impossible to live without a conservatory', words spoken by Ferdinand in Disraeli's novel Henrietta Temple

36

37

THE MUSEUM AS ARRANGED IN 1813.   J. GANDY A.R.A.

Futurism and fantasy

37 **The sublime futurist**
Utopian architecture of the
eighteenth century used the
awesome, top-lit interior as a
constant theme. The crypt of Sir John
Soane's Museum, London, drawn by
J M Gandy, c 1826

Soon after the completion of John Portman's first atrium hotels it was noticed that their interiors were reminiscent of the sets of science-fiction films. Many designers use styling ideas derived from science-fiction illustrators to lend their work the flavour of super-modernity. Portman's spaces, however, are not just styled in this way, they are the embodiment of a train of thought shared by some writers, artists and architects for over two centuries: this is the way things will look in 'the future'. This message from the imagination of visionaries, which has repeated itself for so long, has an undeniable power, and communicates itself to the low- and highbrow alike. Perhaps people unconsciously recognize 'the future' now it has arrived.

The train of thought in question is first discernable at the start of the eighteenth century in the stage designs of the Bibiena family. Seeking to overcome the constraints of small stages in giving illusions of depth, the Bibienas painted backdrops of fantastic architectural interiors, stretching away horizontally and vertically and with prodigious staircases.[1] It is the first evidence of what was to become the 'Architecture of the Sublime!' The artists sought to create a sense of awe similar to that experienced before the scale and power of nature. Their means were the use of super-scaled, crushing masses, and particularly a concentration on gigantic interiors. An interior can somehow convey a sense of the insignificance of man more effectively than an exterior, where the contrast with the real vastness of land and sky undermines the effect. As the description of the inside of the huge planet-building factory of the Magratheans in The Hitchhiker's Guide to the Galaxy puts it.[2]

'Suddenly Arthur had a fairly clear idea of what infinity looked like. It wasn't infinity in fact. Infinity looks flat and uninteresting . . . distance is incomprehensible and therefore meaningless. The chamber into which the aircar emerged was anything but infinite, it was just very, very, very big, so big that it gave the impression of infinity far better than infinity itself.'

Why was there this interest in making man feel insignificant? The 'sublime' movement of the later eighteenth century was infused with a sense of foreboding. For the first time there was widespread concern for the future, and a sense that things would be different and not, perhaps, better. Industrial and political revolution was afoot. The idea of designing the future of man was suddenly in common currency. Simultaneously therefore came the excitement of thinking about Utopian futures, and the fear of change and the possible fall of civilization as it was known. The drawings of Piranesi encapsulate the terror, whilst those of Boullée and Ledoux visualize the vast institutional buildings of the future. They use the architectural language of ancient Rome, thus combining awe for a tremendous civilization, and fear of the collapse which Rome suffered. It is the interiors which move us; they are not just huge, but are seemingly endless, with internal vistas and no view out.

There were some buildings which captured the mood. Sir John Soane was skilled at invoking, in modest buildings, the sublimity of the imagined work of Boullée. Top-lit spaces have layers of surrounding spaces either revealed or hinted at. The sprawling Bank of England complex was made functional by this approach, but Soane's house/museum in Lincoln's Inn Fields encapsulates the fantasy of the style: the sense conveyed is of looking back on the future, with nostalgia for its greatness and regret at its ruin. The institutional buildings devised by, for example, Durand, Dance, Babeuf and Bentham, often had monumental interior spaces[3]. Actual prisons followed Piranesi's imaginary ones at least in having multi-level galleried wings watched from a central domed hall or 'panopticon'.

By the mid-nineteenth century the invention of political and architectural Utopias had become a more literary activity. Industrialisation was changing the face of Europe and America at great speed, but now the mood was one of optimism. Predicting the future, prophesying what would be achieved by the progress in which all believed , became a stock-in-trade for journals like the Illustrated London News. By the end of the century a literary genre, science fiction, had emerged. It combined prediction with a way of telling fables, setting them in imagined futures instead of an imagined past. The fear present in the 'sublime' movement started to return, with the awesome possibility, voiced by writers such as Jules Verne and H G Wells, of travel into the bowels of the earth, invasion from space, or journeys into it.

The genre flourished in the early and mid-twentieth century in illustrated magazines such as Amazing Stories, Astounding Science Fact and Fiction and The Magazine of Fantasy and Science Fiction. Here the writers' and illustrators' minds went to work on the look of the future. Cities were to be vast, but also much more concentrated: the skyscrapers of the day were nothing in comparison. Enormous terraces of buildings enclosed the view completely, with vast spaces crossed by bridges and peopled with aircraft. Huge cities were to be expected below ground, under the sea, in orbit, on the planets. These were, by force of circumstance, totally enclosed. Sheer pressure of population would require the construction of 'endless' three-dimensional cities with no outside. Life amongst its levels would be a claustrophobe's hell.

Film-makers translated these two-dimensional sketches into three. The horrors of a metropolis below ground came to life in the hands of Fritz Lang (Metropolis, 1927). The streamlined brilliance of Vincent Korda's sets for H G Wells' Things to Come (1936) was powerful because they were believable. Of all the psychological progenitors of Portman's work, this is the closest: his Los

Angeles Bonaventure Hotel could be the futurist set of 'Everytown 2036'. The space is free-form and boundless, but enclosed. Light comes from above, but is it natural? Layers of occupied space form a texture up the walls of great apses; bridges leap across the void; trees stand surrealistically on elevated levels; glass elevators glide into vertical infinity. The description fits both set and building.

Writing and film-making continue to model possible futures vividly, while architecture officially stands aloof. Unofficially, however, the interaction is there: many of the set designers are architects. The film designers also feed on a rich fund of architectural imagination dating back to the First World War. Most of its products were not built, but exist in drawings or descriptions as powerful for current designers as those of Piranesi for his contemporaries 200 years ago.

This 'Futurism' embraces the Italians of that name, and also Hugh Ferris, Buckminster Fuller, Archigram, the megastructure movement, Paulo Soleri, and many others.

From the Futurist Sant'Elia came the idea that tall buildings might slope, terracing back level by level, and that elevators, escalators and public transport should be visible and strongly overlaid on buildings: the arteries were to stand out.

Buckminster Fuller's powerful technological mind has long railed against the waste of individual buildings combating the elements. His quest to do more with less includes the enclosure of cities in lightweight membranes, and his space structures have become the obvious technology for atrium envelopes.

Theories about possible urban futures in the early 1960s, when awareness of the 'population explosion' was high, seriously considered concentrated 'core cities' as an alternative to 'ecumenopolis' or world-covering sprawl. Kevin Lynch's scenario in The Future Metropolis (edited by Lloyd Rodwin) suggested a three-mile cube, able to hold 20 million people at generous spacing – a solid city, beyond the mere closeness of buildings.

The megastructure movement was an astonishing phenomenon whilst it lasted. From the mid-1950s to 1970 the avant-garde expected that future cities would consist of vast, three-dimensional permanent frameworks with shorter-life modules slung within them. Megastructures were either static but extensible, even crossing whole continents, or mobile. Archigram, a London group, conjured up images of metal-frame mountains, thrumming with transport-tubes and festooned with life-containing capsules.

These structures would obviously have great depth, far beyond anything considered inhabitable to date. Enclosed volumes within the megastructures would have been on a vast scale.

38

38 **The shape of 'Things to Come'.** Vincent Korda's filmset of Everytown 2036 for the film of H G Wells' novel, 1936

39 **Megastructures imply vast
   interiors**
   Plug-in-City, the Archigram Group,
   1963

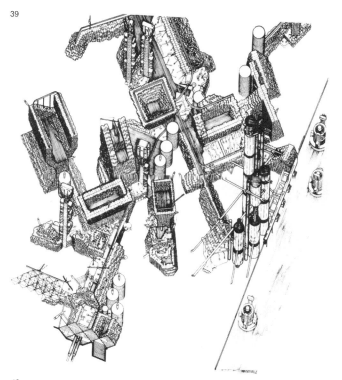

40 **Future cities are under one roof**
   Buckminster Fuller's demonstration
   of his ideas in the US Pavillion, Expo
   67, Montreal

41 **Future buildings** will have dramatic,
   visible circulation systems. Sant
   Elia's images continue to influence:
   his 'Central Station' of 1913

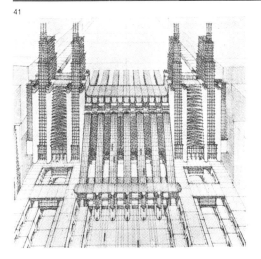

42 Arcology, the thesis of Paulo Soleri
Soleri proposes that we free land by super-concentrating our cities. This scheme is called Arcvillage II. It houses 30,000 at 1754 to the hectare (710 to the acre), is 360 metres high and 420 metres across. Two vast atria feature in this design from the mid 1960s

43 The A-frame megastructure
This recurrent image of superconcentrated development was used by Disney for the Contemporary Resort Hotel at Walt Disney World, Orlando, Florida, 1970

One of the most interesting products of megastructure thinking comes from the constant comparison between proposed megastructures and ocean-liners. Liners crop up again and again as models of self-contained cities, 'cités-paquebots' as the French called them. A project in 1956 by Wladimir Gordeef for a Saharan city has all the attributes of a current Middle-Eastern atrium building. Its compartments open off a communal air-conditioned space containing pools, terraces and gardens. Outer openings were to be kept shut during the day, but were to be opened up at night to the cool air of the desert.

A visionary still proposing 'liner-cities' is Paulo Soleri. His 'arcologies', architecture and ecology in harmony, concentrate cities into compact masses to free the land for nature, agriculture and recreation. The schemes involve huge hollow masses, with inward-facing accommodation, often enclosed by glazing to protect them. First proposed in 1959, the scale and feel of some of the smaller arcologies are now realised in such complexes as Detroit's Renaissance Center (Portman, 1979), and the Houston Center (Periera, from 1978).

Some prototypes did get built, or seriously designed, before the traumatic period 1968-73 when the concept of limitless 'progress' was finally laid aside. Exhibition and fairground architecture (a form of science-fiction) showed the ideas most

42

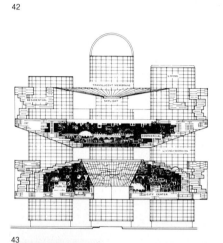

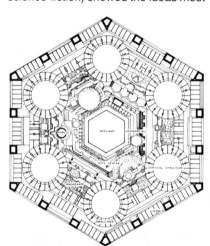

43

44 **The competition winning design for the UN City, Vienna,** in 1970 also used the A-frame megastructure concept. Building Design Partnership proposed two banks of building, leaning together and embracing a multi-level mall of common facilities. The model view shows the futurist interior which results

strongly: as Coney Island was a prototype for Manhattan, so Expo '67 and Disneyworld (1970) were for the megastructure.

Expo '67 featured several structures where exteriors felt internal because they were so wrapped and overhung, and interiors felt external because of their transparency. In the former category are the Theme pavilions and Safdie's Habitat housing; in the latter the United States and German pavilions. Fuller's great bubble, with its trays of space linked by escalators and its small train running through the membrane, demonstrated the enclosed city proposal with great power. Otto and Gutbrod's tent for West Germany was an early example of the potential of fabrics used to enclose space on a grand scale.

Disneyworld featured a whole theme park carried on a square-mile service and access structure, the 'Utilidor'; it also featured Sant'Elian transport—an elevated monorail passing through buildings. The Contemporary Resort Hotel at Disneyworld is a mini-megastructure: a large 'A-frame' carries prefabricated bedroom modules, forming a tent over its atrium lobby. The elevators rise in a central tower, and the monorail glides silently through space.

The competition for a United Nations City in Vienna in 1969-70 produced a late flowering of megastructure proposals. The winning design, by Building Design Partnership, used large inclined walls of offices enclosing a central mall within which were subsidiary buildings. The scale of enclosure, and the interpenetration of spaces within, were of Piranesian magnitude. The scheme was not adopted: one objection was that top officials would not accept inward-facing rooms. A few years later they happily accepted them at the IMF headquarters in Washington DC, a splendid atrium building by Vincent Kling.

44a

44b

The dialogue between architect and 'imagineers' continues. Disney's term for those who invent the future can include the artists, writers and technologists who do so for fun and profit, and those whose work is the actual construction of useful innovative hardware. Norman Foster's brilliant design for the Hong Kong and Shanghai Banking Corporation, Hong Kong, is indebted to the imagery of space hardware as well as of the Chinese culture in which it stands. Of particular note is the acknowledged influence of the Vertical Assembly Building (VAB) at Kennedy Space Centre, Cape Canaveral (Urbahn, Roberts, Seeley and Moran, 1966). This titanic enclosure of 150,000,000 cubic feet has 400-feet tall 'atria' between layers of working floors. The space vehicles are

erected and serviced in these voids, and then rolled out through telescopic doors at either end of the VAB on their way to the launch-pads. A particularly large number of architects have been on tours of Cape Canaveral and this must account for much.

The role of the atrium in the future may well include its use in just those circumstances so far considered only in fantasy. That is the subject of Chapter 8.

1 Galli-Bibiena. See Architetture e Prospettive, 1740, Guisseppe Galli-Bibiena

2 Hitchhiker's Guide to the Galaxy, by Douglas Adams, see Pan Edition, 1979, p 121

3 See Social Purposes in Architecture, Helen Rosenau, Studio Vista, 1970

45 **Acknowledged to be inspired by the Vertical Assembly building** at Cape Canaveral, Foster Associates' Hong Kong and Shanghai Banking Corporation HQ at its conceptual design stage

46 **'Sant Elian transport tubes** flash through the bowels of the subterranean city'. The elevators at Water Tower Place, Chicago, by Warren Platner and Associates, 1975

46

47

5 The contribution of conservationism

A new respect for old buildings

The conservation movement has had a profound and constructive effect on modern architecture. It has helped to soften its dogmatic stance on the relationship between the form and function of a building. Buildings are four-dimensional: not only do they have three dimensions of space, but they respond through time to the demands of the day. This is often more important than their 'fit' to the brief (program) on opening day. A building tailored to a brief whose precision is illusory, runs into obsolescence with alarming speed.

Committed futurists see this as an argument for shorter life, 'disposable' buildings, or for elaborate flexibility.

What makes many older buildings work for new uses is their concentration on the general functions of buildings rather than on the specific needs of their original use. They have good entrances and circulation to give orientation, good structural and thermal performance generally, and provide daylight and air to most areas. Their structures can

take alteration readily, and their sections are usually generous enough to accept modern servicing. The more generalised the old building the more functions it can accommodate.

Conservationism has thus increased respect for older ways of building and caused buildings to be kept rather than to be replaced. It has also led to new buildings borrowing old ideas enthusiastically. The atrium concept has worked in both contexts: old atrium buildings have been restored and used as models for new work; old courtyard buildings have been converted into atrium buildings; existing deep-planned buildings have been made into more useful shallow space by hollowing out atria within them; extensions to respected old buildings have been linked to them by atria, preserving the old façades. Looking at examples of each shows the ingenuity that the concept has released in designers.

Old atrium buildings revived

Several of the milestone buildings in atrium development have been recognized for their value and restored: John Root's Chicago Rookery, George Wyman's Los Angeles Bradbury Building and Manchester's Barton Arcade are examples. The Cleveland Arcade, by John Eisenmann and George Smith, has been restored to magnificence. Its large scale and vivid decoration recall Bunnings', lost Coal Exchange. In St Paul, Minnesota, the old Federal Office Building (1902) has been given a new lease of life as an arts and community centre. This massive Romanesque pile centres on a sky-lit four-storey court with gallery access to the rooms around. The United States Museum of Building is taking over the old Pension Building in Washington, an imposing atrium.

In New York, the massive Federal Archive Building and Appraiser's Warehouse in Greenwich Village has a glass roof over the lower three levels of its court. These lower, atrium floors now house community facilities, such as medical and day-care centres, and space for cultural groups. Upper floors are converted into housing. Much more modest structures have also been rediscovered, such as the London offices at West Halkin Street.

47 **An old shopping arcade successfully revived**
the Grand Arcade, Cleveland, Ohio, 1888, by John Eisenmann and George Smith, restored by Don M Hisaka and Harvey Oppmann, 1982

48 **An atrium rediscovered**
the old Pensions Building, Washington DC once housed presidential inaugurations when the weather was too severe. It is now the National Museum of Building

49 **A Regency atrium**
internal courts at the Pantechnicon, West Halkin Street, London, 1830 have been restored by Michael Haskoll for Capital and Counties Plc (1979)

50 **Coutts Bank, London.** Cross section and roof plan of the 1978 reconstruction by Sir Frederick Gibberd and Partners. The facade bays around this triangular site were retained, with an atrium building inserted behind

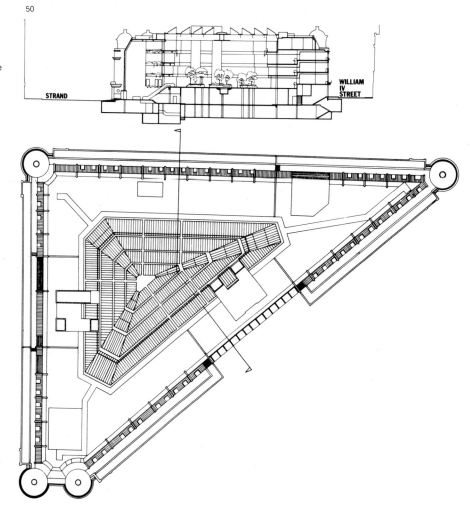

51 **Albert Dock, Liverpool,** Jesse Hartley, 1846. Proposals to convert one block for the Merseyside Maritime Museum involved turning a service court into an atrium Building Design Partnership, 1978 drawing, Peter Shuttleworth

52 **A direct conversion of a lightwell into an atrium**
The Santa Fé or Railway Exchange Building, Chicago by Dan Burnham and Partners, 1903. Conversion proposals by Murphy/Jahn, 1981. The court, originally roofed at third floor, is now to be covered at the top

Courtyards into atria

Two British reconstruction projects illustrate the possibilities of turning old courtyards into atria.

A triangular block development of 1831–5 by John Nash is located on London's Strand. Houses and shops stood along its three street frontages behind unified façades. Service and light courts filled the centre of the block, which was also crossed by a shopping arcade, the Lowther Arcade of 1835, one of the earliest of these eastern imports. In 1904 the arcade and portions of the frontage were demolished and replaced by Coutts Bank. In 1969 road proposals threatened the whole block and Sir Frederick Gibberd proposed a new block in the form of a triangular atrium building straddling the new road. The road proposal died and the pressure to retain the Regency facades proved irresistible. Gibberd's solution was to build the new bank behind the existing Nash frontages, but with the atrium banking-hall he had designed for the new block. It was finished in 1978 and was Britain's first example of the new concept.

Jesse Hartley, the dock engineer and Philip Hardwick, the architect, completed the iron and brick Albert Dock, Liverpool in 1848. Massive flat classical frontages to the dock contrast with more vernacular indented elevations to the roadside. The inset courts were for secure loading and unloading of goods. In 1900 the court of one block was infilled with handling equipment for cold-store use. The 1978 scheme (not yet realised) by Building Design Partnership to convert part of the Dock into the Merseyside Maritime Museum, envisaged making the court into an atrium. Glazed in, the court would provide spectacular circulation with vistas over the City and Port of Liverpool, and space for tall exhibits.

View of top of atrium

View of ground floor of atrium; the original roof frame is retained as a pergola

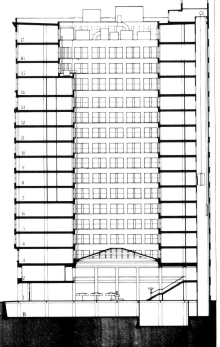
Section before

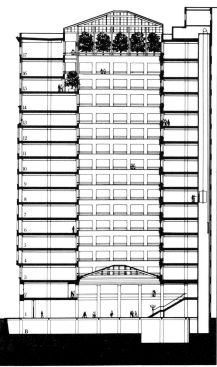
Section after

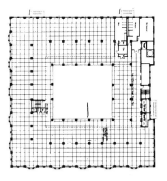

53a **Butler Square, Minneapolis.** A 200 feet deep heroic-scale timber warehouse, converted successfully by hollowing out two atria inside it. The upper floors are offices, the lower two retail

53b The hotel shown on the plan and section is now carried out as offices, 1974–81

53a

53b

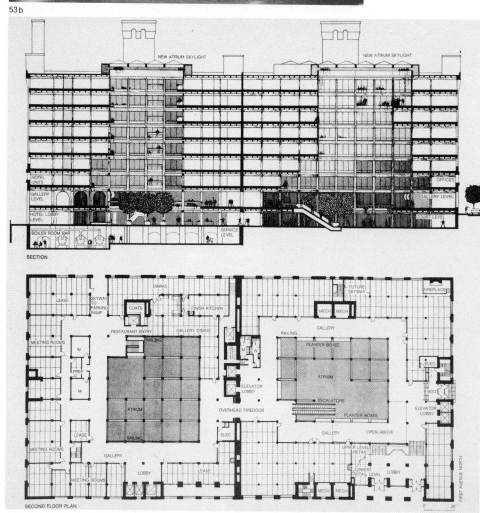

SECTION

SECOND FLOOR PLAN

54 **Central court of the Mercantile warehouse building** in Boston, Massachussetts, where John Sherratt and Associates have converted a cross-wall warehouse into apartments over shopping

Hollowed-out buildings

The Butler warehouse in Minneapolis, built in 1906 by Harry Wild Jones, was one of the firm's many huge repository buildings near the centres of United States cities. Over half a million square feet in nine deep-planned storeys, the structure is all timber apart from the outer walls. Massive Douglas fir framing tapers from 22-inch square columns at the basement to eight-inch at the top floor level. Miller, Hanson, Westerbeck, Bell were architects for the reconstructions done for developer Charles Coyer. Divided into two compartments by a brick wall, the plan was to convert one half into offices and shops, and the other later into an hotel. The first half was finished in 1974 and the rest was also converted into offices by 1981. To get more acceptable plan depths for smaller office suites the great fir frame was hollowed out bodily and the roof made into a skylight. Parts of the centre frame are left behind spacially recalling a Piranesian prison. The character achieved is unique and delightful, and, after initial slow letting in the recession of 1974, the project has proved successful.

The Mercantile Building in Boston was a 100-feet wide, 600-feet long granite and brick warehouse on seven levels. Situated on the waterfront near Faneuil Hall Market it was cut back in length to let the freeway pass, and found itself in a neighbourhood rapidly becoming residential. The block had closely spaced cross walls and excessive depth for

housing. Yet its good character and state of preservation argued for conservation. John Sherrat and Associates won a competition in 1972 for its conversion by the hollowing out of the centre. A 25-foot slice has been cut along the centre-line and sky-lit. Galleries on each side give access to apartments on the upper six floors. Retailers use the street level, and the public can have coffee in a garden-court at the base of the atrium.

The Museum of Natural History and Science, opened in 1977, was created in Louisville, Kentucky, by re-using a set of 1878 warehouses on Main Street. Louis and Henry, the architects for the conversion, incorporated the sturdy, straightforward floors of the warehouses for display. But in order to give the place life and a special character an atrium was introduced. This is not in the centre, to bring light, but at the entrance. The bays immediately behind the old stone façade have been stripped of floors, leaving the frame exposed and the elevation standing like a cut-out. The street paving passes through into this space, in which stand the new entrance, elevators and stairs.

54

55 Charles Englehard Court,
Metropolitan Museum, New York City
by Roche and Dinkeloo, 1980. This is
one of several uses of the atrium at
the museum and connects
extensions whilst retaining old
facades

Sensitive extensions

Often it is necessary to extend an old building and there is great risk that its character and balance will be damaged in the process: important façades could be lost; lighting the interior of existing and extension elements can often be difficult. The question arises: need the new and old elements link in the conventional way?

Two projects demonstrate what can be done. The Metropolitan Museum, New York, planned to extend its American wing. A reconstructed federal period house already existed as an exhibition and museum space. It stood clear of the museum to the north. Architects Roche and Dinkeloo achieved the extension in a remarkable way. The new wing, displaying art, artifacts and interiors, wraps around three sides of the old house, leaving only its fine street façade visible. A large sky-lit court has then been created to link the wing back to the main museum. The Charles Englehard Court, completed in 1980, is a restful garden containing exhibit galleries. Louis Tiffany's house façade has been placed in the wall opposite the federal period house, on its axis, to help create a formal garden. The court acts as visitor centre for the new wing, with bookstall and guides working in a discreet corner.

Chicago's Board of Trade building is one of the city's Art-Deco landmarks. It stands at the end of La Salle Street, a rare closed vista in the city, and soars in set-backs to the statue of Circe on its pyramidal crest. The Board of Trade is the centre of food trading for the world's biggest market. As the trade in wheat, soya and meat has grown, the space on the trading-floor and in brokers' offices has decreased. The Board purchased the rest of the block to extend the building. Murphy/Jahn produced a scheme, completed in 1981, which compliments rather than damages the Deco tower by placing an atrium between old and new.

55

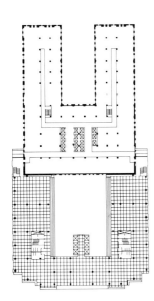

56 **The Board of Trade Building,
Chicago**
Extension by Murphy/Jahn, 1982,
showing the retention of the existing
facade in the new atrium

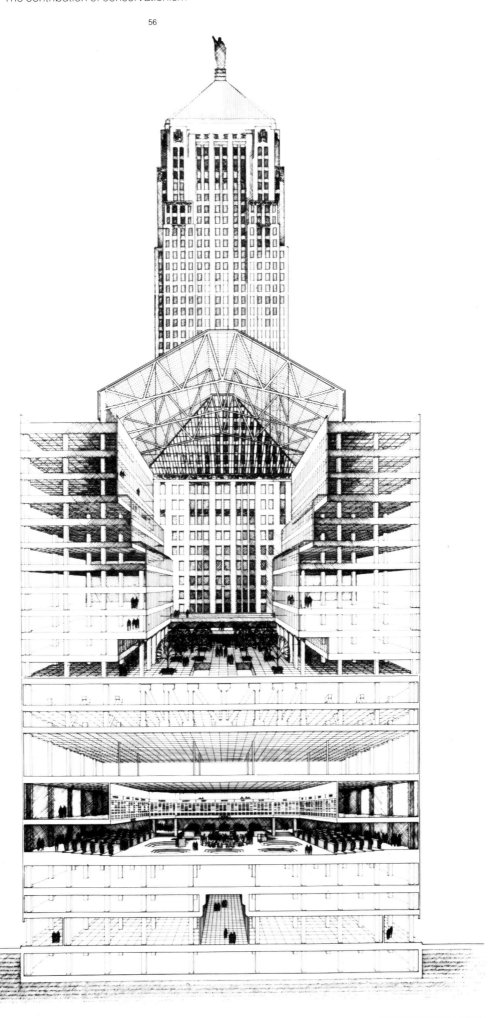

Markets into atria

Redundant market and exchange buildings are a particular problem if their preservation is desired. They are large volumes, often with overlooking office or gallery space, hard to heat and impossible to sub-divide. As prime, useful spaces they could not work. But reconsidered as voids between or around useful spaces they can find a use.

When the Greater London Council proposed to convert the redundant Covent Garden Market into a speciality shopping centre, they first intended to restore it to its original state: three long blocks with open courts between them, rather like Boston's Faneuil Hall Market.

'Keep the roofs,' said the local population, more concerned with comfort and practicality than with historical purity, and they have been proved right. The iron and glass roofs, added in 1874 and 1889, convert the broad spaces between the brick blocks into atria. Although they are not sealed against the weather, the courts are sheltered, and attract thousands to stand and stare, eat or browse, or listen to buskers. The floors of the courts have been opened up to give access to the basements used for additional shops, reinforcing the vertical emphasis given by the soaring roofs. Whilst the space under the roofs earns hardly any rent, it is the key to the earning power of the shops in the three wings and the basement.

57 **Covent Garden Market, London,** converted into a speciality shopping centre by the Greater London Council in 1980. Its atrium spaces make it a focus for street life

57

Manchester's Royal Exchange was the biggest room in the world in its late-Victorian heyday. A cotton exchange, the vast room was built like a Roman bath with huge domes supported on massive piers. The great room was suspended in a multi-purpose building with two floors of shopping below it and offices all around. Abandoned by a declining trade in 1970 the exchange floor was used in 1973 as the site of a temporary festival theatre. This was successful, and the idea was born of siting a new theatre inside the room. By this reversal of concepts—seeing the room as a void rather than as an unusable 'solid'—an asset has been created. Less than one-tenth of the total volume is taken up by the striking theatre. It hovers like a lunar module with its supports buried in the old piers. The atrium now forms a huge foyer, restaurant, exhibition and craft-trade space. Architects Levitt and Bernstein and stage designer Richard Negri conceived it, and its impact has been continuous since 1977. The city has gained not only a theatre but the public room that an atrium can offer.

58

58 Royal Exchange, Manchester, England
The cotton exchange has been converted to a theatre foyer and multi-purpose space, overlooked by offices and a restaurant. The theatre is a 'hightech' module on the old trading floor. Levitt, Bernstein, 1977

59 **Study for the redevelopment of the
Rotebühlplatz,** Stuttgart, Germany,
by Rob Krier, 1974. Krier is one of
many designers who have
rediscovered the value of the
European urban design tradition

59

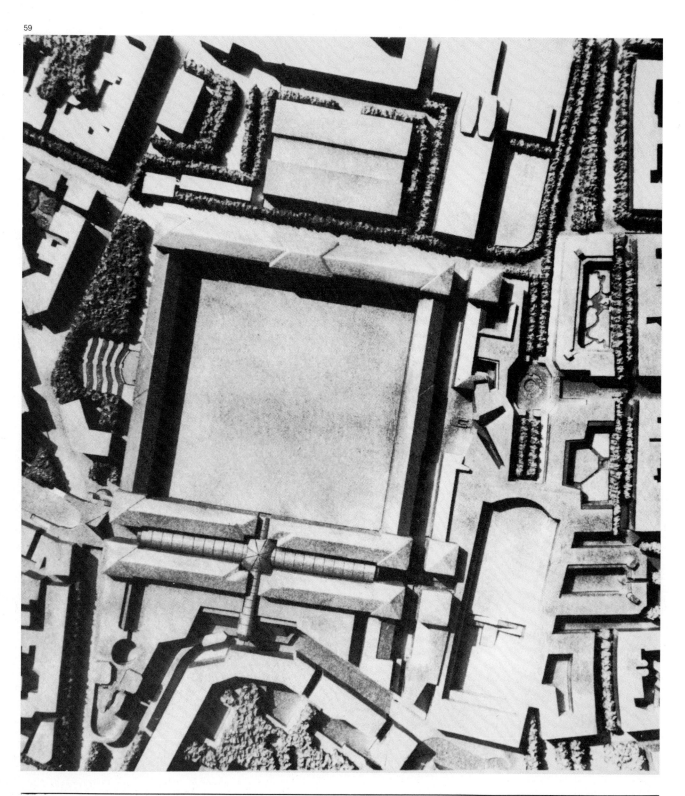

6 The urban design factor

60 **Paris, old and new.** The enclosure, harmony and comfort of nineteenth-century Paris (background) is rejected at La Defense in favour of exposure, disharmony and discomfort

The urban disaster

Modern development has been a disaster for the characters of most established western cities. The well-defined streets and squares and the rich variety of routes criss-crossing the centre are attacked. New buildings disregard street lines and the enclosure of space, leaving a hotchpotch of disparate elements. Towers and slabs reach up and channel strong winds into the excessive spaces left at their feet. The towers challenge established landmarks, disregarding their symbolic value. Major developments take whole blocks or even several blocks, closing all pedestrian routes through them. All this has happened in a period when most cities have had unprecedented control over their own development.

It is fashionable to blame the theories of the early modern architects and planners for this. Corbusier, Gropius, Hilberseimer and others were reacting against the gloomy, congested, smoky city of the early twentieth century when they called for sun, space and greenery to be brought into everyone's lives. They were not suburbanists like Frank Lloyd Wright or the Garden City movement; they wanted to maintain big cities with high densities. Their answer was to set skyscrapers in parkland; they had no time for the street and its culture. They also had no time for the past - all must be swept away to create a brave new world.

In practice in the real world outside their studios, fragments of the idea were applied by modest talents. There was inherently no scope for dialogue between the traditional city and the Corbusian ideal. In cities already densely developed the idea of the free-standing tower was applied to terrible effect. New York's 1916 zoning laws, which led to the consistent, zigguratic city which existed until the end of the Second World War, were modified to allow the introduction of the new amenity plazas. The skyline has been impoverished and the amenity is usually useless - a gloomy and windswept interruption to a formerly strong street. Oppression rather than relief is the result.

For the buildings themselves the ideas also failed. In pursuit of more light and air, buildings rose at optimum angles and with optimum plan shapes. Rules were devised to protect their access to light, and they used huge windows to devour it. For commercial building this was nonsensical. The windows soaked the building in glare and solar heat, and robbed it of the mass to control its temperature. For lighting they were counter-productive: the glare had to be combated by leaving all lights on and applying reflective film to the glass. For air they were useless: windows cannot be opened in tall buildings without unacceptable draught and heat-loss. The whole aesthetic became one of symbolic rather than actual amenity.

60

61a **Land use and built form studies** at Cambridge University looked at the properties of the Fresnel Square. The square is divided into concentric bands of decreasing width outwards. All bands are however of equal area and equal to the area of the central square. The eye finds this hard to perceive; it sees a quadrangle as of apparently greater area than an equal area of pavement around a building

Efficient land use

The first signs of constructive reaction came in that significant period for the atrium, the mid-1960s. Whilst Portman was designing the first Regency Hyatt and St John Wilson the Liverpool Civic Centre, Wilson's colleagues at Cambridge University were making some interesting studies. Professor Sir Leslie Martin and Lionel March published Land Use and Built Form in April 1966 (Cambridge University Press). It set out the relative efficiency of courtyard forms of development compared to tower and slab forms. Using the example of a Fresnel square where each ring is equal in area to the others they demonstrated clearly that land and energy had been wasted in piling up space set back from plot boundaries. The same floor-space could be delivered in relatively low buildings by arranging them around the perimeter of a site. The question of western thought - the free standing solid pavilion or tower - versus eastern - the hollow court - was resolved as a case of mathematical alternatives.

It is a fact of perception that the eye cannot read the rings on a Fresnel square as equal. A quadrangle lawn such as that in a Cambridge college cannot be conceived of as being perhaps no larger in area than the footpath around the outside of the college. The generous set-backs, verges and plazas of the mid-century town-planner were shown to be the mathematical complement to high building: build on the verges and you would have generous courts in return, and lower buildings as well. The thesis amounted to a posthumous vindication of the form of development supplanted by the Ville Radieuse: street-following frontages could deliver space, sunlight and greenery, just as well as towers, and with less expense and discomfort.

The 'land use and built form' theory allowed the reaction in Britain and Europe against high-rise to blossom for housing and city-centre development. The designers who made first use of it for large sites were also the ones to see its potentiality on a tighter scale for atria. Frederick Gibberd built Arundel Great Court in London of six storeys where previously he would have had 15-storey towers. Gibberd then went on to the Coutts building on the Strand. Richard MacCormac laid out public housing on a grand scale at Newport, South Wales, and then developed the multi-atrium office building concept as an urban design and energy-conservation device.

61 a

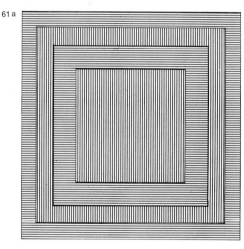

61b The two sites have the same built volume on them. The tower stands on one quarter of the site, leaving three quarters open. The court form building does the opposite and is only one third as tall

61 b

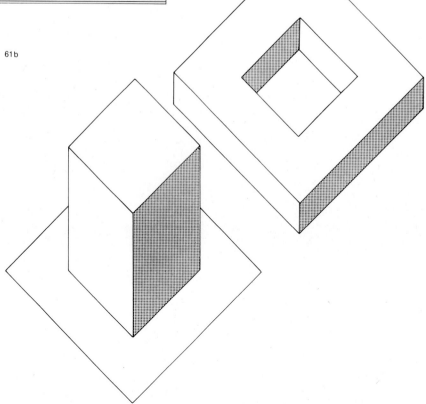

62 **The National Gallery of Art, Washington DC**
    East Building by I M Pei, 1978

Using difficult sites

It is the ability of atrium buildings to deal with complex and unusual site shapes which makes them so useful in urban design.

Washington DC provides good examples. The city has a strict height limit for building – 130 feet on avenues 110 feet wide, and 110 feet on streets 90 feet wide. This rule, enacted in 1910, allows all buildings to be served by fire-fighting ladders, and protects views of the Capitol as the dominant building. Density ratios of 10:1 mean that most buildings are of 12 or 13 storeys, and that they fill the site and follow the frontage. In this unusual (for the United States) straight-jacket, it is hard to deal with the awkward sites created by the l'Enfant plan: its radial avenues crossing gridded streets produce many wedge-shaped areas.

A key site was the wedge between the Mall, Pennsylvania Avenue and 4th Street. Earmarked for an extension to the National Gallery of Art, the new building had the urban-design task of relating to the present gallery, aligning with the Mall, and acting as the last definer of the processional route of Pennsylvania Avenue before it enters the influence of the Capitol itself. An atrium allows the shape to be used, but that is not enough here. The overall site shape is too graceless to produce a strong building form. I M Pei resolved the problem of the building, completed in 1978, by shearing the site in two, creating two sharp triangles which heighten the sharpness of the convergence of the two avenues. In one triangle he placed the galleries; in the other a study centre. The atrium becomes an isosceles triangles bridging between them. The dramatic result and vistas of the city which the building creates make it a masterpiece.

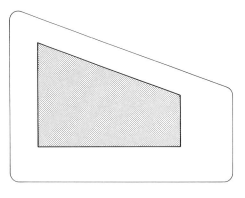

a The site defined by street lines is a characterless wedge

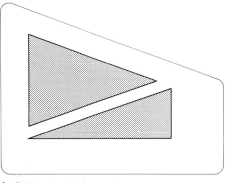

b Pei's inspired stroke was to cleave the trapezoid in two, using the axis of the 1941 West Building as his guide. The larger triangle houses the gallery, the lesser the study centre

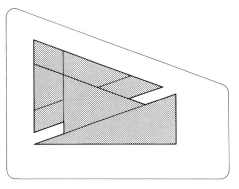

c They are united by overlaying a third triangle, the atrium court

62

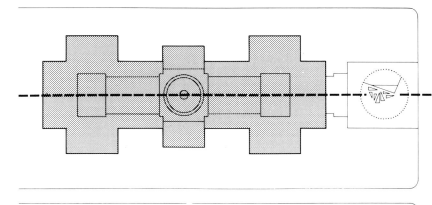

d The completed composition, both stable and dynamic

63

63 **Aerial view of the East Building** with the Capitol beyond

64 **Plan of Embarcadero Center, San Francisco,** California, by John Portman and Associates. The Hyatt Hotel, lower right, sits on the point where the street grid changes direction, skilfully resolving it

64

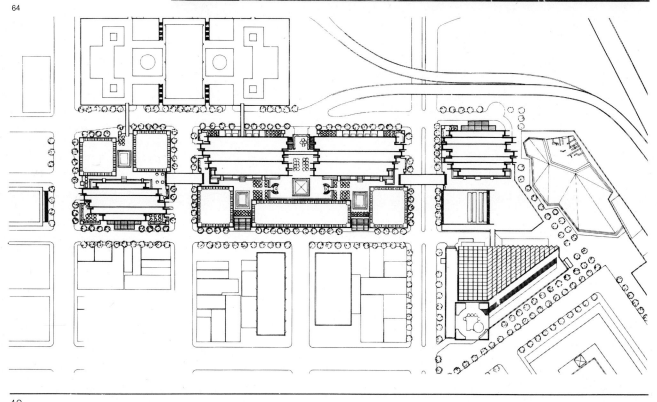

65 **IDS Centre, Minneapolis,**
Johnson/Burgee 1972–5. Section
and plan at skyway level.
See also illustration 3

Also in Washington the International
Monetary Fund headquarters, by Vincent
Kling (1973), demonstrates the atrium's ability
to humanize the thick masses of masonry
which the height limit has created. The
building had to accommodate high-status
staff, the majority of whom rated individual,
perimeter offices. On a full block, the IMF
headquarters could use perimeter planning
concepts, although it still gives up one third of
its permissible floor-space to the central
court. Space is however created which is
shallow enough for individual offices. The
'inlook' into the court is, if anything, more
pleasant than the street view.

In San Francisco the collision between two
street grid patterns creates a string of
triangular sites on Market Street. Most of
these are now filled by 'tower and plaza'

developments, creating a ragged north side to
the street. At its waterfront end John Portman
has put a firm containment on Market Street
with the vertical wall of his Embarcadero
Hyatt Hotel (1974). It is part of the
Embarcadero Center which, however, stands
in the other grid system. Portman resolved
the geometry by using the atrium. Like Pei, he
took it further than just arranging space
around a triangular court. Keeping two sides
vertical, he collapsed the third into a gigantic
lean-to. The cavernous interior is unique and
attracts thousands to use it as a rendezvous.

Places for people

Apart from efficient land use and the
incorporation of awkward sites, atrium
buildings are major elements in urban design
in that they add to the pedestrian space of the
city. They can be routes and destinations,
truly urban spaces. As routes they can
provide mid-block passages and cut-offs,
reviving the intricacy of the older city. They
can also allow and stimulate the development
of pedestrian routes above or below street
level.

In Minneapolis the walkway system is one
level above ground. The 'skyway' system now
links 10 key blocks in the town centre.
providing a winter-proof pedestrian
environment. Major stores, office buildings
and parking garages are connected. The
connected blocks lie each side of Nicolett
Mall, a landscaped street now used only by
buses, and by pedestrians when the weather
is suitable. Dominating Nicolett Mall is the IDS
Center by Philip Johnson and John Burgee
(1975). The IDS Center has the best public
atrium, Crystal Court, built to date. It is a true
piazza: it attracts and holds people by its very
nature. They promenade, people-watch, eat
and shop, as well as move through from place
to place. It is the Minneapolis town square,
and much more effective than its outdoor
alternative could ever be. The reason is not
just the severe climate—although this is what
gave Minneapolis the first indoor shopping
mall and a major turn-of-the-century atrium
building—but, the traffic-free, multi-level
space is more useful and theatrical than
anything since the Italian hill-towns created
the piazza idea.

In Houston, Texas, a movement system is
developing rapidly, this time at a level below
the street. This, in a city without zoning laws,
is less disruptive to the appearance of new
buildings though the routes are inherently
less attractive. Several buildings have atria
which open as far down as the pedestrian
movement level and provide visual relief.
Here, Johnson and Burgee have built Penzoil
Place (1976), a twin-tower office complex with
triangular tent-like atria between the bases of
the towers. The street floor opens to the
basement level. An office tower by Joint
Venture Architects, 1100 Milam Street,
embraces the sidewalk and underground
level. The building's skin is pulled away from
the tower at the fourth level and stretched to
the kerb-line all around. The public pass
through this air-conditioned skirt freely.

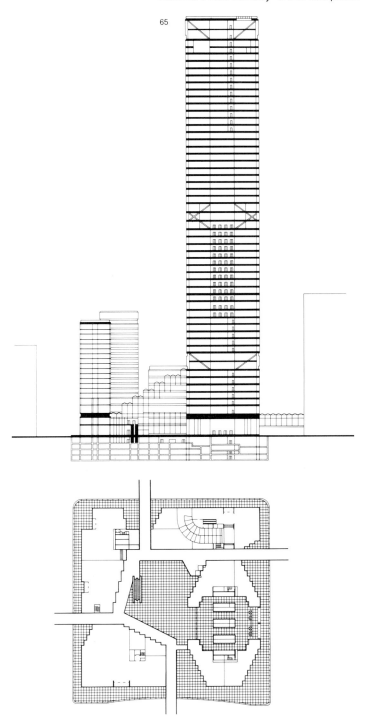

65

66 **Civic Center, Scarborough, Ontario,** Raymond Moriyama 1976. The town square inside the town hall

67 **The indoor equivalent of nearby Paley Park,** the Market at Citicorp, New York. Hugh Stubbins, 1978. *See 167 for plan and section*

68 **Atrium lobby at Pennzoil Place, Houston,** by Johnson/Burgee, 1976; a cool oasis

The enormous Eaton Center in Toronto acts as an urban movement system in itself. This galleria centre is parallel to Yonge Street and has subway access. Designed by Bregman and Hamman with Ebehard Ziedler, it was completed in 1979. Its cathedral-like space runs between offices and parking levels above four levels of shopping. Other atrium buildings are rising nearby. The Parkin Partnership's Bell Canada complex is split in two and reconnected by a bridging atrium. The vista through the glass bridge directs the eye to Trinity Church and an entrance to the Eaton Center.

As public places in their own right, and not as elements in movement systems, several splendid examples of atrium buildings exist.

The Civic Center for Scarborough, Ontario, by Raymond Moriyama (1976) achieves what Colin St John Wilson planned for Liverpool. Open decks of offices are accessed by the public from a central atrium. The central space here is circular and open for one quarter of its circumference to a park outside.

Together these spaces work as a civic focus for ceremonies ranging from weddings to political events. The atrium at Citicorp in midtown New York, is like a small park. Completed by Hugh Stubbins and Emery Roth in 1978, a vast tower floats on its core and four columns over the centre of the site. To one side is an outdoor plaza with a wedge-shaped church fitting under the tower base. To the other is a seven-level courtyard building embracing the tower. In the lower two levels, subway and ground, are speciality food shops ringing a landscaped patio and gallery; on the tiled floors are wire tables and chairs ready for any stroller or prospective customer to settle down. It is an up-market fast-food centre and is a success in commercial and urban terms.

Mention should also be made here of a remarkable conversion atrium at the Chemical Bank building on Park Avenue, New York. The bank have added a glasshouse-style podium atrium to enclose a former draughty plaza at the base of their tower block. It was designed by Haines, Lundberg, Waehler and completed in 1981.

The threat of introversion
Atria can do more harm than good in the urban environment when they are designed to be completely introspective, with blank street frontages. Many poor examples exist, by Portman, Caudill Rowlett and Scott, (CRS), Skidmore, Owings and Merrill (SOM) and other designers, who have handled the idea better elsewhere. It may be pragmatic to recognize streets as intended for cars and undesirables only, but it also makes that condemnation self-fulfilling.

66

67

68

69

69 **Eaton Center, Toronto,** the
apotheosis of the Galleria concept,
the street as a people's cathedral.
Bregmann and Hamman/Zeidler
Partnership 1977–79.
*See also the photograph on the
jacket of this book*

Site plan and section of Eaton
Center. The city flows through it on
several levels

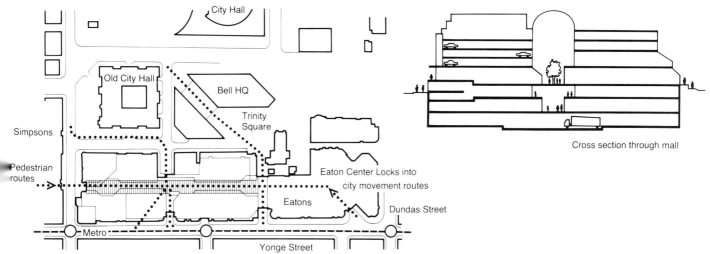

City Hall

Old City Hall

Bell HQ

Trinity
Square

Simpsons

Pedestrian
routes

Eatons

Eaton Center Locks into
city movement routes

Dundas Street

Metro

Yonge Street

Cross section through mall

70 **Kaufmannshaus, Hamburg, Germany,** where a series of atrium or arcade buildings has appeared in one part of the inner city in the last few years. A sheltered street life is now possible and economic revival has resulted

Atria as urban renewal catalysts

Most of the projects mentioned in the previous section have had a dramatic effect on the city centres in which they were built. Since Gruen's Midtown Plaza in Rochester in the 1950s, the idea of using a single project to spark off general city-centre revitalization has been proved workable. The IDS Center was the making of Minneapolis; the Eaton Center recreated its area of Toronto.

The major example of a city reborn in the 1960s and 1970s is Atlanta, Georgia. A combination of aggressive development of the airport (Hartfield) and airline (Delta), and the provision of stunning hotel, conference and exhibition facilities (the Peachtree and

70

Omni Centers) have changed the city's image. Atlanta now ranks third in the United States convention business and attracts new company headquarters continually.

The Peachtree Center was John Portman's vision. His Merchandise Mart started the whole enterprise in 1961. In the following 20 years six city blocks have become connected and animated by a complex pattern of functions and public spaces. It is arguable that the quality of the public spaces created has determined the success of Peachtree Center. Portman aimed far higher than conventional developers before him, and created unique environments: major and minor public atria now connect via pleasant indoor and outdoor routes. From the start Portman saw his atria as city squares, with fountains, sculptures and cafés overlooked by meeting-rooms and living spaces, in this case, hotel bedrooms. The only criticism must be the ambivalence towards the city-street frontages. Most commercial life is engulfed by the interior world, leaving the streets for service functions rather than human ones.

When Portman had set the standard at this altogether higher level than was usual for commercial development, the competition had to respond in kind. Several major complexes have resulted: the Omni Center by Thompson, Ventulett, Stainback (1976), with its arenas, convention facilities, hotels and offices, is centred on a three-acre bridging atrium, the largest yet built, and one which over-reached itself in many ways; and Peachtree Summit, by Toombs, Amisano and Wells (1977), is a cluster of triangular towers with linked lobbies of atrium scale. These two isolated developments await the completion of the MARTA rapid transit to tie them back to the city and encourage the building up of the voids around them.

The use-mixing ability of atria as urban renewal catalysts does not operate only at the mega-scale of Atlanta. By employing them at the smallest workable scale it is possible to generate intricate, ground-covering development for multiple use. Richard MacCormac demonstrated this in a study done in 1980 for a site in East London. The Spitalfields Study is based on the 'courtyard array' concept developed by the Cambridge University Land Use and Built Form Research Group. Court size is minimal, sufficient to light conventional depth floor-space in a four- or five-storey development. The site thus takes three rows of atria in its depth. The central ones are connected to form a mall, and the outer rows are for more private or communal uses. Commercial space in the lower layers is topped by a 'crust' of housing, particularly on the southern flank. The whole development is likened by MacCormac to the Venetian pedestrian network away from the canals, in this case the bounding traffic streets. A large surface area is provided for the public and for enterprises to interact in a compact and congenial environment. A volume of adaptable space is stacked close to the ground for sub-division and use by the wide variety of activities for which the area is noted.

The urban design factor

71 **Multiple atria in mixed use**
A 1980 study by Richard MacCormac for a large site in Spitalfields, east London. The plan and section show how buildings mass around an array of many courts which are linked at street level into routes.

72 **The Winter Garden, Niagara Falls,** New York, by Cesar Pelli; an atrium waiting for its surrounding building

This mini-atrium approach makes many small, leftover sites usable. Its ability to light space from inside the block overcomes the lack of light on boundary lines which limits many city sites.

A radical use of the atrium to create development is in Niagara Falls, New York. Following the principle of Victorian developers who laid out a park and then sold frontage plots, Caesar Pelli has created a lush Winter Garden on redevelopment land: the great greenhouse is designed to attract and accept buildings which would plug into its flanks. Eventually it will be a typical atrium, but with mixed ownership and styles of buildings around it. Here is a city really using its civic role to improve the public domain.

In the atrium concept there is therefore a powerful urban design tool. The attrition of character in established cities can be reversed. People-centred environments of surpassing attractiveness can be created which can set in train the revival of city centres. Those centres will survive only on their social and cultural attraction: mere utility does not justify them in the electronic age. They are needed as civilizing elements, to draw inhabitants out of their wired-up hermitages. They must therefore be supremely civilized.

71
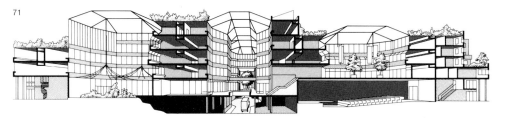

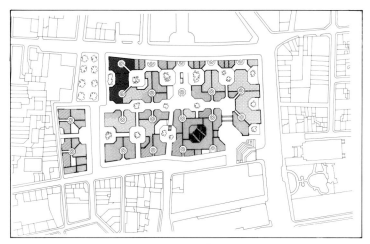
72

53

7 Energy and atria

In dealing with the energy implications of atria two of the four functions listed are discussed: shelter and economy. The quality of comfort enjoyed in the built environment is a function of its cost. That cost is in part capital, but is increasingly an operating expense. The degree to which comfort depends on consuming non-renewable fuel resources is disturbing; reducing this vulnerability is one of the major challenges of the next several decades. Atrium building is one of the strategies for getting more comfort for less energy-cost.

Coming in from the cold (or from the heat)

Because cities have usually been composed of discrete buildings put up by private- or state-owners, the public domain has been the 'leftovers', the outdoors. Cities first appeared in the benign climate of the Mediterranean where the model of open streets and squares separating buildings became established. The public spaces usually were as comfortable as the buildings, which existed largely only for privacy and security. Public life was lived in the open, with shade from a colonnade around the agora. As the expanding world population moved into hotter, colder or wetter latitudes it scarcely modified its approach to creating shelter. The public domain just became less comfortable and even uninhabitable. Some cultures used arcades and canopies to shelter people from sun, rain and snow. Others used planting to shade and cool streets. The rapidly built cities of the industrial revolution did neither, and

suffered. Only in the Islamic world was there a method for merging the 'solids' of buildings with the 'voids' of streets to create a comfortable city.

Buckminster Fuller has compared the traditional western city with the radiator of an engine: a vast, reticulated surface designed to maximize the rate of heat transfer. The citizens pay to put heat in or pump it out of their own little projection of the city surface, condemned to this expensive behaviour by their economic and political systems. As they act independently, their shelters must be self-contained and detached from each other. It is within this context that arcades appeared in the nineteenth century: both sides belonged to one developer. Anything else, such as Fuller's city-covering domes, could only come from an all-powerful state.

A glimpse of ways forward has come from the most extreme climates man has chosen to inhabit. The sub-arctic communities of Scandinavia have developed very economical methods of heating and insulation. They have also looked at enclosing whole sections of towns. Ralph Erskine's schemes are of particular interest (see Architectural Design, May 1960). It is no accident that Minneapolis has atrium buildings: it has the coldest, snowiest winters of any big city in the United States. At the hot end of the spectrum the cities of Atlanta and Houston were the first to try out air-conditioned covered space. In 1960 Houston first roofed a stadium, the Astrodome.

With the roofing of spaces between buildings came the revelation not only that more comfortable 'outdoor' spaces were created, but that the cost of keeping comfortable inside the adjacent buildings fell dramatically. A study by Hastings and Ruberg (Progressive Architecture, April 1980, p. 114) of the effects of putting glass canopies across existing streets found that the street canopy cut adjacent building heat-losses by 57 per cent. The canopy let the building frontages and street pavements store solar heat in winter, and acted as a draught lobby, cutting air heat-loss from movements in and out of the buildings. In summer the shading effect was valuable, with induced air movement if ventilators in the canopy were opened.

74

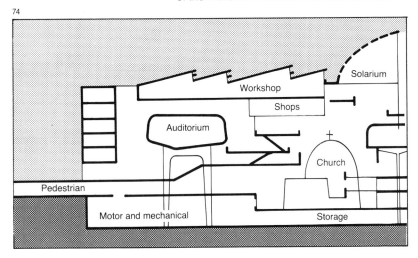

75 Buffer thinking
Illustrations from the Guardian
newspaper 'Community of tomorrow'
competition winner, by Terry Farrell,
Ralph Lebens and David Clarke

75

1 ENERGY CONSCIOUS DESIGN: Should have as its starting point THERMAL COMFORT

a) PRINCIPLES OF HEAT LOSS

b) THE PROBLEM: In a poorly insulated building: No convection loss but still DISCOMFORT

c) THE SOLUTION: Ideal room temperature at 17°C with efficient insulation (using BUFFER ZONES) will provide a comfortable THERMAL ENVIRONMENT

Thermostat can be set this low and comfort achieved.

2 DESIGNING WITH THE CLIMATE MEANS Maximizing the benefits of wind and sun

a) Sun
b) Wind

Use winter sun to heat house & domestic hot water

Summer sun heats domestic water and creates solar chimney

BUFFER THINKING means using shape of building, landform and trees to provide sheltered areas

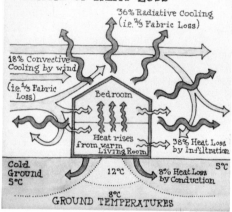

3 THE INEFFICIENT HOUSE: PATHS OF HEAT LOSS

36% Radiative Cooling (i.e. ⅔ Fabric Loss)

18% Convective Cooling by wind (i.e. ⅓ Fabric Loss)

Bedroom

Heat rises from warm Living Room

38% Heat Loss by Infiltration

Cold Ground 5°C

8% Heat Loss by Conduction

GROUND TEMPERATURES

4 THE ENERGY EFFICIENT HOUSE

BUFFER THINKING means: Trapping air and using its good insulating properties to reduce heat loss from building.

Winds

Living Room

BUFFER ZONE

Bedroom

Air in buffer heated to reduce heat loss

Perimeter insulation assists in stabilizing ground temp.

Sit house ½ in ground to gain from constant ground temperature

well insulated walls

SOLAR CHIMNEY

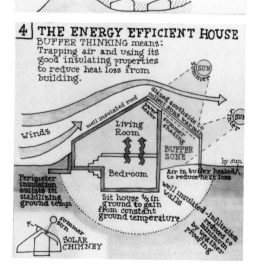

5 TYPICAL 5-PERSON HOUSE

UPPER LEVEL   LOWER

SECTION

North

89·5 m² Parker Morris standard. cost = £150/m²

Saving of 11·2 m² on Parker Morris

Saving allows a 33m² buffer zone @ £50/m² to give same total cost as Parker Morris but 22 m² additional space

Developments in material science have produced: the low cost twin-wall extruded polycarbonate which can be used to provide cheap buffer zone space, Enormous developments in glass technology to control heat losses and other improved properties.

6 BUFFER HOUSING

Gently curved terraces by varying hollow/storage party walls

Buffer Zone of trees and built up land

Various temperatures in protected zones

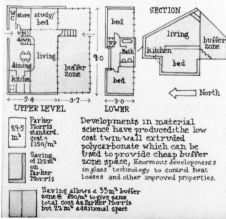

7 BUFFER THINKING TO DEVELOP WORK SPACES Broad views & access to surrounding countryside are not essential to work spaces, so they are partially sunken to increase visual amenities for housing and reduce heating & cooling loads on work areas.

OFFICE SPACES where the buffer is the core space which also provides visual and leisure amenities.

Summer sun can be blocked

Winter

North wind

built up land form

offices   buffer amenity space

MANUFACTURING SPACES where the buffers are the ancillary offices stores and amenities

amenity spaces & stores

delivery access at intervals   FACTORY   offices or stores

8 BUFFER THINKING TO DEVELOP NEW KINDS OF COMMUNITY SPACES Public capital is used to provide buffer zones between schools, shops and small offices. These would be covered over to produce an arcade and sheltered village squares.

green house florist

Wind buffer zone provided by shops

Covered arcade portions can be opened up to direct sunlight

South Buffer Greenhouses, florists schools, restaurants etc. Portions of South Buffer removed to allow access to air and direct sun.

Buffer thinking

What the 'street canopy' or any other covered area outside the fully habitable space achieves is a buffer effect. The full force of external climate—air temperature, radiation, wind and water—no longer falls on the membrane protecting the occupants. Its main force is dissipated on the buffer surface.

Terry Farrell and Ralph Lebens, British architect and engineer respectively, have pulled together all aspects of the effect into a thesis they call 'buffer thinking'. The winning entry in a 1980 Guardian newspaper competition to describe the community of tomorrow, Farrell and Lebens' thesis suggested how effective buffering could be, and in how many ways such control could be achieved. They illustrate the results of planning to use shelter from earth and landscape, passive solar gain, and the air-entraining virtues of glazed buffer spaces: wherever possible buildings are oriented with long sides north and south; polar sides are buried in the earth or sheltered by planted mounds; solar sides have conservatory buffer zones outside the fully habitable space; and double-banked accommodation is achieved each side of sun-scooping arcades, or around atria.

The energy economy of buffer spaces is only fully achieved if no attempt is made to keep the spaces themselves comfortable all year round. They are lightly constructed and are colder in winter, hotter in summer than the fully comfort-conditioned spaces they protect. Uses in the buffer zone need therefore to be seasonally appropriate. In winter, for example, cafés would be for use by people dressed for outdoors; in summer, resort wear would be better. Buildings with expensively heated and cooled atria are, therefore, missing the energy point.

Many recent buildings exist which use a complete double-wall concept to provide the buffer effect. Arup Associates have used the concept in Britain and in South Africa. Sir Basil Spence used it at the Scottish Widows Insurance headquarters in Edinburgh. The Hooker building at Niagara Falls, completed in 1981 by Cannon Design Inc., is the most dramatic example in the United States. Several of these designs recover solar heat from the cavity for re-use in winter, and use the space as a return-air plenum to do so. Nevertheless, it is an expensive idea: two walls cost more than one, even if both are simpler and less substantial than one alone would have been.

Farrell and Leben's illustrations show limited runs of double-walled buffer zone, used only where it can do most good. On the south side it is cost-effective. On the north side, landscape shelter is better. The atrium concept tries to use as little outer surface to buffer as much inner surface as possible. In a cube-shaped atrium with roof-glazing, the roof area buffers four times as much wall. The savings on wall-insulation and waterproofing can probably pay for the roof.

In an attempt to reduce building energy-use several countries have introduced wall-insulation standards for non-residential buildings. This is simple to administer, but can have a stifling effect on design innovation. The British Building Regulations (Part FF) do however recognize the beneficial effect of unheated buffer space. Walls do not need to have specific insulation value where they divide fully heated space from partially or completely unheated enclosed space. Unheated space does not need insulation from outside. Thus a glazed atrium or conservatory can have minimal walls between it and occupied space and be within the regulations.

75

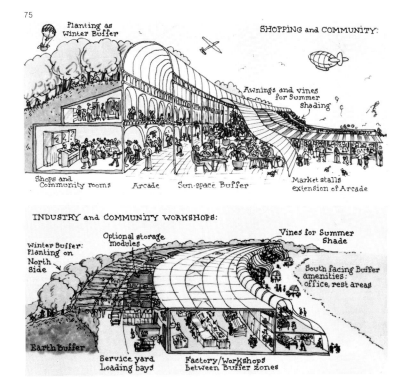

76a Three double wall designs by Arup Associates
Section, British Sugar Offices, Peterborough, England. The inner wall is part of the partitioning system and can be glazed or solid at will. Air drawn from the basement storage area ventilates the wall cavity. A cool climate solution

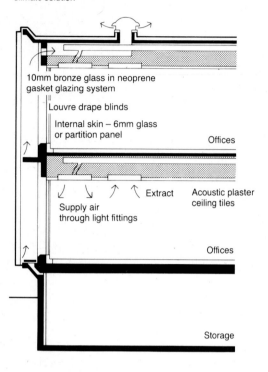

10mm bronze glass in neoprene gasket glazing system

Louvre drape blinds

Internal skin – 6mm glass or partition panel

Offices

Extract

Acoustic plaster ceiling tiles

Supply air through light fittings

Offices

Storage

76b Plan and detail, IBM building, Johannesburg. In a warm, sunny climate, an outer skin used as a heat shield. The outer skin is heat-absorbing glass, naturally ventilated to cool it

Lower typical floor

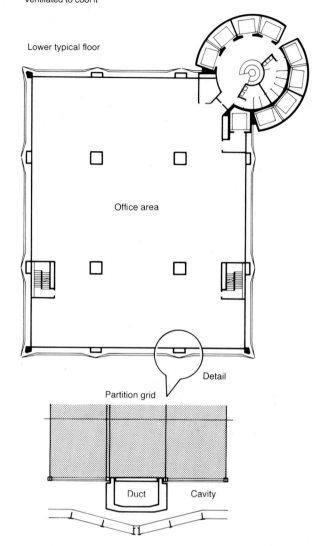

Office area

Detail

Partition grid

Duct   Cavity

76c Plan and section, office block in Farnborough, England, 1983. A double wall is used on the solar elevations only and the cavity used as a duct routeway for supply air. The outer skin is in the Pilkington Planar System of frameless, silicone-sealed glass

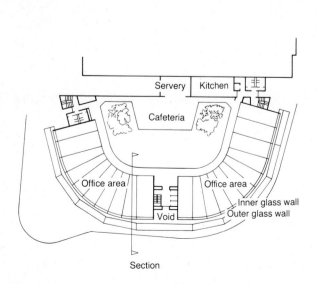

Servery   Kitchen

Cafeteria

Office area   Office area

Inner glass wall
Outer glass wall

Void

Section

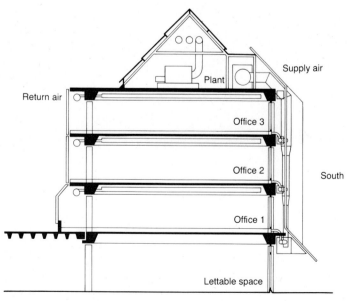

Return air

Plant

Supply air

Office 3

Office 2

South

Office 1

Lettable space

77a/b **Plan and section, Children's Hospital of Philadelphia** by Harbeson, Hough, Livingston, Larsen. The open side of the court faces south and collects largely winter sun

77c The atrium at CHOP, which is used as a restaurant and entrance hall, as well as a return-air plenum. Note the ducts below the roof

An American example of the potential is the Children's Hospital of Philadelphia (CHOP) by Harbeson, Hough, Livingston, Larson (H2L2). A U-shaped plan surrounds a south-facing atrium. Outer walls to the street are smooth, heavily insulated and minimally windowed. Walls to the atrium are light partitions, highly glazed and modelled. CHOP's defensive outer wall thus contrasts markedly with the airy interior court. The court is overlooked by play-spaces, treatment-rooms and circulation galleries. The floor of the court is used as a restaurant. CHOP uses the atrium as a return-air plenum and passive solar collector. Summer overheating is avoided by shading built into the roof and south wall, and by venting rather than recycling air from the court.

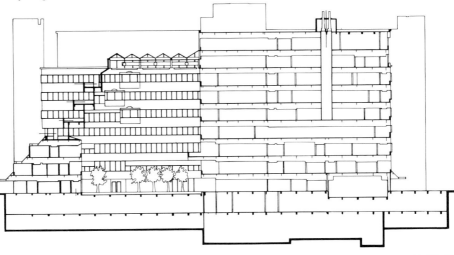

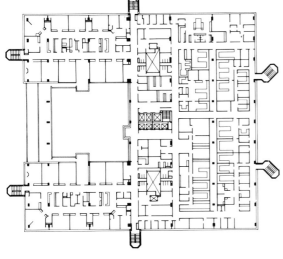

78

A splendid European example of buffer thinking is the University of Trondheim, Norway. Architect Henning Larsen completed the first phase of the campus in 1979, ten years after winning a design competition.

Three-storey blocks of accommodation stand each side of a 7.2 metres wide street running east–west. It is glazed in, as are short 'transepts' giving entrance to the street from outside. The galleria thus formed is unheated, but allows large simple windows to the buildings. Summer sun is stopped by yellow fabric blinds above those windows. Venting the roof in summer removes heat and induces breezes in the buffer zone; in winter it is warm enough for social life between classes.

Sheltered streets are created in Canada's more dispersed University of Alberta. The HUB building was built in the early 1970s. Barton Myers' design provided buffering to student flats and a social focus for them, as well as connecting other buildings together.

Passive solar design
Buffer thinking uses passive solar heat collection as one of its methods, although by no means the only one. In cloudy northern Europe the air-infiltration protection and 'tea cosy' effect of trapped air is often more important. Where sunshine hours permit, however, the atrium can be a passive solar collector of great value. CHOP uses it to collect solar warmed air.

78 **The street inside the HUB housing building,** University of Alberta, Edmonton, by Diamond and Myers

79 **University of Trondheim,** Norway, plans at ground and first floor, and cross sections. The campus can grow and retain its minimal surface and continuous shelter

79

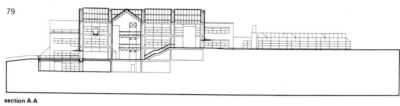

section A-A

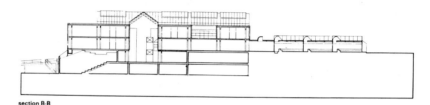

section B-B

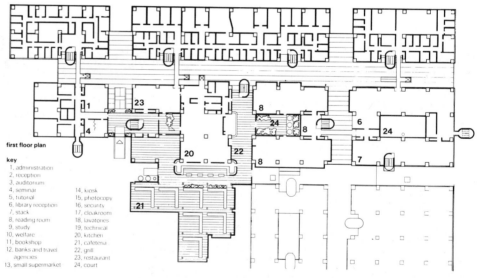

first floor plan

key
1. administration
2. reception
3. auditorium
4. seminar
5. tutorial
6. library reception
7. stack
8. reading room
9. study
10. welfare
11. bookshop
12. banks and travel agencies
13. small supermarket
14. kiosk
15. photocopy
16. security
17. cloakroom
18. lavatories
19. technical
20. kitchen
21. cafeteria
22. grill
23. restaurant
24. court

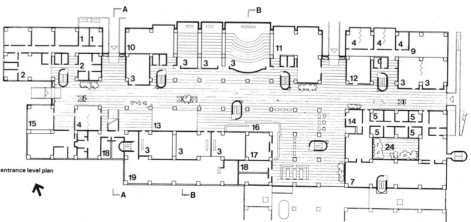

entrance level plan

80a **Section, Solar Energy Research Institute Headquarters,** Golden, Colorado. The building steps down a south-facing slope, its wings connected by linear atria

80b Model view
See 114 for details of solar courts

The Solar Energy Research Institute Headquarters (SERI) at Golden, Colorado, (projected for 1984), promises to exploit every technology available. Table Mountain Architects and Engineers (a joint venture involving CRS and Dubin Bloome Associates) have organized the plan on buffer thinking lines. The site is earth-sheltered by being on a south-facing bowl-slope. Rows of blocks run east–west, accessed and separated by linear atria. These have been dubbed 'solar courts' to avoid the connotation of luxury in a government building. The stepped blocks give the sun easy access to the south wall of each series of buildings. Various passive solar collectors—Trombe walls, phase-change salt banks, water-walls—will collect heat here

without the need for outer glass layers. Operable shutters on the outside of the glass roofs will be used to trap heat on winter nights, radiate it outwards on summer nights, and limit solar penetration on summer days.

The fans which remove smoke from the courts in any fire emergency will be run on summer nights to draw cool air through the structure.

SERI's atria are designed to be used as completely as possible to achieve all their advantages. They will provide a humanized scale, circulation routes and orientation, amenities, and contact with nature as well as energy collection and conservation.

80a
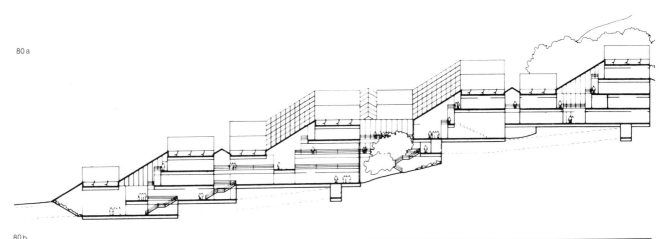

80b

81 **A concept for daylit building** form by Dean Hawkes and Richard MacCormac. Using models the authors developed a module of space able to be naturally lit to office background illumination levels for the months of April to September in the UK; the court form thus eliminates summer cooling loads and collects and conserves winter heat

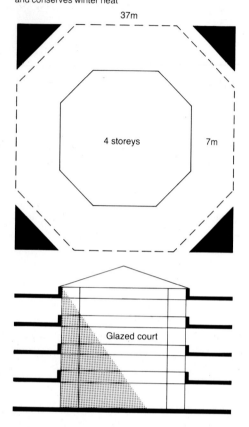

37m

4 storeys

7m

Glazed court

a The generic form

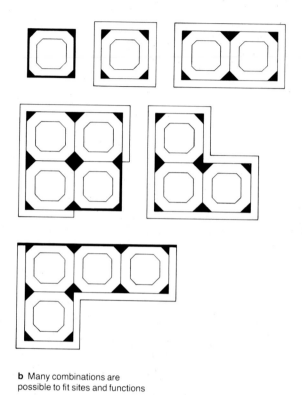

b Many combinations are possible to fit sites and functions

c Study for a multi-module building on a rural site; plan and section; tapered courts perform well

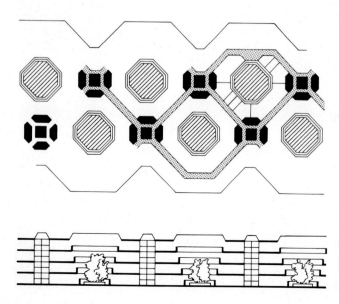

d Sketch of court interior

82 **Tennessee Valley Authority building,** Chattanooga, Tennessee. Model of central, light collecting atrium. *See also 101*

83 **Bullocks Store, Oakridge Mall, San José,** California. The atrium under its fabric roof saves lighting and cooling power

Daylighting

In non-residential building in the developed countries a high proportion of delivered energy goes to provide artificial light. This uses the premium energy source, electricity, and represents a disproportionate percentage of the primary energy used. For the past 30 years, since the introduction of fluorescent light, buildings have been planned to rely on this rather than on daylight, and the discipline of daylight-based planning has been lost. Deeper-planned buildings had shorter perimeter walls and saved heat energy that way. The price trend for energy now suggests that daylighting will often be more economic, though heat losses and gains through the windows make it marginal. If these heat problems can be reduced, daylighting has even more to offer.

Three examples can illustrate the range of daylighting options using atria. First, the studies by Dean Hawkes and Richard MacCormac (RIBA Journal, June 1978) based on the minimum size court needed for daylighting surrounding space, have

82

83

suggested a discipline for building up multi-court layouts. Totally introverted buildings, lit only from the court, show remarkably low energy needs for heat or light. Back-to-back, multi-court developments also work well.

Secondly, at Chattanooga, Tennessee, the Tennessee Valley Authority is building a new headquarters of one million square feet. Designed in 1979, the architects were Caudill, Rowlett, Scott, the Architects Collaborative, and Van der Ryn, Calthorpe and Partners. The vast low-rise building uses many techniques of energy conservation as a demonstration of responsibility to its energy customers. Deep, open floor areas are used, stacked five or six high each side of a linear atrium. The unusual feature is the incorporation in the floor-edge design of curved, reflecting light scoops. These bounce sky-light across office ceilings as background illumination. The roof of the atrium is shielded by sun-following motorized louvres. Sun-following heliostats and 'sunducts' are installed in several other buildings in the United States. In sunny locations such installations may allow deep-planning to use natural light.

Bullocks department stores in the San Francisco Bay area have adopted the atrium as a daylighting device par excellence. The architect of their San José store (1978) was Virgil Carter, with Geiger Berger as structural engineers. A central court of 18,000 square feet is roofed in 'teflon' coated glass-fibre fabric and used as a normal part of the store. In the equable climate of the area, comfort conditions are achieved with very little effort. However, $18,000 a year are being saved on lighting. The roof is 16 per cent translucent when single layer, seven per cent when double. This delivers adequate light levels to the courtyard floor and surrounding spaces. The limited translucence resists solar heat and reflects artificial light well at night.

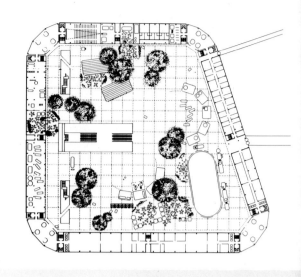

8 Tomorrow's atria

84 The unrealized but surely prophetic Hammersmith project
Foster Associates. Plan and part section

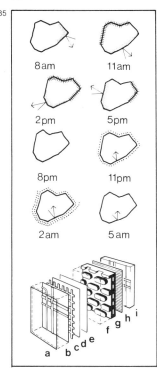

85

8am   11am

2pm   5pm

8pm   11pm

2am   5am

a b c d e f g h i

85 The polyvalent wall
A speculation by Chrysalis architects on the form and performance of a controllable solid-state 'glass'. Above: a typical wall response on a sunny spring day. Below; the structure of the wall

a Silica weather skin and deposition substrate

b Sensor and control logic layer, external

c Photo-electric grid

d Thermal sheet radiator/selective absorber

e Electro-reflective deposition

f Micropore gas flow layers

g Electro-reflective deposition

h Sensor and control logic layer, internal

i Silica deposition substrate and inner skin

86 The 'Climatroffice', a study for a 'building in a bag' by Buckminster Fuller and Norman Foster

The age of the atrium building has just begun. A few hundred have been created in the first 15 years after their revival in 1967, and several thousand are now on the drawing-boards of architects and students of architecture. In the next 50 years, as the world tries to accommodate an increase in population of four billion, more buildings will be built than already exist. Much of this new building could exploit the possibilities of the atrium form, both the tried and proven possibilities illustrated throughout this book, and the yet untapped potential. There is potential in this form for the design of individual buildings, more potential for the urban design possibilities and yet more for the kind of cities we can create for the future.

The individual building

The potential for individual buildings ranges from the single house to the most complex and sophisticated development. The atrium house shows signs of becoming popular. Patio and courtyard house planning has long been valued for combining access to sun and air with total privacy. Enclosing the court brings enhanced passive solar performance and a year-round gain in living space. John Hix's Maximum Space House, (see **30a**) where a glasshouse is used as the house and garden enclosure, flexibly divided, takes the principle a stage further. It could attract self-sufficiency seekers of the post-industrial West.

86

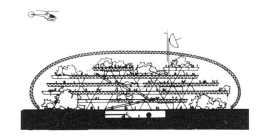

For larger buildings the focal space created by an atrium is attractive because it acts as a place where the occupants can be together. School, office and industrial buildings gain a place where everyone enters and to which they repair at break times, encouraging group spirit and combating the fragmentation of decentralized organizations. The environmental benefits are a bonus.

Few designs yet exploit the fact that the outer envelope and the outline of occupied spaces need no longer automatically follow each other's form: inside a minimal surface envelope accommodation can be freely disposed. Conversely, highly 'rational' space arrangements can be enclosed in a free-form envelope which answers the urban design needs of the site, or has a purely sculptural motive. The volume 'lost' between skin and space will still perform its many climatic, social and aesthetic tasks if intelligently disposed. Studies for such 'buildings in bags' have been done (see **86**), but no firm guidelines evolved. Hertzberger's seminal Centraal Beheer building (see **5**) shows the possible internal feel of such buildings, though its exterior is a form-following wrapper.

Moves towards the detachment of occupied space boundaries from the envelope are coming in the multi-atrium designs now in construction. The Solar Energy Research Institute (see **80**) and John Andrews' Intelsat headquarters in Washington DC both arrange their spaces looking out into atria on all sides. Exterior walls are merely there for potential expansion: if windowed they will look into future atria.

Progress in glass technology will encourage further experiments. Development is in progress to achieve more selective glass behaviour, either accepting daylight but rejecting solar heat, or accepting solar heat but improving retention of longer wavelength internal heat. Photochromic glasses, which react to sunlight are a probability, admitting a higher percentage of light when skies are cloudy, but darkening or reflecting when the sun appears. More speculative is the concept of the 'polyvalent wall', of glass-based material able to change its transmission characteristics under control.

87 **Hammersmith project,** model
photograph showing fabric roof

Using atrium space

Advances in thinking about the possible use of atrium spaces can be anticipated. Almost any activity needing a large-volume enclosure is a candidate for atrium location, with supporting smaller spaces or even compatible but unrelated activities forming the walls of the space. Single-use leisure buildings were early candidates for development. Already hotel atrium spaces are incorporating sports and pool areas as well as the dining and bar spaces they have long enclosed. Holiday Inns have dubbed their atrium hotels 'Holidomes'. With ozone sterilization of water an indoor pool can be compatible with other atrium functions. In Florida, the Burdine's chain of department stores is using atrium spaces with open 'matrix' structures in them to provide a distinctive circulation and sales environment.

Theatre and concert use of atria is consistent with some forms of performance. It would bring indoors the street-theatre and busking traditions, both of which can develop to high levels of quality in perfect outdoor climates like that of San Francisco. Exhibition and even theme-park development could combine

its large and small spaces in atrium form: the Air and Space Museum in Washington DC (Helmuth, Obata, Kassabaum, 1976) has shown the spatial possibilities . In the Trocadero development in Piccadilly, London (Fitzroy Robinson, 1983), the same concept is evolving into an indoor theme-park.

Atria can become the public rooms of a city, functioning as do the agora buildings in Dutch new towns. From its earliest days Edbrooke's Brown Palace Hotel, Denver (see **11**) used its grand atrium as a special event space. Public balls are regularly held in it, Indian pow-wows have used it, and a cattle market has taken place inside with prize animals living in the space for a week. The sadly superseded development at Hammersmith, London designed by Foster Associates in 1979 had this potential. An atrium of 160,000 square metres was to be formed by a ring of four office buildings carrying a fabric roof. The floor of the space roofed a major transport interchange for buses and underground railways. The space was to be a public garden, event-space and commercial centre.

87

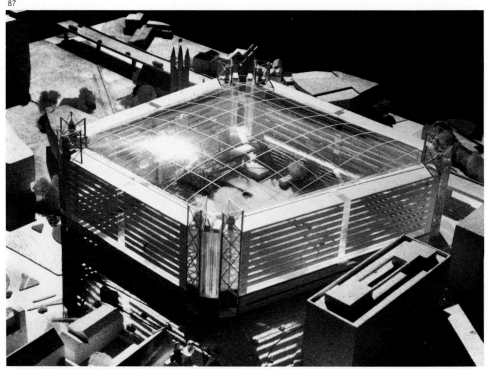

88 **Project for the roofing of Stephensplatz,** Vienna, by Gruppe M

89 **Roofed spaces between parallel new blocks,** proposals from 'Camera Solaris'

88

89
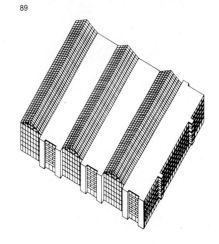
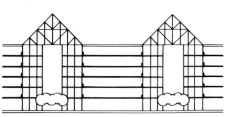

90 Building on the acceptance of Disney's urban model are these proposals for major development in downtown Miami, Florida, by John Portman. A monorail service for the city glides through a linear atrium

Several entrepreneurs regarded it as a potential goldmine, ensuring good trading conditions for perimeter stores and also for stalls and features in the open space. This concept will be realized somewhere in the not-too-distant future, perhaps particularly in relation to transport terminals.

Urban design potential

Beyond the scale of the individual building or development comes the way atria can affect the relationships between buildings. In new developments several changes can be made if city authorities can encourage them in the interest of a more comfortable city. The spaces both between new blocks, and between old and new buildings can be enclosed: roofing of existing streets, where pedestrianized, is not impractical where buildings are of similar heights. This would finally equalize the contest between older but unsheltered shopping streets, and the fully enclosed centres.

Atrium buildings have the ability to be totally introverted, with blank external walls. This

means they can relate to other buildings by solid contact along party walls on as many as three sides (one open side would be essential for construction access). Development on this principle can, on the smaller scale, allow infilling of difficult sites, and on the larger scale, allow dense continuous development over large blocks by incremental growth rather than by one-off development.

Authorities can do more than adjust their zoning requirements to permit and encourage atrium development. They can build free-standing atria to attract surrounding buildings as has been done at Niagara Falls (see p. 53). This is the modern equivalent of the method by which the Parisians created their grand boulevards and squares, and the Victorians their city parks. The former built the frontage and let individuals build behind it; the latter sold perimeter house-plots on the park to pay for it.

90

91 Prebuilding public circulation For new centres development could proceed by first building galleria/atrium spaces, then selling frontages for development. The public space outlasts generations of development

a Prebuilt atrium/galleria

b Development comes alongside

c Redevelopment occurs in due course

91

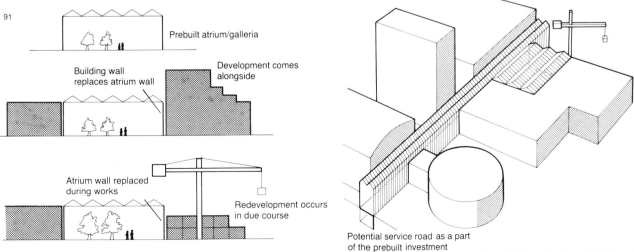

Prebuilt atrium/galleria

Building wall replaces atrium wall

Development comes alongside

Atrium wall replaced during works

Redevelopment occurs in due course

Potential service road as a part of the prebuilt investment

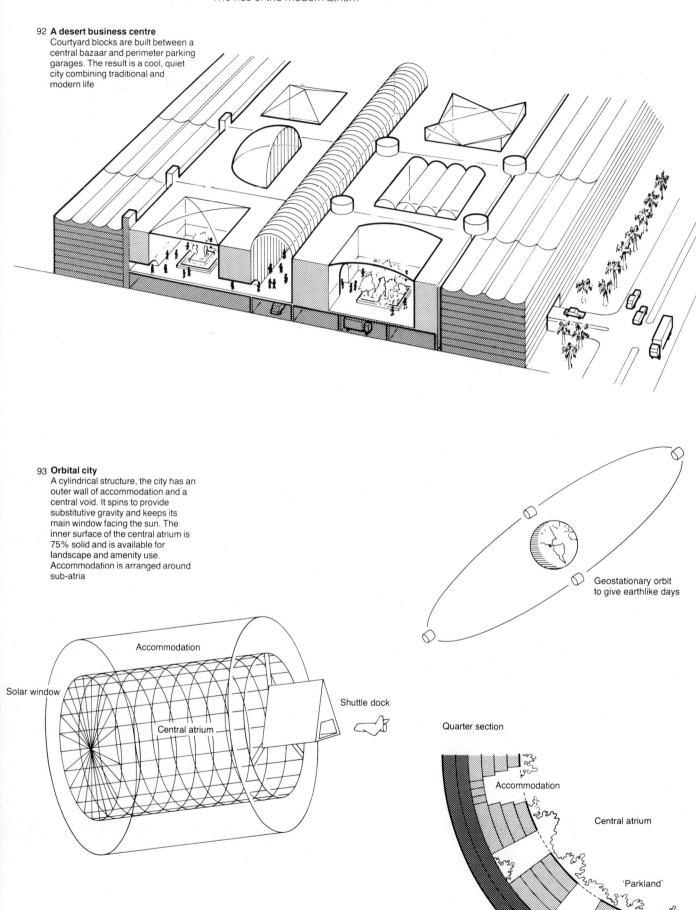

92 A desert business centre
Courtyard blocks are built between a
central bazaar and perimeter parking
garages. The result is a cool, quiet
city combining traditional and
modern life

93 Orbital city
A cylindrical structure, the city has an
outer wall of accommodation and a
central void. It spins to provide
substitutive gravity and keeps its
main window facing the sun. The
inner surface of the central atrium is
75% solid and is available for
landscape and amenity use.
Accommodation is arranged around
sub-atria

Geostationary orbit
to give earthlike days

Accommodation

Solar window

Shuttle dock

Central atrium

Quarter section

Accommodation

Central atrium

'Parkland'

Shielding

Plant a
ducts

94 Arboretum at Sohio Base Operation Center, Prudhoe Bay, Alaska, 1972. The center consists of linked atrium buildings, one of which contains this garden. Architects were Wallace, Floyd, Ellenzweig, Moore, Inc

94

95 **Pit cities.** Two versions which might appear: the artic colony, built in a worked-out ore pit, and the floating atoll city in tropical waters. The atoll uses ocean thermal energy conversion. Both have central atria enclosed by air-supported fabric

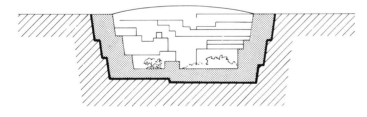

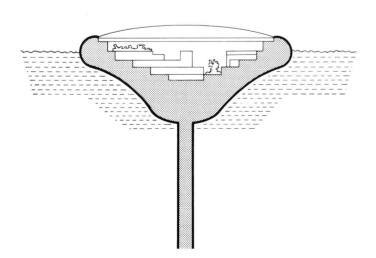

New city forms

There are going to be many wholly new settlements to be built for the expanding world population. Most of them will be in the developing world where the pressure or the resources exist. Some will be in places not previously considered habitable.

Atrium development can be a useful principle for new urban forms, especially where defence against the elements is important.

The new cities of the oil-rich Middle East display a general disregard for climate and for their cultural tradition. Western concepts, only moderately suitable even for temperate latitudes, have been adopted as a symbol of modernity and because the consultants employed were using their own cultural background rather than that of their clients.

An up-dated approach to the traditional Islamic city is conceivable using atrium principles. The potential development of a business centre is shown in **92**). A development like this could grow and change incrementally. Schemes for enclosed cities based on huge air-supported or geodesic domes are not conceivable in terms of free market forces. Build-up must be gradual, change continuous and expansion possible. The pragmatic possibilities of covering city centres by abutting atrium buildings bear examination.

The most inhospitable corners of the earth, and beyond into space, will be colonized during the next 50 years. Arctic cities, to exploit minerals, floating cities based on ocean thermal power, fish-farming and ocean minerals, undersea cities for similar goals, communities on the moon or in earth orbit-all these need to provide for human needs beyond mere life support. Thinking about habitability of space vehicles suggests that there must be some spatial release for people, beyond the infinite and therefore meaningless view into the black void. An internal perspective, of similar scale and nature to that on earth, would be ideal.

Notional orbital colonies have been sketched, combining a pseudo-gravitational field with this desire for some 'inner space'.

The same principles apply on earth to communities in hostile environments. The 1972 British Petroleum/Sohio Prudhoe Bay complex on Alaska's north slope has atrium courts within each of several buildings. One acts as an arboretum. Outward view is often of blizzard or arctic night, whilst the indoor vista is bright with artificial light and colourful with flowers and trees. The architects were Wallace, Floyd, Ellenzweig, Moore, Inc. One can envisage the winning of coal from the Canadian and Russian Arctic leading to development below ground level, sheltered in the huge pits left behind. Inward-looking complexes are but a development of the old Chinese pit-houses, dug into the soft loess soil (see **95**). Floating or submerged communities will also need massive outer shells to defend themselves against pressure or storm, and can only create humane environments if they open up internal volumes.

Thus there is a multivalent future for the concept of atrium building. It is a way of thinking about the built environment which can only prosper in the years to come.

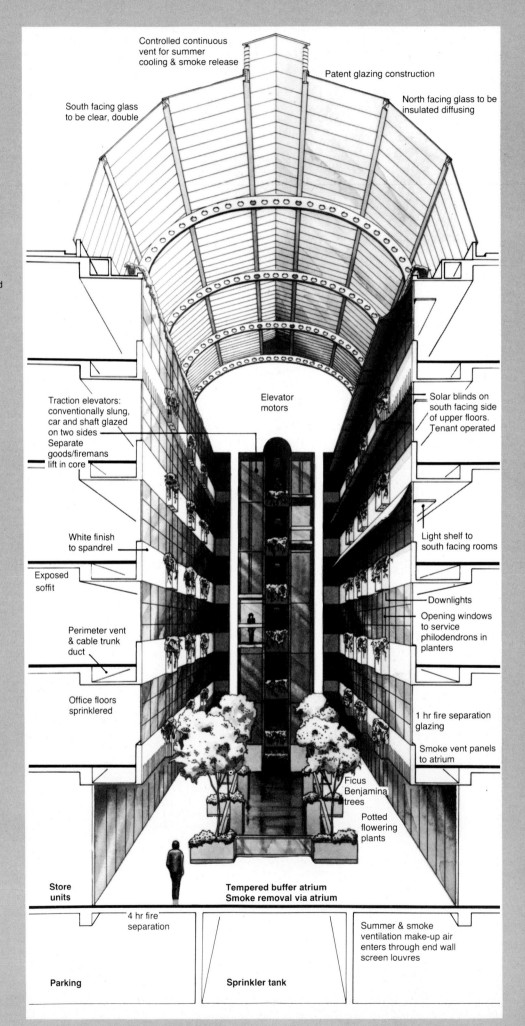

96 **66 Oxford Street, Manchester, England.** Section through proposed atrium with construction notes. Building Design Partnership, 1982

Controlled continuous vent for summer cooling & smoke release

Patent glazing construction

South facing glass to be clear, double

North facing glass to be insulated diffusing

Traction elevators: conventionally slung, car and shaft glazed on two sides
Separate goods/firemans lift in core

Elevator motors

Solar blinds on south facing side of upper floors. Tenant operated

White finish to spandrel

Light shelf to south facing rooms

Exposed soffit

Downlights

Opening windows to service philodendrons in planters

Perimeter vent & cable trunk duct

Office floors sprinklered

1 hr fire separation glazing

Smoke vent panels to atrium

Ficus Benjamina trees

Potted flowering plants

Store units

Tempered buffer atrium
Smoke removal via atrium

4 hr fire separation

Summer & smoke ventilation make-up air enters through end wall screen louvres

Parking

Sprinkler tank

Part two

Constructing the atrium

This part of the book is structured to enable a designer to consider all the major technical factors affecting thinking at the formative stage. It contains six chapters which cover those aspects of design which are particular to atrium buildings, and where innovative techniques and design approaches are involved.

The chapters can be read as separate packages in any order. The design aspects they cover do, however, strongly interact. The economics chapter (14) embraces all the others to show the synthesis of costs and benefits.

The chapters are in order of their potential significance for the basic form of an atrium building. There will be many cases where brief (program) or design aims put the emphasis differently. It is the contention here, however, that if criteria of maximum functional advantage are used to guide decision-making then the role of the atrium in environmental control of the building is paramount. To work as a significant climate modifier and source of daylight the atrium form must follow that function. The next most significant influence is the strategy taken to avoid fire hazard: atria reduce a buildings natural compartmentation and introduce new and powerful natural ventilation patterns. Life-safety dictates certain choices.

Next in influence are the structures and skins used to enclose the atrium space and the circulation system included in the atrium. These will greatly determine the look and experience of the place. Finally, the use of plants and other landscape elements: atria are quasi-outdoor spaces and their character can range from that of a garden to that of a grand salon. Successful landscaping brings the atrium to life.

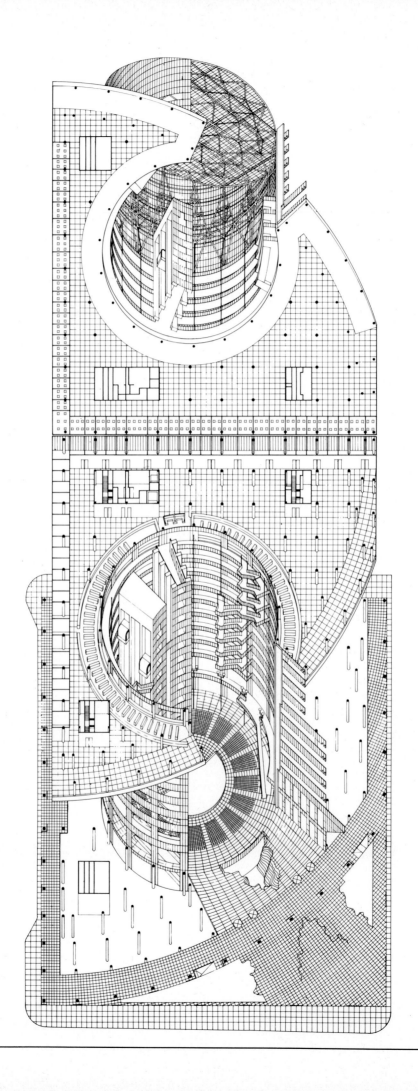

9 Shaping and servicing

97 **State of Illinois Building, Chicago,** Murphy/Jahn 1983. A bold example of the plasticity of form encouraged by the use of the atrium. One million square feet of offices sit above 150,000 square feet of shopping, connected to two transit lines. Visitors to state agencies will rise in the rotunda space to visit the appropriate gallery level

Basic building form decisions

As outlined in Chapter 7, a significant reason for the success of the atrium in the 1970s was its promise to lower demand for artificial energy. But few early atria exploited the potential to the full. They were visual statements rather than integrated energy systems. There remains much scope for developing the contribution of atria to reduced building energy use. To realize the potential, however, atrium buildings need to be designed very much with energy in mind. It can become the dominant form-giver in the design process.

This chapter will deal with the built form implications of obtaining those potential servicing benefits: extensive daylighting without the conductive and radiant heat loss or gain of conventional buildings; reduced air heat loss by using the atrium as a second skin; collection or rejection of solar heat as required by the building's use and climate location.

Obtaining the lighting benefits involves shaping the atrium as a daylight collector and distributor, and arranging the space around it to take advantage of this. Similarly, obtaining the thermal and ventilation benefits involves orienting and shaping the atrium to give shade or collect heat, as required, and using the volume intelligently in your air-handling strategy. The basic configuration of the building will be influenced by these considerations.

Plan-depth
The decision to seek useful daylighting of occupied space has a profound effect on built form for non-domestic buildings. It represents a reversal of the trend towards simpler plan shapes and deeper floor-plans, with smaller windows, which was the hallmark of development until the early 1970s. Even now many atrium buildings are still basically artificially lit and deep-planned, using the atrium for visual release rather than daylight.

Getting the full benefit means reducing the width or increasing the height of occupied space until all useful areas can be given at least a satisfactory ambient level of light naturally. With conventional floor-to-floor heights and window design this means space

widths of about 12 metres. Higher storeys and the introduction of reflecting devices can increase this. Raising ceiling heights from 2.7 metres to 3.6 metres can allow good light up to 9 metres into the plan. There is a trade-off between plan depth and storey-height within an overall volume. Shallow-plan space may not need deep service volume between ceiling and floor levels as the space can be served from the perimeter. The volume of an atrium may thus be offset by reduced floor-to-floor heights. Increasing ceiling heights to daylight deeper floor-plans reduces the number of floors in a given height, and also increases the 'interstitial' volume needed to ventilate the space. If deeper space suits the function better than shallow space, these trade-offs should be investigated. If all ambient light can be provided naturally, during daylight hours, the thermal consequences will be significant in temperate climates. Cooling loads will be greatly reduced, and a heat-requiring building may result, able to benefit from the heating potential of the atrium.

An alternative strategy is the use of deeper floor-plans, lighting a proportion naturally, and the balance artificially. The heat-surplus core will then provide for the needs of the heat-deficit perimeters. Balancing exercises can be done to find the right mixture for the task, and to decide whether a heat-deficit design, with a warming atrium, is preferable to a heat-surplus design with a cooling atrium.

Basic thermodynamics means that providing a certain amount of heat will always be more economic than providing the same amount of cooling.

Arranging the space
The space width selected will need to be coiled and stacked on the site to achieve the area required or permitted. The atrium will be the void described by the pattern of coiling and stacking selected. A productive way of considering the form of building most suited to the context is to use the 'double-skin' idea (see Chapter 7) as a conceptual tool. The outer envelope of the building can then be considered quite separately from the pattern of occupied space. The desirable outer envelope form can be considered from the point of view of urban design factors and solar access to this and neighbouring sites.

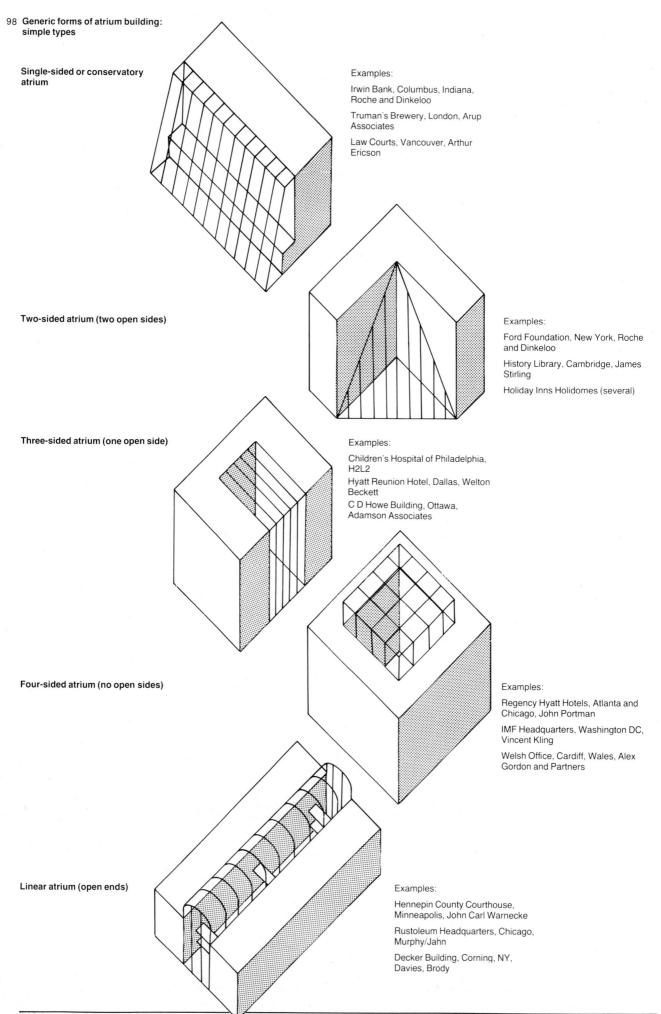

98 **Generic forms of atrium building:
simple types**

**Single-sided or conservatory
atrium**

Examples:

Irwin Bank, Columbus, Indiana,
Roche and Dinkeloo

Truman's Brewery, London, Arup
Associates

Law Courts, Vancouver, Arthur
Ericson

Two-sided atrium (two open sides)

Examples:

Ford Foundation, New York, Roche
and Dinkeloo

History Library, Cambridge, James
Stirling

Holiday Inns Holidomes (several)

Three-sided atrium (one open side)

Examples:

Children's Hospital of Philadelphia,
H2L2

Hyatt Reunion Hotel, Dallas, Welton
Beckett

C D Howe Building, Ottawa,
Adamson Associates

Four-sided atrium (no open sides)

Examples:

Regency Hyatt Hotels, Atlanta and
Chicago, John Portman

IMF Headquarters, Washington DC,
Vincent Kling

Welsh Office, Cardiff, Wales, Alex
Gordon and Partners

Linear atrium (open ends)

Examples:

Hennepin County Courthouse,
Minneapolis, John Carl Warnecke

Rustoleum Headquarters, Chicago,
Murphy/Jahn

Decker Building, Corning, NY,
Davies, Brody

99 Generic forms of atrium building:
complex types

Bridging atrium, between multiple buildings

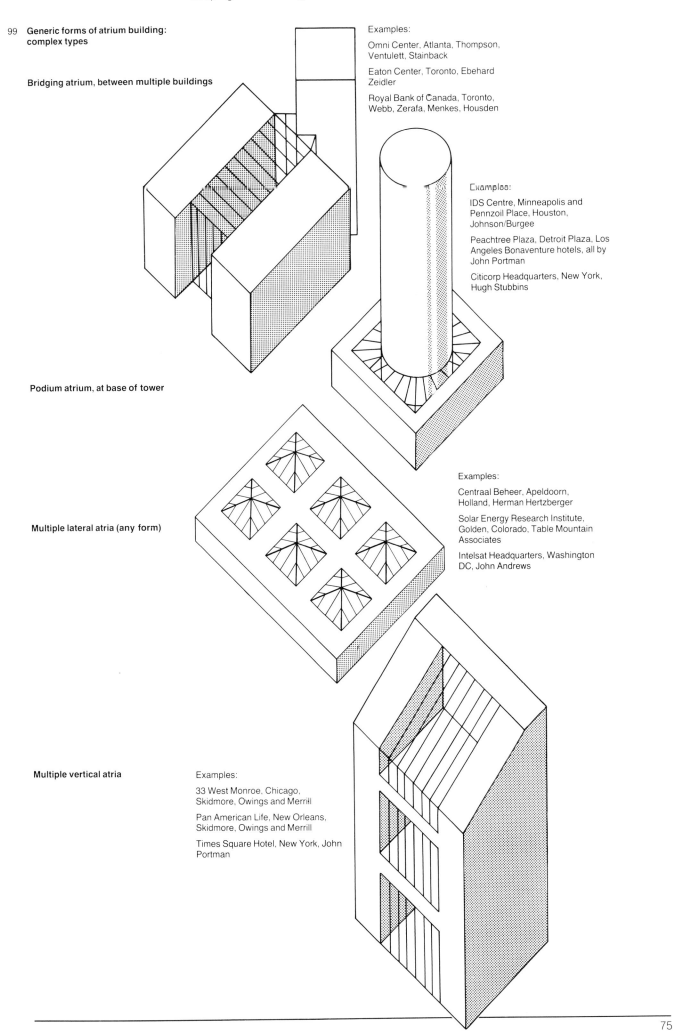

Examples:

Omni Center, Atlanta, Thompson,
Ventulett, Stainback

Eaton Center, Toronto, Ebehard
Zeidler

Royal Bank of Canada, Toronto,
Webb, Zerafa, Menkes, Housden

Examples:

IDS Centre, Minneapolis and
Pennzoil Place, Houston,
Johnson/Burgee

Peachtree Plaza, Detroit Plaza, Los
Angeles Bonaventure hotels, all by
John Portman

Citicorp Headquarters, New York,
Hugh Stubbins

Podium atrium, at base of tower

Multiple lateral atria (any form)

Examples:

Centraal Beheer, Apeldoorn,
Holland, Herman Hertzberger

Solar Energy Research Institute,
Golden, Colorado, Table Mountain
Associates

Intelsat Headquarters, Washington
DC, John Andrews

Multiple vertical atria

Examples:

33 West Monroe, Chicago,
Skidmore, Owings and Merrill

Pan American Life, New Orleans,
Skidmore, Owings and Merrill

Times Square Hotel, New York, John
Portman

Any excess volume within the acceptable envelope compared to the usable space needed will be a measure of the scope for the use of atria. The double-skin can be retained as the concept develops, or the inner and outer skins merged where the accommodation touches the envelope, in the interests of economy.

Decisions on the disposition of atria should be related to whether a warming or cooling atrium is required, and the climate in which it stands. Most light is available from above, in all latitudes, and a skylight will be the most cost-effective way to collect daylight.

Collecting sunlight for warming will also be simple through a skylight, but the most heat will be collected when least needed, in summer. An equator-facing glazed side wall is very desirable in cool temperate latitudes, to collect lower-angle sunlight. In warmer latitudes it may be preferable to a roof-light as it can be shaded from high-angle solar-penetration and deliver considerable quantities of reflected light. Skylights can, of course, be shaped and oriented to exclude or admit sunlight.

East- and west-facing atrium side walls are not recommended unless specific vista opportunities are important. They admit low-angle sunlight in summer and are hard to shade. In winter they lose heat far more than equator-oriented walls. Polar-oriented walls are valuable in very warm latitudes as they deliver sky-light without solar penetration. Between the tropics some shade against high-angle sun crossing into the polar half of the sky is necessary.

Shaping and fenestrating the atrium is thus very similar to the design of a room and its windows, but on a large scale: in cool latitudes solar admittance is sought; in warm climates, it is avoided. This avoidance pattern must also be followed if the building is deep-planned and has a heat surplus, regardless of climate.

Generic forms
Part I revealed the variety of forms which atrium buildings can take. At the conceptual design stage it is worth considering options systematically. Five simple and four complex forms which have emerged are shown in **98** and **99**, and examples noted. Many other hybrid arrangements are possible by elaborating from one or more of these generic forms.

The 'pure' forms, one-, two-, three-, four-sided and linear atria, can be applied to small, single buildings as well as to large complexes. The complex forms are more appropriate to higher-density, larger-scale development. Very tight sites are least likely to find atrium options possible, whilst generous sites may respond to multiple horizontal forms; large but compact low-rise complexes can thus be created, with extensive day-lit space on each level. The unlit 'cross-overs' in multiple court forms can be used for service cores. They can be avoided by linking usable spaces corner to corner, as at John Andrews' Intelsat headquarters, Washington DC, or by using multiple linear atria with linking bridges as at E H Ziedler's Mackenzie Health Center, Edmonton, both now under construction.

Formal freedom
The wide range of functional built form strategies available should not however lead the designer to assume that one of these combinations of internally generated factors must alone determine the overall building shape. Amongst the flaws of tower or slab building in the twentieth century has been the inability of these forms to respond sympathetically to the urban context. Internal criteria have been seen as paramount in shaping buildings, and mismatches between the resultant form and the context have at best been moderated by the use of suitable materials and treatment. Atrium buildings, as discussed in Chapter 6, can respond to context by being more plastic in their outline and massing. The choice of basic form may well be determined by the desirable external implications, and the design can then be worked up to obtain the most functional advantage possible.

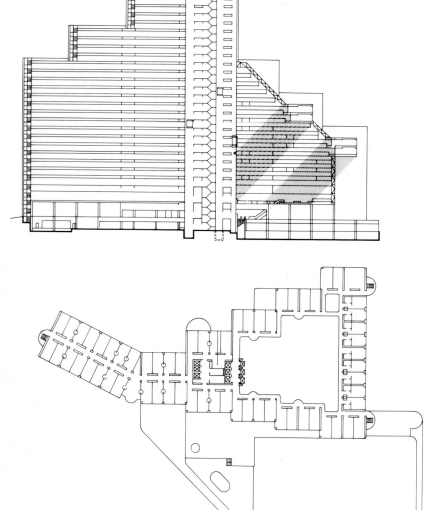

100 **Hyatt Regency Hotel, Dallas,** Welton Beckett and Associates, 1979. A three-sided atrium like the State of Illinois building, serving to demonstrate the range of ideas which are encompassed in each generic form

Despite the recognition of generic atrium building forms, the genre is particularly open to elaboration. Once the outline of occupied space is separated from the building envelope, internal spaces can be freely modelled without the risk of economic consequences that might otherwise arise. Evidence of the form-making potential of atrium building is growing. Once the designer gains confidence in the approach, scope for originality is considerable without necessitating the sacrifice of servicing advantages.

Lighting

Daylighting is the key

One of the strongest contributions which atria can make to energy conservation in buildings is in allowing the use of daylight to be re-established. The cost of artificial lighting, directly in power consumption and indirectly in the cost of removing the heat released, may now be higher than the cost of daylight, and is likely to be so for a considerable period. The energy cost of daylight lies in the low insulation and shading value of glass, causing heat loss and gain. If atrium planning can reduce or remove the thermal cost,

101 **Artificial sky facility**
Pilkington's Limited, St Helen's, England. Instrumented models are placed inside, for overcast sky performance readings

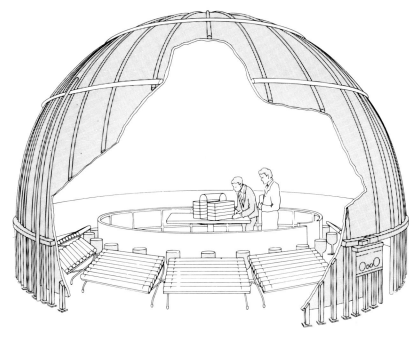

daylighting gains a clear advantage. If it can also allow the large, compact floor-plans which come with 'deep planning', the best of both worlds is achieved.

Good daylighting means lighting of the right quality, delivered to the greatest plan-depth possible. Quality rather than quantity counts; low glare and contrast are most desirable. The quality of light now sought for working spaces presents the greatest challenge: residential or leisure buildings have less critical requirements and are now lit for character rather than performance. Office-type spaces are discovering a changing need for light-quality under the impacts of energy costs and the advance of office electronics. A consensus of opinion is emerging that light

can best be delivered as a combination of two components known as ambient light and task light. Task light is that needed to provide the right level of acuity at the heart of the work-place; ambient light provides background illumination. The ratio of background to foreground light must not be too great, or contrast problems will result. Background or ambient levels of between one-half and two-thirds of task levels are ideal. For offices this means ambient levels of between 300 and 500 lux. A high proportion of this can usually be achieved with daylighting in a well-designed building.

For electronic offices with staff using visual display units, a separate task-lighting component is not usually needed: the task is self-illuminating. The way in which the ambient component is delivered becomes more critical since reflections of bright sources in the VDU screen are disabling. Ceiling-mounted luminaires and bright windows are equally problematic, and indirect light appears to offer greatest comfort. The integration of natural and artificial lighting strategies is discussed further below.

Daylighting-calculation techniques exists for conventionally planned buildings. These methods do not work for atrium buildings and new tools are still in development. The reason for the difference is that conventional calculation assumes direct daylighting from the sky and allows for internal reflection within the room. In an atrium building daylight entering a room may be on its second or third diffuse reflection from surfaces within the atrium. Computer techniques may emerge to model this complex behaviour, but at present the best method is the use of physical models: large-scale models of the rooms and atrium proposed, with reflectivities as proposed, are studied under 'artificial sky' conditions and delivered light is measured. Artificial skies exist in the laboratories of several glass companies, schools of architecture, and energy research centres. The technique sounds laborious and costly, but it is worthwhile for major projects. The modelling technique enables the designer to manipulate the three main components in atrium daylighting: how the light is admitted to the atrium; how it reflects inside the atrium to reach all parts; and how it is finally collected by the space around the atrium and delivered to the 'working plane'.

Admitting light into the atrium

The strongest influence on the way light can be admitted into an atrium should be the climate in which it stands. Quite different approaches are valid in climates where skies are often cloudy from those where they are usually clear, and between equable, temperate climates and those with extremes of daily and annual conditions.

For the temperate, often overcast climate of Britain and the rest of Northern Europe, daylighting expectations must be based on the cloudy sky. Indeed a standard overcast sky (the CIE sky) has been adopted for calculation and model-testing purposes. It has a mean brightness of 5,000 lux but is brighter at the crown of the sky than at the horizon. The ideal atrium in these circumstances would be largely top-lit, and with a clear, unobstructed glazed roof to achieve the maximum transmission of light. Diffuse light from all parts of the sky would enter the atrium in this way. When sunny conditions do occur, diffusion of light to rooms on the shaded side of the atrium will need to be provided for.

In sunny climates daylighting is difficult to achieve successfully with direct light. Sunlight is too harsh and shadow too dark. Sunlight must either be excluded by shades or converted to diffuse light. Where the sky is usually bright even with cloud, polar roof-light will deliver plenty of useful diffuse light. A 'sawtooth' roof-configuration can be used, with solar sides perhaps reflecting sunlight into the glazed non-solar sides (see **102c**). Where skies are usually cloudless, there is very little light to be collected from the sky-vault, and sunlight must be captured and diffused. Passive or active shading devices can be used. A passive approach is to use solar-facing glazing in a sawtooth roof and fix external shades at an angle to exclude summer sun-rays, but instead to reflect the rays up onto the underside of the roof and thence down into the atrium; winter sun will enter directly, to bounce downwards off the roof.

Active shading can be the right solution in a warm climate or one with extreme seasonal variations. For the TVA building in

102 **Light collecting atrium roof forms**

a Lantern light for cloudy
 temperate climates

b Solar sawtooth, for sunny
 temperate climates

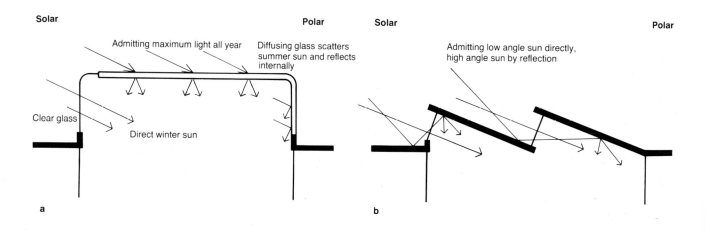

a

b

c Polar sawtooth, for sunny
 warm climates

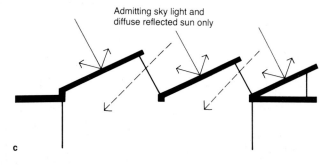

c

Chattanooga small external shade-vanes were investigated, motorized, and controlled by sun-following photocells and micro-processors. Vanes are mirrored one side, white the other. The vanes maximize the amount of light delivered at each season, diffusing it for distribution (see below), and also form a winter night-shutter.

In very hot, desert conditions, only a small amount of light transmission is needed to give adequate daylight levels. Most sun must be excluded and any admitted must be converted to diffuse light. A fabric roof can be an effective element here, transmitting between five and 15 per cent of sunlight, but as a diffuse glow like an overcast sky (see p. 91 ff.).

Heat admitted with sunlight will cause some build-up of hot air below the roof, and this is best allowed for by raising the roof clear of surrounding accommodation and creating a lantern or monitor (102a). (See p. 84 ff. for discussion of the thermal strategies.) The lantern will also be able to collect light from the sides, and in northern climates this can be valuable. Side-glazing can be less obstructed by framing than roof-glazing, and even though the overcast sky is less bright, any sun is more likely to enter the atrium through side-glazing. Solar-shading to prevent overheating of occupied space is best left to the windows inside the atrium, as shading in the roof itself would greatly reduce the transmission of diffuse light in the more normal overcast conditions.

d-g Active shaded rooflight proposed for TVA Headquarters Chattanooga, Tennessee, showing four main operating modes. It proved uneconomic in practice

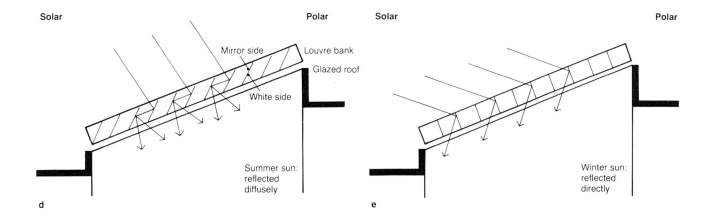

Solar — Polar

Mirror side · Louvre bank · Glazed roof · White side

Summer sun: reflected diffusely

d

Solar — Polar

Winter sun: reflected directly

e

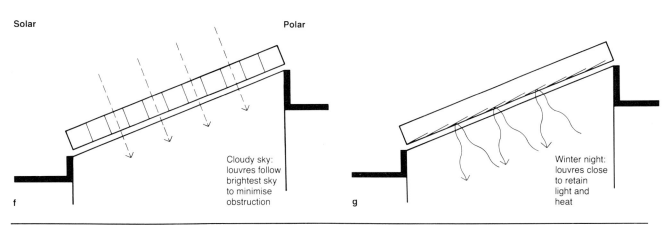

Solar — Polar

Cloudy sky: louvres follow brightest sky to minimise obstruction

f

Winter night: louvres close to retain light and heat

g

Distributing light within the atrium

The atrium acts as a 'light duct'. Openings into occupied spaces are its outlets, but it is the walls of the duct which determine the 'pressure' achieved and how much light gets to the bottom and into the lowest storeys of the building.

The first, strategic design decision is the proportions of the court itself—its aspect ratio. The ratio between its width, length and depth will govern the rate of decay of light levels in the court: the less bright the sky, the wider will a court need to be in order to deliver a useful level of light to the lowest storey.

However, the reflectivity of the sides is very important: there can be enormous variation in performance depending on how reflective the walls are. For the lower storeys lit from an atrium, their 'sky' is the reflective wall opposite them. If walls are of floor-to-ceiling glass, or are completely open, very little light will bounce off them to travel downwards to lower storeys. At the theoretical opposite extreme, if there are no openings, and a highly reflective surface to the walls, light would bounce down the duct as it does inside an optical glass fibre, losing little intensity. Light should ideally be drawn off for each storey only to the extent necessary, with the rest reflected back for further transmission downwards.

The logical outcome of this concept is that fenestration for each floor level should differ. At the top storey there need be very little window, reinforced with collecting devices, and, lower down, progressively more glass until full glazing is used at the lowest level. This is no more unusual a concept than the concept that windows should vary from elevation to elevation with differing orientation. Climatically responsive architecture has these varations and capitalizes upon them. A possible atrium wall elevation with progressive glazing from top to bottom is shown in **103c**.

As an alternative to varying the glass area from floor to floor, types of glass could be varied. Reflective glass of differing strengths could be used, finishing with clear glass at the lowest level. This is less effective as a

103 Distributing daylight

a The amount of direct light reaching the floor of an atrium depends on its proportions

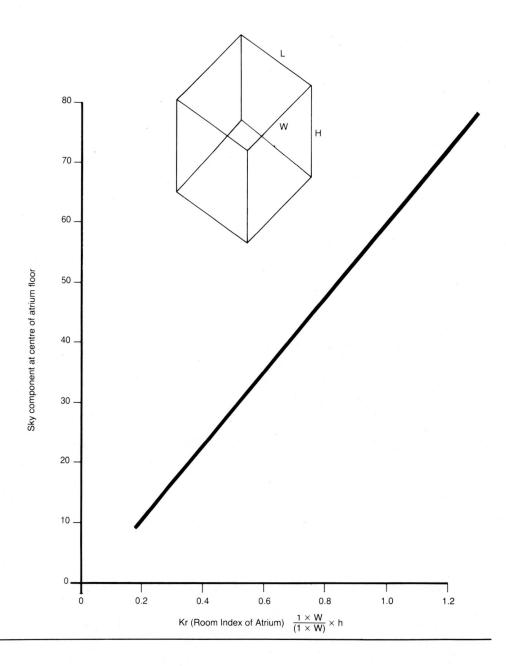

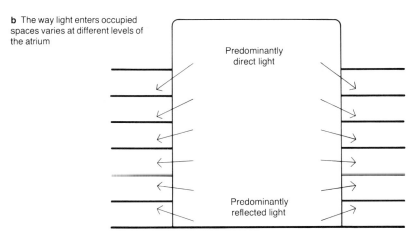

b The way light enters occupied spaces varies at different levels of the atrium

strategy, as specular reflection is a less efficient way to bounce light down the duct. Diffuse reflection, from white tile, render, metal or laminate surfaces is more effective. Diffusing glasses exist and can be used to transmit part and reflect part of the light. The ratio of diffusing and clear glass would then vary from top to bottom of the atrium.

Landscaping within the atrium can conflict with daylighting performance. Planting on balcony levels has a very low reflectivity, and absorbs light otherwise destined for lower floors. Planting is a welcome feature, but should be located to minimize such losses of light: the floor of the atrium is available without great penalties. Plants themselves need high light levels (see Chapter 13) but should not have problems in any atrium designed for daylighting adjacent space.

c The amount of reflected light available for lower storeys can be enhanced by selective design of the walls at each level

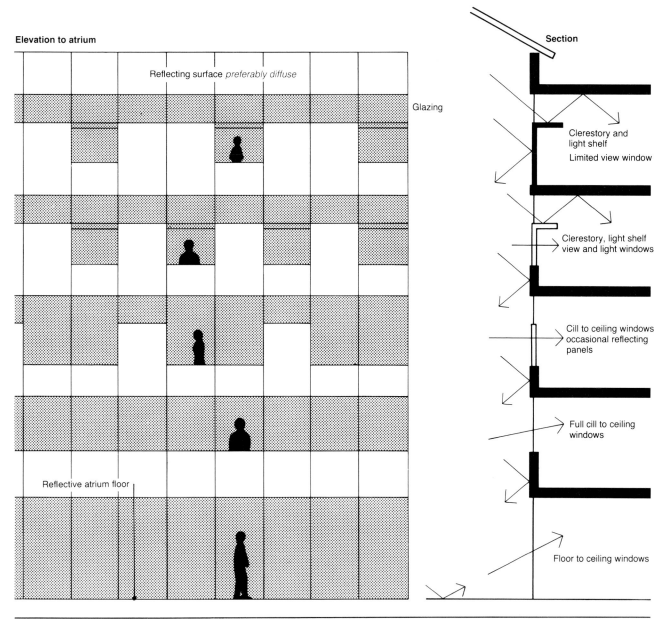

Collecting light into the occupied space

From a conventional window, or unglazed opening, light levels within a room fall off quite rapidly. Useful levels of light are hard to achieve at between four and five metres from a window in conventional room heights, virtually regardless of window brightness. Indeed, sheer window brightness is a negative feature, causing glare and gloom effects. Ideally a window should allow view generally, but direct much of its light upwards onto the ceiling, to bounce further into the room and reduce contrasts.

This inversion of natural law can only be achieved by reflection. Indeed the light that can be used in an atrium building has already been reflected many times—in the roof, and from upper side walls.

The idea of the 'light shelf' is being revived, for external and atrium use. A light shelf is a horizontal or inclined baffle in the window, placed just above eye level but as far below ceiling level as possible. Sunlight and diffuse light are stopped from passing straight to the floor close to the window, and reflected back onto the ceiling. Much more even distribution of light within the room is achieved, and views of the bright upper part of the window are cut off, easing contrast problems (see **104**).

The shape and finish of a light shelf can vary widely. Horizontal matt white shelves will scatter diffuse light effectively. Angled or curved specular reflectors can throw sun-light even further into a room—but their performance is not noticeably better than matt white surfaces when dealing with diffuse light.

There is an argument for allowing each light shelf to 'see' a slice of the atrium roof since that is the brightest source of light. Many atria have stepped sections, with floors moving closer together further down the court. This gives each floor a window jutting into the light, without shading the floor below. Where little useful reflection is provided by the walls of the atrium, this is useful, but only increases the brightness at the front of the rooms; with light shelves it is more effective. Stepped sections have disadvantages too: floors get deeper towards the base of the block, exactly where least daylight is available to them. More artificial light might thus be used rather than less. They are also structurally problematic.

Quite complex light-collecting window profiles can be constructed inside an atrium without the costs normally associated with external windows. They can be of partition-standard construction only, single-glazed and not weathered in any way.

There is the question of the maintenance factor in daylighting, with all the reflecting and transmitting surfaces to be kept clean. This need not be a serious problem. Internal features like light shelves and atrium windows are accessible and keep cleaner than external features. Artificial light systems, of course, also need periodic cleaning to maintain their efficiency.

104 Daylighting occupied space

The most important determinant of the depth of useful daylight penetration is ceiling height. A good ambient level can be obtained twice as far in with a ceiling height increase from 2·7m *9ft* to 3·6m *12ft*. The window head can remain low without much loss of light at the back of the room

The light shelf concept works well in direct light. It redistributes light from front to back of a room, also reducing contrast and intercepting solar gain

Stepping floor edges can work similarly in atria, giving each floor a view of the skylight. Reflective flooring at this point bounces light deeper into the room

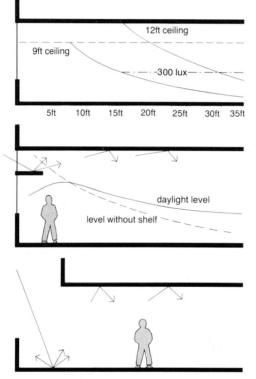

105 Lockheed Missiles and Space Company, Building 157, Sunnyvale, California, by Leo A Daly, Architects and Engineers. This cross section shows deep floors being successfully lit by the use of a high, sloped ceilings and light shelves. Ninety per cent of the useful illumination comes from clerestorey and light shelves. The atrium provides about half as much light as the outside walls

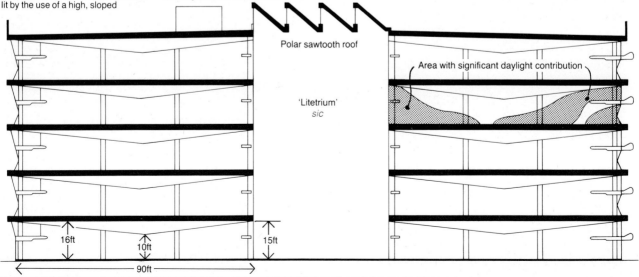

106 High performance concept
(Lockheed building) with shaped light
shelf defining perimeter offices
without loss of light to interior space

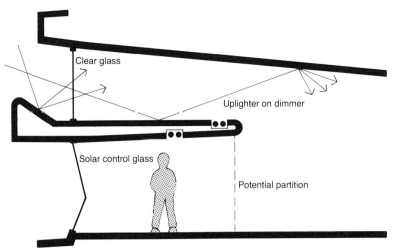

Clear glass

Uplighter on dimmer

Solar control glass

Potential partition

107a Integrating natural and artificial ambient lighting

1 Most daylight admitted at clerestorey and bounced off light shelf

2 85% (min) reflective ceiling, preferably structural as a heat sink

3 View windows shaded to reduce reflection on VDUs

4 Uplighter on automatic dimmer, varying output with daylight level

5 Uplighter for constant ambient light. Light shelf and shaded window are less necessary lower down an atrium where light enters room at all angles and without sky brightness

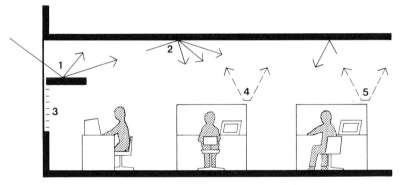

107b Section parallel to window wall
showing use of deep beams in
direction of daylight flow. Artificial
ambient sources are in coves on
beams as an alternative to floor
based uplighters. Automatic dimmer
control can be used to balance
artificial with natural contribution

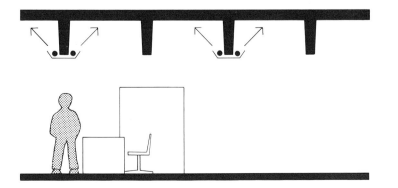

Integrating natural and artificial light

Full benefit will not be gained from daylighting unless the artificial lighting system and the internal finishes of the occupied space are considered together with it. The daylighting concept outlined has delivered diffuse light, laterally, and upwards onto the ceiling for reflection onto the working plane. The artificial light should ideally perform similarly, and the ceiling be designed to accept both.

Up-lighting, the idea of bouncing light off the ceiling rather than delivering it direct from a luminaire, can be as efficient as down-lighting given appropriate design. The reflection factor of the ceiling replaces the losses caused by diffusing or louvering the light. A flat, matt, ceiling will reflect well if white and clean. A textured ceiling loses efficiency but gains interest. A coffered or heavily modelled ceiling will work much less well unless given careful attention. The up-lighting concept often goes with the use of an exposed structural ceiling, all services being in an elevated floor. Unless a flat-slab structure is used, beams should be arranged to run perpendicular to the windows, to provide adequate reflecting surfaces to channel the light deeper into the room.

Finally, daylight and artificial light must be interlinked by control systems to obtain the full economy potential. Some artificial light will always be on in any building, to light parts which daylight never adequately reaches. But in a building planned for daylighting, over half the working area should be able to derive all its ambient light naturally, and the rest needs only partial topping-up during daylight hours.

As daylight fades, at the end of the day or in poor weather, so artificial sources should come into use progressively, from the centre of the plan outwards. Automatic controls are preferable for ambient light, as personal controls is preferable for task light. Fittings can be ganged together in banks parallel to window walls, or individually operated by sensors. Switching on and off artificial sources is undesirable: it is distracting, creates a sense of gloom after a switch-off even if measured light levels are 'sufficient', and, with some discharge light sources, is not workable owing to their slow start-up.

Dimmers are now advancing in sophistication with micro-electronics: each fitting can adjust its level imperceptibly from fully off to fully on, balancing daylight performance and using the minimum possible power.

Used skilfully, daylighting techniques need present no constraints on the usefulness of the building, and can deliver cost-in-use economies as well as enhanced character and quality in the interior. Close and early co-operation between architect, interior and lighting designers, environmental and structural engineers and cost consultant is the way to develop any such concept to achieve the potential.

Climate control

It should be stated at the outset that most atrium buildings above domestic scale cannot operate without mechanical and electrical systems. Fire safety (see Chapter 10) requires detection and control systems, usually involving pumped air. Making use of the passive thermal advantages of atria often involves coupling them with artificial heating, cooling and ventilation systems. An atrium building is not therefore, except in the most benign climates and on a small scale, a candidate for a complete 'natural energy' approach. In very hot climates its best service is to improve the performance of a totally artificial environment system. In the terms used by a recent analyst, Dean Hawkes in The Architecture of Energy, (1982) an atrium building can be 'selective', using natural energy techniques to the reasonable limit for the building purpose and location, then completing the task with mechanical, electrical and electronic systems.

Atria involve two natural phenomena which can work for and against comfort: the greenhouse and stack effects. The greenhouse effect is caused by the fact that short-wave heat radiation from the sun will pass through glazing to warm interior surfaces. The re-radiated heat will then be at a longer wavelength and will not pass back through the glass. Solar heat is thus captured, with positive winter effects and negative

summer ones. The stack effect is the result of the action of pressure differences with altitude: air will always move from a lower opening to an upper one in any enclosed volume. Wind movement over the openings will enhance the suction effect. Combined with the buoyancy of air warmed by the greenhouse effect there will be strong stratification of air by temperature in a tall closed volume, and an equally strong upward draught when openings are made. Working with these two effects makes climate-control simple; working against them can be costly or even impracticable.

There are two basic questions to be answered before servicing strategies can be discussed. First, what is the climate of the site? Secondly, what is the thermal nature of the building use? What is sought is evidence to make a choice between an atrium which normally collects heat (the warming atrium), one which normally rejects heat (the cooling atrium), and one which attempts to do both at different seasons (the convertible atrium).

The climate is the obvious deciding factor: buildings in cool temperate climates generally need heat for most of the year; buildings in the tropics, constant cooling; and buildings in continental climates, heat in winter, cooling in summer. However, the nature of the building's form and use can change the contribution sought from the atrium from the obvious. Deep-plan buildings for shopping or

108 Geoffrey Bateman building, Sacramento, California 1981. An atrium building with comprehensive energy conscious design features. Office of the State Architect

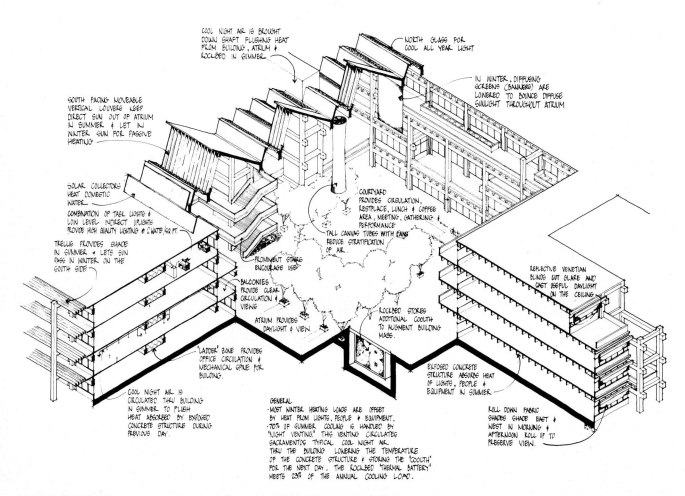

office use have year-round heat surpluses, at least in their core areas; they may even be in total surplus in northern winters. An atrium in this context will only aggravate matters if it collects solar heat: it would be better if it acted to dispose surplus internal heat. If an office building is re-planned to be shallow enough to lose its high electric lighting load it will then, in the same climate, need warming by its atrium. Consider the interaction of building use and climate before selecting the atrium thermal strategy.

A further basic decision, before the strategy can be turned into a design, is on the degree of comfort required in the atrium space itself. Four steps in comfort-control can be considered, from a simple unenclosed canopy, to enclosure without comfort-control–the basic buffer space–enclosure with partial control to help plants survive–the tempered buffer space–to enclosure achieving full human comfort standards. The basic buffer delivers most energy saving. The full-comfort atrium delivers the least saving, but still probably has no net energy cost compared to the alternative of not having it at all.

The possible nature of the barrier between surrounding space and the atrium will vary as the atrium comfort standard rises, as will the advisable nature of the atrium envelope, and the possible air-handling concepts. The air-handling concepts which can be considered are

1 Complete separation between occupied space ventilation and the atrium.

2 Intake of primary air via the atrium, the rest separate.

3 Exhaust of used, clean air into the atrium, the rest separate.

4 Use of the atrium as a supply air plenum to occupied spaces.

5 Use of the atrium as a return air plenum.

Advantages and disadvantages of each mode in warming, cooling and convertible atria of differing comfort levels are listed in **109**.

109 Atrium thermal type selection

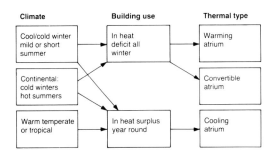

Climate	Building use	Thermal type
Cool/cold winter mild or short summer	In heat deficit all winter	Warming atrium
Continental: cold winters hot summers		Convertible atrium
Warm temperate or tropical	In heat surplus year round	Cooling atrium

111 Ventilation mode selection

	Canopy	Buffer	Temp buffer	Full comfort	Thermal type
No vent relationship	Norm	Norm	Possible	NA / Behaves as separate room	Warming Convertible Cooling
Intake via atrium	No effect	OK Summer / NA / OK winter	OK summer / NA / OK winter	NA	Warming Convertible Cooling
Exhaust to atrium	Slight effect	Useful	Useful	NA	Warming Convertible Cooling
Atrium as supply plenum	NA	NA	NA	Possible / Useful	Warming Convertible Cooling
Atrium as return plenum	NA	NA	Collects solar / Useful	Useful	Warming Convertible Cooling

110 Comfort type selection

Performance level	Comfort type	Examples
Shelter and shade no air containment	Canopy	Galleria, Milan Brunel Plaza, Swindon Antoine Graves houses, Atlanta
Winter air containment, shelter and shade. Summer natural ventilation no heating	Buffer	Trondheim University Swansea Quadrant Centre
Heating only to ensure minimum of 7°C or 13°C wide fluctuations	Tempered buffer	Atria North, Toronto Children's Hospital of Philadelphia Gregory Bateson Building, Sacramento
Servicing to normal occupied space standard	Full comfort	Royal Bank, Toronto Coutts Bank, London Hyatt Hotel, O'Hare, Chicago

112 Insulation and shading decisions

Thermal type	Canopy	Buffer	Temp buffer	Full comfort	Insulation location
Warming	Normal as for exterior walls *shadable in summer*		Lowered	No wall needed	Internal atrium walls
	None	To choice	Raised	Highly *shadable*	External atrium skin
Convertible	Normal external wall		Lowered	No wall needed	Internal atrium walls
	None *externally shadable in summer*	To choice	Raised	High	External atrium skin
Cooling	None	None	None	No wall needed	Internal atrium walls
	Shading only	None *externally shaded*	None	None	External atrium skin

The warming atrium

A warming buffer atrium will be designed to admit sun freely and will therefore generally be at least five degrees C warmer than outside air temperatures, except in prolonged cloudy periods. Even in cloudy periods it will be one or two degrees C warmer than outside in the daytime, due to heat flow into it from surrounding accommodation. It will therefore have the effect of shortening the heating season in the surrounding accommodation and reducing fuel need, although there will be negligible reduction in the heating system size needed to meet peak demands. In this it is like all other ambient energy systems.

Warming atria are the type of most interest to the countries of Northern Europe, which share winters of varied severity, cool, cloudy springs and autumns, and short, erratic summers. Heating may be needed for nine months of the year, and warm weather is welcome if it comes. Air conditioning is only essential here where building planning, construction or special use generates a need.

As the first two factors are under the designer's control the tendency since the start of the energy crisis has been to plan to reduce the amount of electricity needed for lighting or cooling, at the price, if necessary, of a greater heat need. Heat can be provided at lower primary energy cost, or the need obviated by greater insulation or by ambient energy collection.

Form and fabric

Building forms in this climate zone can be low-rise and well-spaced generally, because of the low (by world standards) development densities permitted. This accords with the low sun angles in Northern Europe. Since these low sun angles, down to 10 degrees above the horizon, are sought in building, it is desirable to have glazed side walls to the atrium facing within 20 degrees of noon. If only roof-glazing is possible, a south-facing monitor form permits collection of the most sun. Heavy solar penetration is acceptable if full atrium comfort is not being sought. If it is, then a south-facing wall can be shaded most easily to exclude higher-angle sun.

113 The warming atrium

a and **b** show a ventilation strategy for a buffer atrium. In winter it is slightly warmed by exhausting air into it after heat recovery. In summer it is cooled by movement of exhaust air plus any supplementary natural ventilation

c and **d** show a strategy for a tempered buffer atrium. Less ductwork is needed but more heat (except in sunny climates) as the whole atrium is warmed in winter

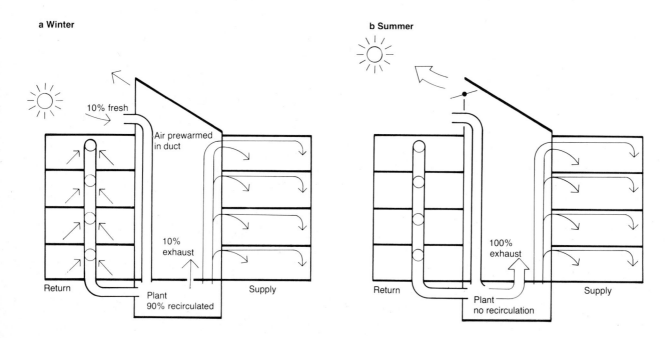

a Winter

10% fresh

Air prewarmed in duct

10% exhaust

Return

Plant 90% recirculated

Supply

b Summer

100% exhaust

Return

Plant no recirculation

Supply

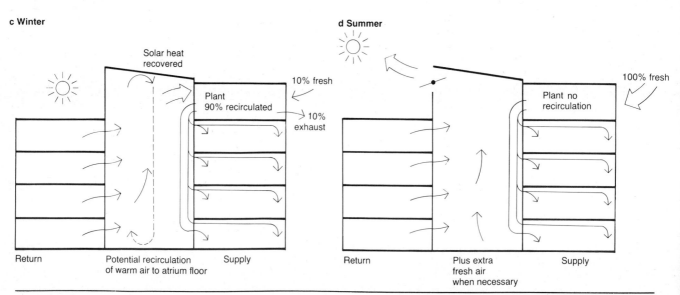

c Winter

Solar heat recovered

Plant 90% recirculated

10% fresh

10% exhaust

Return

Potential recirculation of warm air to atrium floor

Supply

d Summer

100% fresh

Plant no recirculation

Return

Plus extra fresh air when necessary

Supply

Thermal storage capacity in the internal atrium walls and floor is desirable. It will slow the build-up of heat when the sun is shining, and spread the warmth over short cloudy periods. A Swedish study by Goran Lundquist (in Camera Solaris, Stockholm, 1980) shows a benefit of two degrees C in overnight low temperature where thermal capacity is provided, and a converse reduction of two degrees C in periods of peak temperature. Walls should be light rather than dark in colour: daylight reflection will save higher-grade energy than will heat absorption.

The amount of insulation required in atrium surrounding walls depends on the comfort needed in the atrium and the insulation provided in the atrium envelope. High insulation in the atrium envelope will always be desirable in a warming atrium. It is least important on sun-facing side walls or monitors, but particularly important on roofs: heat migrates more rapidly upwards than sideways, as warm air presses against the roof. Open night skies in winter can suck radiant heat from an atrium, cooling it to below outside temperature. An alternative to insulated glazing, which has lower light transmission if thermally efficient, is the use of night-shutters. These can be of fabric or folding sheet material, and will be very cost-effective, especially if a full-comfort atrium is sought.

Ventilation in winter
Air circulation in winter is desirable even in a passive buffer atrium. Still air will stratify with cold air ponding at the level people pass through, and with any warm air pressing against the roof and cooling. If the atrium and occupied space are uncoupled for normal ventilation, effective air-mixing can be achieved by using a low-velocity fan to pull air down a duct. The duct can be a simple fabric sock hanging in the space. It will be effective and can be decorative too.

If comfort for plants is sought, it is worth considering some coupling of the atrium and building ventilation systems. Discharging clean exhaust air into the atrium, after heat-recovery, will provide a useful few degrees of warming at no cost to the building. Assistance with maintaining background temperatures in a tempered buffer atrium can also be achieved by siting the plant room below the floor of the atrium to give the benefit of its heat gain. Back-up heating, to run over winter weekends and holidays to keep the atrium temperature above minimum, will be needed (see also p. 149 ff.).

If full comfort is sought, the atrium is no longer strictly a buffer space. Solar penetration must be more selective and ventilation more sophisticated. Using the atrium as a part of the building ventilation system is then advisable, and the best results will be achieved if it is a return air plenum. Solar pick-up can then be collected, and any food smells controlled: atria are often used for dining. Warming an atrium by any other methods is problematic: injecting warm air into the inhabited levels of an otherwise cold atrium will lead to periodic dumping of cold air from above, and the escape of the warmed bubble of air; radiant heating is an option, but is not beneficial to plants.

Summer modes
When summer does eventually come the warming atrium must be able to cope. This is achieved in two ways. First, the occupied space around a buffer atrium can be economically shaded by internal-type blinds placed on the atrium side of the glazing.

Venetian blinds preserve daylight delivery; internal shading blinds to the atrium itself are only needed if higher comfort is sought in the atrium. Secondly, the greenhouse and stack effects can be used to induce ventilation, either of the atrium alone or of the whole building. Summer ventilation strategies are shown in **113b/d**. Shade and ventilation can be combined in the 'solar chimney' concept, which is useful for a comfortable atrium. In all atria to which sun is admitted it will be necessary to provide a reservoir volume at the top of the space to collect hot air. This should be above occupied levels, or, if not at the top of the building, on a plant room level.

The heat can be recovered, re-circulated or released, and the reservoir will also perform a smoke-control function (see p. 101) Many of the early atrium buildings do not have this reservoir and as a result some of the levels are almost uninhabitable.

114 **Solar chimney**
If increased exhaust power is needed in summer, an insulated blind hung behind glass will induce strong convection which can be used to pull air out of the atrium

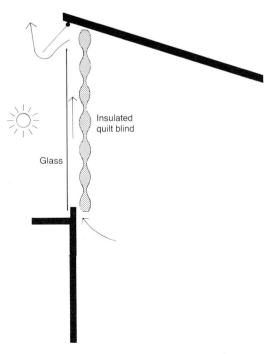

Insulated
quilt blind

Glass

115 **Warming atria: computer studies of performance.** While no complete models of atrium behaviour exist as yet, programs used for conventional building analysis can show the effects of different arrangements and constructions of atria. The ESP program has been used here, and the graphs are of external as against atrium air temperatures in typical weeks in the UK. Atrium temperatures are assumed even. In fact stratification will occur without air circulation

a January 13-19. Four-sided buffer atrium, top lit, single glazed, insulated walls to accommodation, leakage air change only

Weak winter sun raises atrium temperatures 2°C to 4°C above outside, when combined with heat lost from accommodation and the increased effectiveness of insulation due to the preservation of still surface air layers

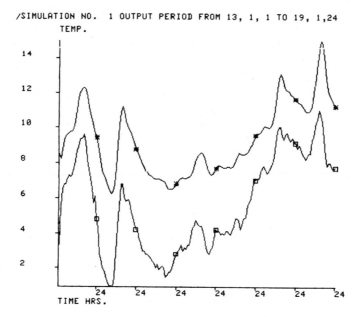

/SIMULATION NO. 1 OUTPUT PERIOD FROM 13, 1, 1 TO 19, 1,24
   TEMP.

b **January 13-19.** Three-sided buffer atrium, southside and toplit, double glazed, insulated walls to accommodation, leakage air change only. With increased glazing area the winter solar benefit is less than in the toplit atrium, and depends on double glazing to show any benefit. A 1.5°C to 3°C overnight gain is seen, though with greater diurnal swings in temperature

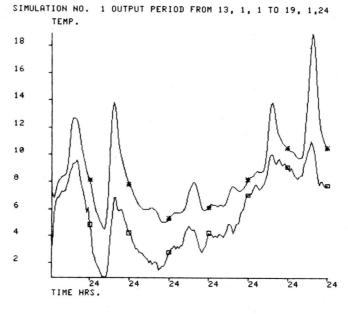

SIMULATION NO. 1 OUTPUT PERIOD FROM 13, 1, 1 TO 19, 1,24
   TEMP.

c **March 6-12.** Three sided buffer atrium, southside and toplit, specification as above. In mid-season overnight gains of 4°C to 6°C are achieved, greatly reducing heating loads. Midday temperatures in the atrium are passing 20°C however and before long will need to be vented off. A solid atrium roof on the same model reduces midday temperatures by 4-5°C

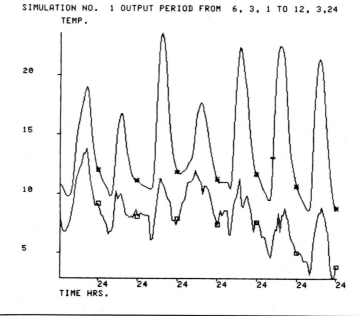

SIMULATION NO. 1 OUTPUT PERIOD FROM 6, 3, 1 TO 12, 3,24
   TEMP.

The convertible atrium

The convertible atrium should work very much as a warming atrium in winter, but have more substantial defences against over-heating in summer. This is the case even when full comfort is not sought in the atrium itself, since solar impact on the atrium interior will lead to heat build-up in the occupied space, and to impractical ventilation rates in the atrium. The basic need is for external shading to the atrium glazing. This can be fixed to admit low-angle sun in winter but to exclude high-angle sun in summer, or it can be operable. Operable shading is able to deliver more benefits, but at higher cost: it provides winter-night insulation and admits more daylight. Such shading shutters may be able to substitute for some of the insulation capacity of the envelope.

The Solar Energy Research Institute (SERI) building, Colorado, is in a classic continental climate, and has high insulation. Its atria are prototypes of the convertible form. An additional summer-night strategy used at SERI is the pulling of cool air through the hollow building fabric using the atrium smoke-removal fans. Pre-cooling the exposed structure reduces radiant temperatures next day, and therefore allows higher air temperatures to be tolerated.

A lower-cost operable device is a variant of the solar chimney. An insulated quilt can be hung below polar-oriented glazing in winter, and swung to shade solar-oriented glass in summer.

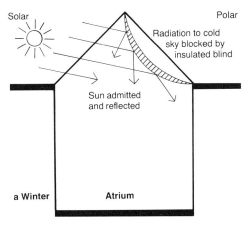

a A passive device, an insulated blind hanging from the atrium apex. In winter it substitutes for double glazing and acts as a solar reflector

a Winter   Atrium

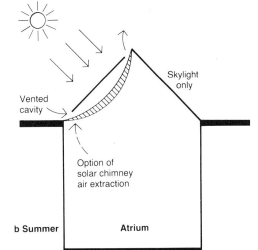

b In summer it is moved to the solar side and excludes direct sun

b Summer   Atrium

c-f Active concepts at the Solar Energy Research Institute (SERI) where multiple linear atria are shaded by external louvres

c In winter these capture sun

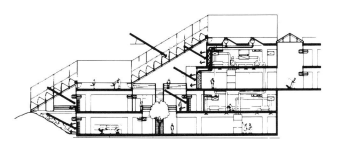

d In summer the louvres open vertically at night to radiate heat

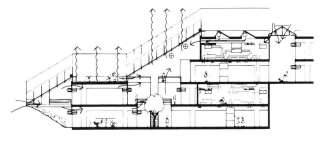

e On winter nights the louvres close to trap heat and prevent frost

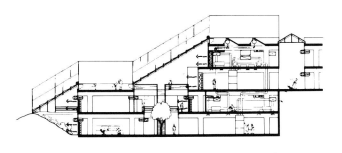

f On sunny summer days the louvres intercept sun. Natural cross ventilation removes heat and induces air movement through accommodation

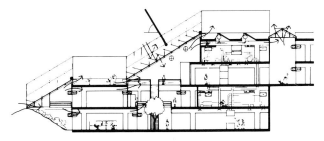

117 The cooling atrium

a High technology—the atrium as supply plenum. Using figures from the Atlanta Regency Hyatt hotel: atrium volume—3 million cu. ft; plant inputs 190,000 cfm into the atrium; 830 guest room plants each draw 90 cfm from the atrium and circulate 300 cfm (210 cfm room air recirculated); 90 cfm is exhausted via each bathroom, drawing a total of 75,000 cfm from the atrium; 115,000 cfm is recirculated from the top via a shaft in the elevator core

Air enters the atrium from a ring duct below the lowest guestroom level and rises in spirals, circulating all atrium air about four times per hour. Guestrooms have local control to heat or cool primary air. When rooms are unoccupied bathroom extract continues

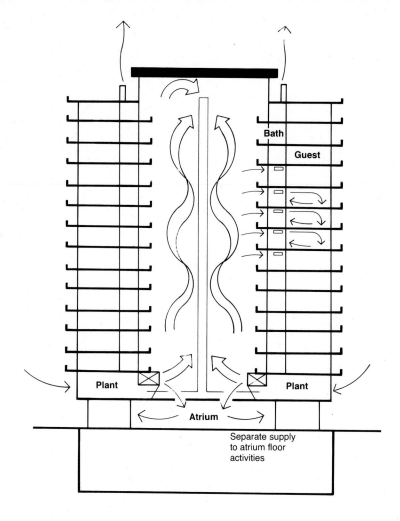

b Intermediate technology – the atrium as solar powered extract duct. Where generous cross ventilation is appropriate a large solar chimney atop the atrium can induce occupant-controlled cross ventilation in otherwise still air conditions

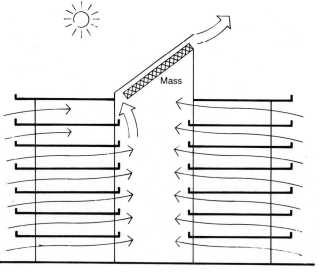

c Solar collector roof. Rooftop arrays of collectors for powering air conditioning can cross atrium roofs without excluding daylight

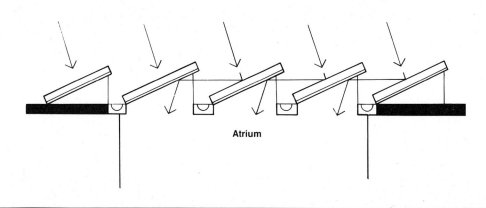

The cooling atrium

Where the climate or the nature of the building use requires continuous defence against high air temperatures, high humidity and strong sunshine, the atrium needs to behave as a shading device and a store of cool air. There are humid climates and cultures where acceptable comfort is achieved by strong cross-ventilation: an atrium can provide the 'fan power' to induce cross-ventilation of the occupied space using the stack effect, windscoops or solar chimneys. The majority of atrium buildings in warm and hot climates are, however, being built as part of 'exclusive' climate-control strategies, with air conditioning.

The ideal basic disposition of a cooling atrium is the reverse of that of a warming atrium. Sun must be excluded, except for 'accent lighting', and so glazing must either be fully shaded or polar-oriented. Sheer sky brightness in sunny climates may suggest indirect daylighting, diffusion by reflection, tinted glazing or fabric structures.

During the daytime the atrium needs to behave like a chest-freezer, holding a supply of cooled air. Where the diurnal temperature range is high this supply can be night air from the previous night, held as a thermal buffer and not used primarily for ventilation. This approach follows the open-air courtyard strategy of Islamic architecture: night air collects in deep courts and cools the walls, slowing the rate of heat build-up the next day. More commonly the atrium acts as a supply or return plenum.

The supply-plenum strategy is of value in this context and is used by Portman and his engineer Britt Alderman for their atrium hotels in warm climates. The primary air supply for the whole building is pumped into a shaded atrium (see **117**). Portman has used the concept with input either at the top or at the centre of the section with equal effectiveness, though smoke-extraction needs suggest input at the base. He has found that air temperature in the atrium varies only four degrees F from base to top when air in the space is circulated in this manner.

It is possible to see the supply-plenum concept working for many building types. Office space with local distribution plant could draw air from the tempered atrium supply. It follows that the atrium is fully comfortable, and that space can be opened up to it from each side if desirable for any reason. Smoke-control strategies must be compatible (see p. 101 ff.). If the floor of the atrium is used for dining, as is often the case in hotels, offices and shopping complexes, the flow of air must not allow the migration of food odour to other levels.

Insulation of the external skin of cooling atria is not very important: air temperature differences are not as extreme; condensation on the outside of glazing is uncommon as an issue. Heat-rejection is achievable very effectively by mass, shading and reflection, rather than by insulation.

The large roof areas of atrium buildings offer substantial opportunities for the siting of active solar collectors. This is especially true in hot, sunny climates where solar-facing roof-slopes need not be glazed. Hot water supply, and, in favourable circumstances, solar-powered air conditioning, can be fed from arrays on the atrium and building roof.

The atrium as a duct

There are savings in construction costs where the atrium performs as a supply or return air duct for the building. It is also sensible to route those services which are ducted via the atrium: in this way they do not take up usable floor area, can be prefabricated in large elements, and are accessible for maintenance and for modification. Plant-room location under the atrium floor or on the roof-top to one side of the atrium allows for this economical supply- and return-routing. Examples of bold sculptural use of ducting in atria are to be seen in the Eaton Center, Toronto and in the Rustoleum headquarters, Chicago by Murphy/Jahn (1978).

Calculating performance

Throughout this section reference has been made to the calculation of the amount of insulation, shading and other factors required to meet the climatic needs of the building. Full computer modelling of the thermal performance of atrium buildings is still to be achieved. The models developed for conventional-scale spaces have been stretched, and are performing usefully. In the United States the program DOE2 is relied upon. In Sweden the BRIS program is used. In England theoretical work is in progress at the Martin Centre, University of Cambridge, to produce a full model of the behaviour of atria. But however good the analytical tools become, the starting-point for design will continue to be informed intuition.

10 Design for fire safety

The challenge

Of all the technical issues arising in the design of atrium buildings, fire safety is the most challenging. Atrium buildings break with orthodox concepts of safety: without careful design they will probably not be safe. Even when a design has been achieved which the designers consider will perform adequately, consent must be obtained from the relevant authorities. Since codes and regulations have usually evolved to meet the orthodox approach to design, obtaining consent can be a taxing process: the most effective method is to consider fire safety from first principles, and to share your thinking from the start with experts and with the people who can give or withhold permission.

Why do atrium buildings present fundamental safety problems? Fire and smoke can spread vertically with great rapidity if openings in the floors are not properly enclosed. Assuming they are, the layered nature of a conventional building where space is divided by floors, provides resistance to the growth of fire, escape routes away from the affected floor and refuge in unaffected floors.

This is, of course, an idealized picture. In reality compartmented buildings also have inherent weaknesses. A fire in an unoccupied space can be undetected before it becomes too large to control easily. The miriad cavities and ducts in a modern building can provide concealed routes for fire to spread throughout a structure almost before it breaks out into visibility. The maze of partitions and corridors can make escape difficult and make finding the seat of the fire harder. But all these hazards are well understood and the best practice at any time and place can be prescribed clearly to the designer. An atrium, however, appears to some people to throw the safety advantages of cellular design out of the window; the hazards an ill-conceived atrium building might present are shown in **118**. It is little wonder that the first reaction of the fire department to a proposal to erect an atrium building is often one of extreme caution.

There are, in fact, answers to all the problems posed. An atrium building can be as safe as a conventional one. That hundreds of atrium buildings now exist, many in cities with highly sophisticated and tough fire departments, is proof that safety measures can be incorporated convincingly by competent designers. John Portman's experience reveals that fire departments can welcome atrium buildings. With proper detection, fire- and smoke-control systems the buildings offer superior visibility and clarity of escape routes, as well as ease of discovery and access to the fire. It is argued that the huge air volume in the atrium cools flame, dilutes smoke and sustains life. This is only true to a certain degree and whilst recognized by the 1981 United States NFPA Code[1] is not yet universally accepted.

This paradox of the atrium principle being apparently anathema to some and acceptable to others, is the result of the wide range of design possibilities within the concept, as well as of the varied experience and attitudes of authorities. The truth is that no two atrium buildings are the same. They are as individual in their fire behaviour as conventional buildings. Also, whilst the phenomenon of fire is universal, its effects vary depending on the climate and environment of different countries. National codes therefore differ, and grounds for seeking exemptions for unusual designs must reflect these differences. It has taken 17 years to evolve a national code for atrium buildings in the United States, the only country that has one to date. Even now there will be debate on its correctness—the number of variables is so great. The most productive result of these years of discussion has been to divert many designers and fire officers from merely squabbling about code interpretation to considering pure performance standards.

What is the level of risk in the building? How is the quantity of smoke to be limited? How is the smoke to be controlled and removed? How has the necessity for total evacuation been avoided? How is fire-spread limited? The discussion goes to the first principles of the nature of fire, the psychology of people in emergencies, and the workings of the building's plan and systems.

First, the consultancy team needs to work closely together. Safety measures will influence the whole plan, structure, systems and cost of the project.

The fire at the Hyatt O'Hare

Debate about the fire safety of atrium buildings recurs largely in the vacuum of hypothesis. There have been very few incidents from which to learn what really happens. Burning curtains on an upper gallery in the atrium of the Atlanta Regency Hyatt were extinguished by the fire brigade without any panic, smoke-logging, or evacuation. Sprinklers have knocked down incipient fires in hotel rooms, also without problems.

A major fire did occur in the Regency Hyatt O'Hare in Chicago on March 2nd, 1973. A lot was learned from this incident: at the time a theoretical study of atrium fire behaviour was underway on behalf of New York City Fire Department who were considering an application for a new hotel, and the O'Hare fire was studied by the same team.

The fire started in the Blue Max nightclub on lobby level, below one side of the bedroom court. It was deliberately started, while the club was unoccupied; a major fire developed as the club was not sprinklered. Smoke poured into the atrium from the open side of the club. The automatic extract system was inoperative as it had been disconnected for maintenance. Neither the re-circulation-based system nor the summer-time cross-ventilation fans under the skylight were operational. Smoke gradually logged the atrium down to the bedroom level directly above the lobby. Guests were evacuated and no-one was hurt in spite of the smoke-logging. However, many guests claimed not to have heard alarms; some who did went for the lifts in the central tower rather than the stairs, which were not easily identified. Smoke entered some of the bedrooms. The dilution of combustion products afforded by the atrium volume, even in these adverse circumstances, reduced the smoke hazard.

The 1973 report (unpublished), by P R De Cicco and S Ifshan, noted the faults in the design and management of the hotel, and these lessons have been incorporated in subsequent designs, and in the Hyatt O'Hare. Sprinklers now cover all spaces opening into the atrium. One smoke-extract system is always operational. Stairs are more clearly indicated, both in their locations and in instructions on the doors of each room.

The fire at the IMF headquarters

An example which illustrates just how much smoke can be produced from a small fire, and how inadequate control measures can be, is the fire which occurred at the IMF building, in the centre of Washington DC. The IMF building is a 13-storey atrium office building. Used by top executives of the Fund, its floor-space is almost entirely sub-divided into cellular offices with glass walls to the atrium. On the evening of May 13th, 1977, after all staff had left the building, fire broke out in one 150-square foot office on the tenth floor.

By the time fire-fighters arrived the window between the affected office and the atrium had broken due to the fire, and smoke was entering the atrium at a great rate. Smoke detectors spotted the fire, and released six spring-loaded panels in the roof-glazing to vent the smoke. Only two worked since the springs were rusted or strained; the other four were later opened manually. The atrium HVAC system, which included smoke-purging facilities, had been switched off and the fire-fighters could not discover how to activate it without the building engineer.

Smoke from the one burning room quickly filled the top three storeys of the 100 by 140 feet space in spite of the venting, and continued to bank downwards reaching the floor of the atrium at one stage. There was no significant 'reservoir' volume in the glazing above the highest floor. Sprinklers situated under the plastic glazed roof never got hot enough to release. They would have been counterproductive anyway, serving only to cool and mix the smoke with the clear atrium air. By the time the smoke was cleared, by portable smoke-ejection fans on the atrium floor, $300,000-worth of damage had been caused by the smoke, although none of it had entered other occupied spaces.

As a consequence the fire department considered that such buildings should have automatic smoke-extraction fans available at all times. As will be seen below (p. 101) a properly engineered natural venting system would also have prevented much of the damage.

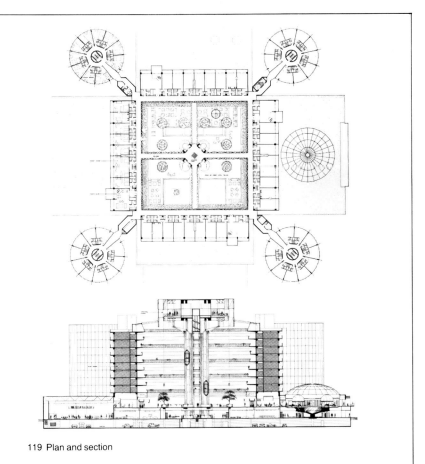

119 Plan and section

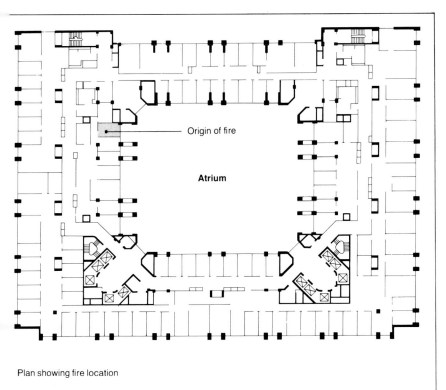

Origin of fire

Atrium

Plan showing fire location

Service-engineering concepts will be particularly deeply affected.

Secondly, bring in experienced specialist fire consultants: not only can they help the design team to choose an effective strategy, but they can build a bridge of understanding between designers and fire-fighters. Thirdly, and most importantly, involve the fire authority from an early stage. Develop the essential thinking in discussion, so that not only does the scheme work, but the fire department is identified with it. Visit examples of similar projects with members of the fire department—it is often only then that the physical reality of the sort of building under discussion comes home to those fresh to it. Use models to investigate fire-fighting approaches.

After having established rapport with the working officers of the fire authority, you must be prepared to present your thinking to committees and councils. Here you will probably be dealing with laymen, and clear presentations are needed, both verbal and visual, of all the principles at stake. There can be a problem in creating precedents. This means that the case must be handled with legal and administrative precision. The authority will be reluctant to allow new precedents to be set, and may well respond legalistically as well as technically.

The problem of getting permission differs in developing and long-established contexts. It could be said that Portman's original atrium was achievable because Atlanta at the time was just beginning to develop on a large scale. New people and attitudes were arriving, and an open, non-rigid view was taken of the concept. In some countries the act of getting approval is purely political, and designers will be seeking to test themselves in order to achieve peace of mind, insurability and safety from legal pursuit rather than to convince anyone else. Local customs and lifestyles will create differences both in the hazards and in the reaction of people to emergencies. Think them through before developing the design and the argument for it.

This chapter will consider the special features of atrium building design for fire safety under three headings: means of escape, smoke-control, and fire-control. The subject of means of escape interacts strongly with the whole planning and circulation concept of the building and should be considered from day one. Smoke-control strategies are part of the ventilation concept as a whole, and equally fundamental to the idea of the building. Fire-control measures and fire-fighting provisions will take their slice of the budget. The financial effect of all these precautions is discussed in Chapter 14. All sections will discuss first principles as these may well be the basis of the debate on consent.

Means of escape

Basic principles
The basic principle in escape-planning is that occupants of a building must be able to turn their backs on a fire and reach a place of safety by their own unaided efforts. The 'place of safety' may be the ground outside, or, in large building complexes, a part of the building completely isolated from the spread of the fire; the escape route is between the place where the fire starts and the place of safety. This must be a protected route, unlikely to be affected by smoke or flames before evacuation is complete.

Staged escape
A fire may start in virtually any part of a building although it is normally assumed that one will not start in the protected routes themselves or in toilet (restroom) areas. If it starts in a small room its occupants should be able to get through the door whilst the fire is still very small. If it starts in a large room it may grow quickly and block the path to the door, so that a second door giving an alternative route is needed.

Escape from the affected room must be very quick: the production of toxic smoke can render a room uninhabitable in a very short time. The travel distance acceptable before leaving the affected space will depend on the use of the space and such factors as the fire-load, the type of combustibles present, the toxicity of smoke, the degree of crowding or obstruction in the space, and whether it is

Once people have left the directly affected or endangered spaces they should be on the second leg of their escape, in a protected route. There may be three stages to this: a corridor or other room before a stair is reached, then the stair itself, and finally the route to the outside or refuge. If initial escape is through another room or conventional corridor, this is still part of the unprotected route; the fire risk in that room or corridor should, therefore, be very small. Corridor and door widths should accommodate expected traffic and respond to its increasing density towards the door to the stairway.

Stairways suitable for escape must be of non-combustible construction, have no fire risk in them, and must be sufficiently structurally separated from the rest of the building to keep fire at bay during the escape period. Doors into them must be fire resistant and self-closing. High fire-risk rooms should not open directly into escape stairways.

Stairways have to be wide enough and designed and lit to allow safe movement by the anticipated number of evacuees. This number will vary depending on whether evacuation of the whole compartment, or only of the fire floor and the one above it is necessary.

Smoke-entry to staircases must be prevented by design. Natural ventilation can only keep a stair clear in favourable atmospheric conditions if two opposite walls are external and have large permanent openings.

121 Principles of fire escape planning

a Travel distances in unprotected space follow these generally accepted figures. Actual routes must be measured, not radii

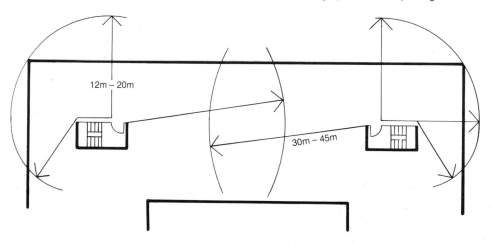

12m – 20m

30m – 45m

publicly accessible. The travel distances normally accepted are between 12 to 20 metres where only one direction of movement is possible, and 30 to 45 metres to the nearest escape where a choice of routes is available. Office and commercial buildings with low fire risks will obtain the higher figures. Hotels or other places where sleeping people may need to be aroused in endangered rooms will have far lower acceptable travel distance through unprotected space. In some codes increased travel distances within the fire-affected area are allowed if the space is sprinklered. This is questionable. Heat risk may be reduced, but sprinklers cause mixing of smoke and clear air, endangering visibility and breathing sooner unless coupled with smoke-extraction systems.

Mechanical pressurization is more effective and gives freedom of stair location: a small over-pressure developed in the stair by a special air supply will hold smoke at bay. It is effective even when several doors are open. Design criteria are given in British Standard 5588. In tall buildings and in extreme climates stair-shafts may have to be divided into stages to reduce the effect of natural pressure gradients in the shaft.

In the final stage of escape, at the base of the stair, a protected route to open air at ground level must exist, wide enough to clear people from the stair and avoid congestion. There is no need to limit travel distances in the stair or final route since there is no fire danger within them.

Use of the familiar route

All of the above is straightforward and is accepted in forms of varied detail around the world. Problems arise immediately in all multi-storey buildings and especially in mall or atrium buildings.

In an emergency people tend to use the route they know. Occupants of office buildings can be trained by fire drills, but visitors to shopping, leisure or resort buildings only generally know the way they came in. For most of them this means the grand, unobstructed way in, and a ride in an elevator or on an escalator. Elevators are usually considered to be unsafe in fire: their shafts can be smoke routes, and their controls are vulnerable to heat. Protected elevators can be designed in pressurized shafts, and may figure in the future, but present practice suggests: 'don't use the elevators'. In a normal multi-storey building evacuees will eventually find the stairs. They should open, in or adjacent to the familiar elevator lobby, so that at least the escape corridor layout on each floor is the one used for normal purposes. With an atrium this may not always be the case. It is therefore necessary to intercept movement to the elevators by locating stairs on the familiar route and signing them very clearly.

Circulation concepts

There are various ways of laying out the circulation of different types of atrium building in order to ensure that evacuees find a protected staircase quickly and are not exposed to smoke (see **122**). These layout principles apply whether accommodation is open to the atrium, or screened from it. Smoke-control is simpler when screening is used, and escape via gallery-circulation is then protected from smoke if the fire is not in the atrium itself. The risks from heat radiation through glass screens will need to be considered.

Some authorities prefer external gallery escape routes to atrium galleries. The Continental 'fluchtbalcon' or flight balcony, is provided, usually by cantilevering floor-edges a metre or so beyond the outer wall. The balconies also serve as sun-breakers, maintenance routes, and, if slightly enlarged and screened, patios for hotel rooms or flats. However, they too have their dangers.

It is sometimes essential to use the atrium floor itself as part of the protected escape route. In shopping developments this is the normal route with the capacity to handle crowds. It can usually be of non-combustible construction, have no fire-load and have an effective smoke-control system. It is tempting, where other accommodation is stacked above such a space, to discharge staircases into the mall. This is done at Henning Larsen's Trondheim University. It is not without risk, although partially accepted by the NFPA. The fire could be on the lowest level, and considerably more time will elapse before people emerge from the stair base compared to direct escape from the mall floor level. And time is risk.

The Los Angeles Bonaventure Hotel has fire-shutters to enclose routes from the base of its stair-shafts to the outside. They are normally open to the atrium. This too is undesirable: smoke-detector-activated shutters are sensitive and can be dangerous; heat-detector-activated shutters would not drop until conditions were already far too dangerous for escape.

b Protected routes are of fire resistant construction, vented or pressurized. There is no travel distance limit, but protection must extend all the way to the exterior, or to a 'place of safety', a completely protected compartment

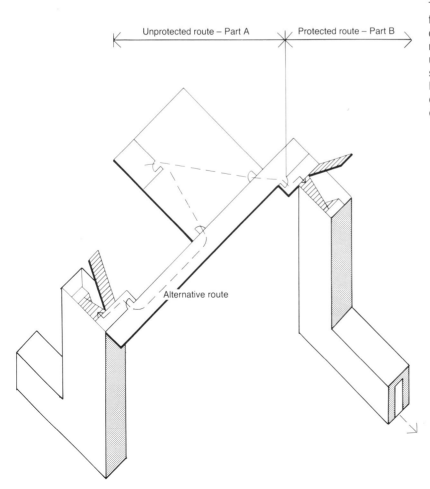

Unprotected route – Part A   Protected route – Part B

Alternative route

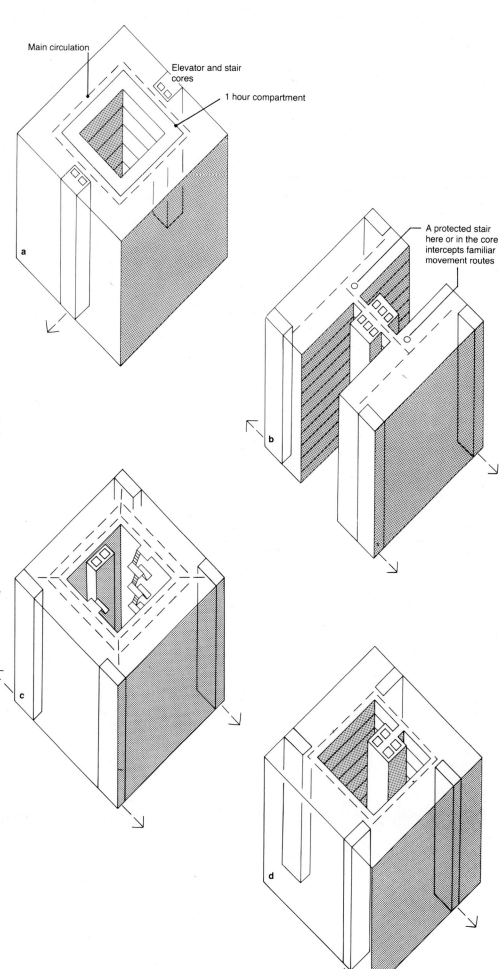

Main circulation

Elevator and stair cores

1 hour compartment

a

A protected stair here or in the core intercepts familiar movement routes

b

c

d

122 Circulation and escape options

a Complete separation of circulation from atrium
Ring circulation inboard from atrium. Office space overlooking atrium compartmented. No safety issues

Example: Welsh Office, Cardiff, Wales Alex Gordon and Partners

b Mixed Circulation
Main elevators in the atrium; escape stairs remote. Familiar routes need interrupting with fire stairs

Example: Galleria II, Houston, Texas Helmuth, Obata, Kassabaum

c Alternative Circulation
Elevators and unprotected stairs in atrium circulation both around atrium edge and inboard. Fire stairs remote. Clear signing and emergency drills advisable

Example: Toronto Metropolitan Library
Raymond Moriyama

d All circulation via atrium
Stairs in protected shafts but accessed only via atrium galleries. Galleries must be shielded from smoke invasion and heat radiation by active and passive measures

Example: Hyatt Hotel, Atlanta John Portman Associates

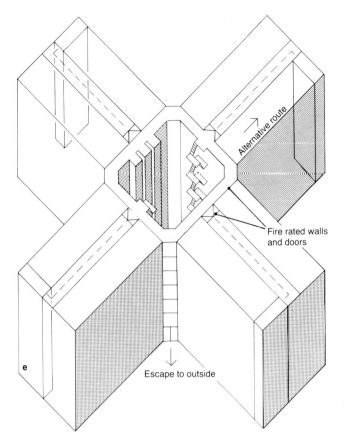

e Atrium as protected route
If the whole atrium is of incombustible construction, contains no fire load, is separated from all accommodation and pressurized, in emergencies it can act as a protected escape route as well as everyday circulation

Example: none known

f Atrium floor as part of escape route. An atrium floor may be a safe final escape route from the base of stair shafts if smoke is kept away from the floor and there is a choice of routes out

Example: Trondheim University
Henning Larsen

g Radiation hazard with glass screened galleries. Where escape is via internal or external galleries or balconies care must be taken to protect people from heat radiation. Whilst glass can contain smoke and fire for a period it allows radiation to pass through. Unless considerable balcony width is provided, consider an opaque spandrel panel to cill height, allowing people to crawl safely by in emergency. An alternative is intumescent laminated glazing, which goes opaque in fire and thus blocks radiation

h The 'fluchtbalcon' concept
External galleries (900 mm min) can lead to external or internal stairs. A choice of routes must be given but there are no travel distance problems.

A drawback: by encouraging the opening of exterior doors the fire is often drawn more rapidly through the building and up its external walls

Example: Saxon Court Offices, Milton Keynes, UK
MKDC

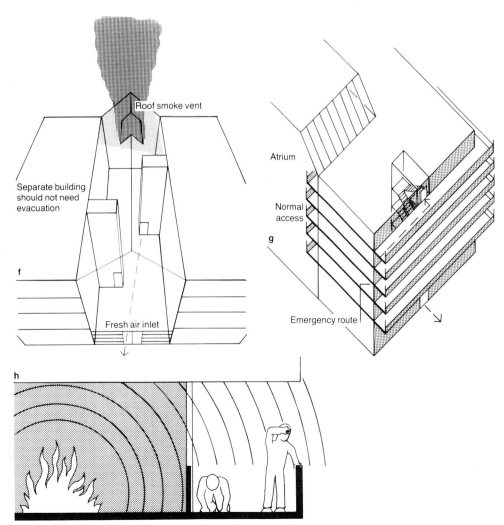

123 Smoke production

Production of smoke by a fire

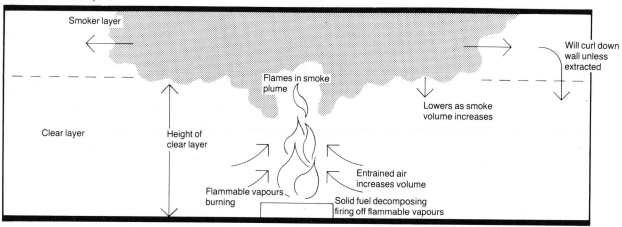

Variables determining smoke output
Y=distance from fire to underside of smoke layer (metres)
P=perimeter of fire (metres)

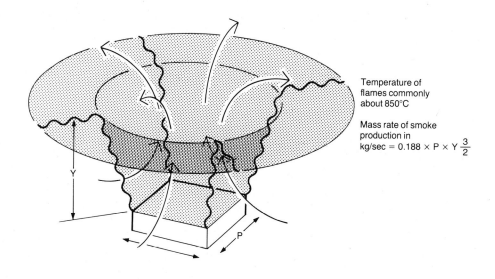

Temperature of flames commonly about 850°C

Mass rate of smoke production in
$kg/sec = 0.188 \times P \times Y^{\frac{3}{2}}$

Typical smoke expansion in tall space. Smoke temperature is assumed to be 300°C by the time it reaches the smoke layer. In a tall atrium cooling to ambient generally occurs after 18 m rise. Volume stops increasing

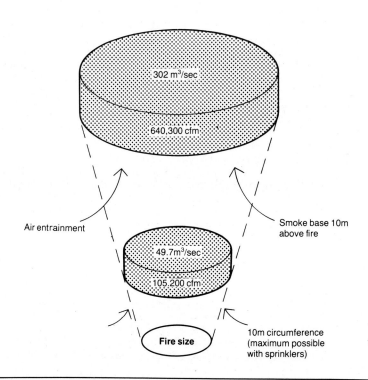

302 m³/sec
640,300 cfm

Air entrainment

Smoke base 10m above fire

49.7m³/sec
105.200 cfm

Fire size

10m circumference (maximum possible with sprinklers)

Smoke-control

Smoke is the first and most rapidly developed threat to life in fire. Control methods are highly desirable in any building to give maximum time for safe escape from the affected floor; they are essential in open-sided atrium buildings to prevent the need for total evacuation.

Smoke production

It is necessary to look at the nature of smoke before the use of control strategies can be understood. Smoke consists of 'the airborne solid and liquid particulates and gases evolved when material undergoes pyrolisis or combustion' (ASTM-EJ 1979). The chemistry of a fire is very complicated. There can be many different reactions occuring simul-taneously, with the products of some combining to initate others. The result is a range of gases, small droplets of tars and other condensates, and larger solid particles.

When inflammable material is heated, usually by adjacent burning material, hot, volatile combustible gases are produced. These ignite so that above the fire is a column of flames and hot, smoky gases. It has a strong upward movement because its density is lower than that of the cold surrounding air. Natural convection set up by the fire draws air into the bottom of the combustion zone. Some of the air supplies oxygen to the fire, but most is simply heated and entrained in the smoke, becoming an inseparable part of the expanding plume.

The quantities of smoke produced by a fire can be calculated. For a given size of fire the gases directly produced by burning are but a small component of the smoke volume produced. Entrained air forms the great majority of the volume. The smoke quantity can therefore be assessed from the perimeter length of the fire, along which air is being entrained, and from the height of the plume before it reaches the underside of the cloud below the ceiling of the space involved. Of these two factors the plume height is the more important. Volumes produced are prodigious, and the dilution effect of the atrium is relatively small.

Expansion and air-entrainment do not, however, continue indefinitely. The smoke will eventually rise and cool to the same temperature as the surrounding air. It will then form a stagnant layer, prey to any air currents in the space. In practice it will usually be carried on up by hot smoke from below. The height at which stagnation takes place depends on the heat of the fire. For a three by three metre (five megawatt) fire the height will be about 20 metres above it.

Smoke-control and extraction

Some form of smoke-control will be essential to prevent an atrium and all connected space smoke-logging. Smoke-control, by venting or extracting smoke to keep occupied spaces clear, can only be achieved if smoke quantities are limited, which means limiting fire-size. This is discussed in the section on fire-control (p. 109) in more detail, but for most buildings it involves sprinklers, allowing a maximum fire-size of three by three metres between their spray heads.

Alternative strategies for handling smoke and excluding it from occupied space involve combinations of two concepts: Is the atrium open-sided or enclosed? Is smoke-removal to be via the atrium or away from it? Buffer atria will be enclosed entirely with no permanent use on the atrium floor and therefore no serious risk of fire starting in the atrium. In buffer atrium buildings smoke-control may not be essential if the accommodation wall to the atrium is sealed. As it will usually be openable, control will be needed. With a full-comfort atrium, surrounding space is rarely entirely screened off, and sometimes entirely open, and there is usually activity on the atrium floor. Choices arise from these factors.

Extraction away from the atrium

There is a psychological and physical advantage in extracting smoke away from the atrium. The signs of fire are largely limited to the fire floor, reducing the desire to evacuate other levels. This strategy is economically feasible if the fire-risk and load on the atrium floor are minimal; otherwise smoke from that source would need extraction too, and duplicate systems would be involved. A buffer atrium is likely to be acceptable for this strategy, or a 'comfortable' open-sided atrium used scrupulously for circulation only.

Smoke reservoirs will be needed above all accommodation, connected to extraction. A reservoir is the volume between the underside of the structure or closed ceiling and a safe height above people's heads. Suspended screens limit sideways spread of smoke. Partitioning of floor-space will need to respect the reservoir concept. Full-height partitions create separate reservoirs which will need connecting to extraction systems or vents. This extraction strategy is ideally matched with the use of the atrium as a supply plenum.

Extraction via the atrium

This can be a choice for buffer atrium buildings, compatible with using the buffer as a return air plenum or exhaust. It will be obligatory for comfortable atria where there is fire-load within the atrium. Where floors are open to the atrium and open-planned, reservoirs will not be needed as smoke can move freely into the atrium. Partitioned rooms will need vented reservoirs. Screened floors will need full reservoirs, with controlled vents into the atrium, which can all work as part of the return-air system.

Once smoke enters the atrium it can expand freely as it rises. Much greater volumes must be extracted compared to the alternative route. The physics of rising smoke also enables open-sided floors to defend themselves against smoke-entry. Up to atrium heights of about 20 metres smoke should lift itself unaided out of roof vents in temperate climates.

Dilution is not enough

It is sometimes argued that the sheer volume of large atria has a diluting effect on smoke, increasing visibility for escape and reducing toxicity. In association with adequate fire size limitation and smoke removal measures this may be so. Without them no atrium is big enough to dilute smoke appreciably

Example:

Assume a fire size of 3m × 3m, with a 5mw heat output (a normal maximum size for a sprinklered building). Smoke will rise in the atrium and expand for at least 12m before cooling to ambient temperature

Smoke mass produced 94kg/sec
Smoke volume produced 75m^2/sec at 21°C

Probably optical smoke density=10
Acceptable density for 5m visibility is 0.2

Dilution factor is therefore 50 times
Air volume required to dilute this smoke is:
50×75m^3/sec=3750m^3/sec, or 225,000m^3/min; 8 million cfm

This represents several times the volume of the largest atria built and is required to dilute only one minute's smoke production

Inadequate reservoir height or vent area leading to smoke invasion of upper floors

Plume expansion pushes smoke into upper floors

15°

Smoke plume expands at approximately 15° to vertical

In tall atria (over 20m) lateral smoke spread can occur due to cool smoke moving with air currents

Uncontrolled fire size producing smoke in unhandlable quantities

125 **Smoke extraction away from the atrium**

a Fire A, in open sided floor, fire size controlled by sprinklers

b Smoke reservoir between structure and safe height ventilation, less if powered. Ceilings should be open type unless plenum extract is used

c Edge screen to atrium, containing smoke reservoir (can be toughened glass)

d Builder's work duct used as normal return air shaft. All extract plant capacity concentrated on fire floor. Return from other floors cut off

e Supply air only to non-fire floors. Air spills to atrium defending non-fire floors against stray smoke

f Make-up air enters fire floor below smoke layer, avoiding creation of turbulence

g Fire B shown as an alternative in a screened floor with perimeter venting

h Perimeter vent must be high enough to obtain reservoir, or be powered

i Make-up air must enter fire floor through screen but below smoke layer

j Atrium must have minimal fire load to avoid duplicate smoke extract system

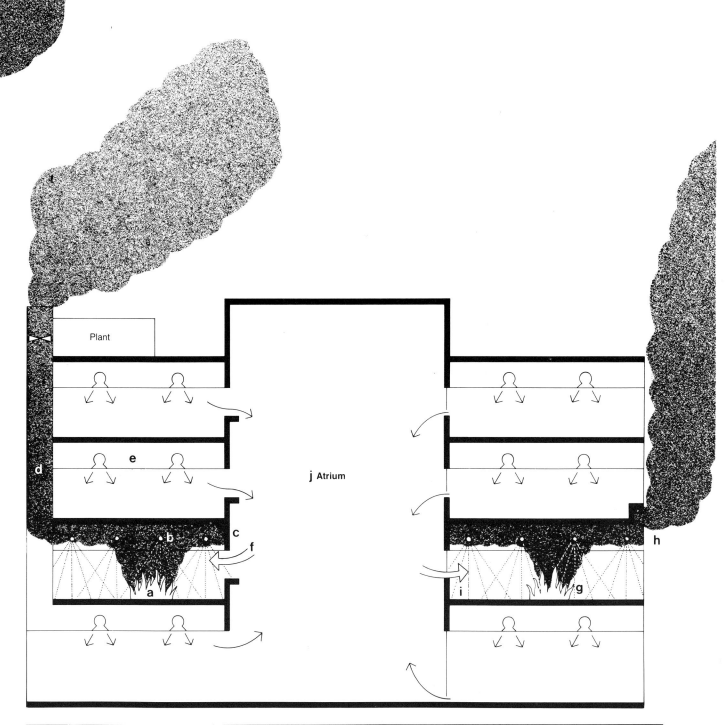

Constructing the atrium

126 Smoke extraction via the atrium, open sided floors

a Fire size controlled by sprinklers

b Smoke vented to atrium. No edge screens must obstruct flow

c Edge screen preventing smoke invasion from fire on lower floors

d Smoke plume spreading at 15° from vertical, contained by floor edges

e Non-fire floors on air supply only, no supply to fire floor

f Atrium smoke reservoir; effective depth measured from highest exposed floor to centreline of vent; 1.7m minimum for natural lift

g Vents open automatically on detection of smoke in the fire floor

h Make-up fresh air introduced via atrium floor, or as low as possible

i Alternative floor edge profiles, preventing smoke

J Light shelves must not cut the 20° angle

k Set back floor edges protect themselves

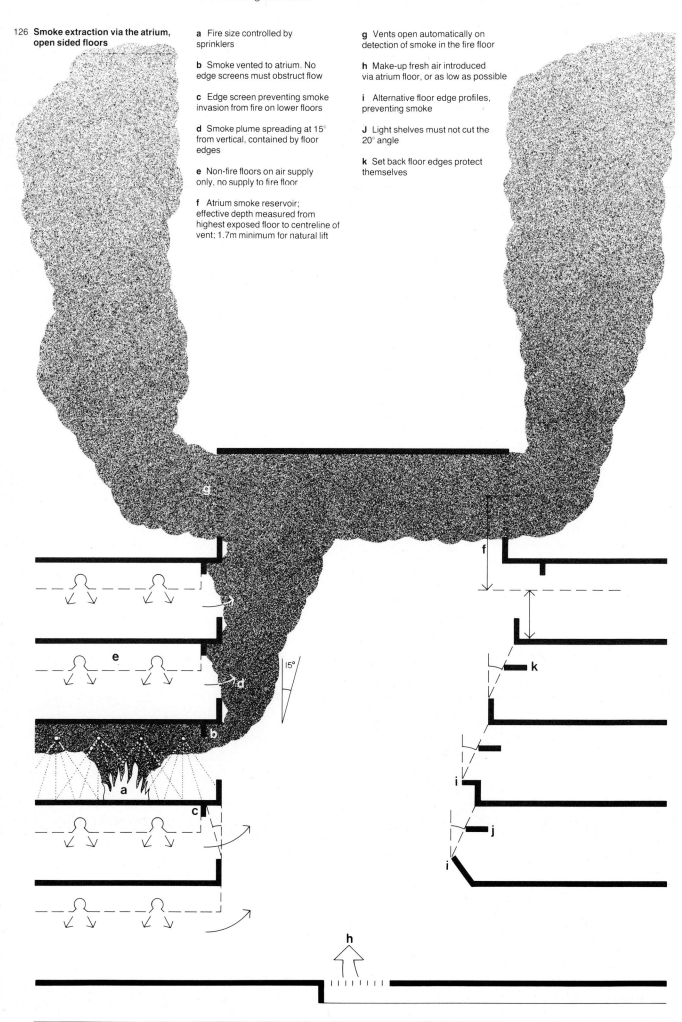

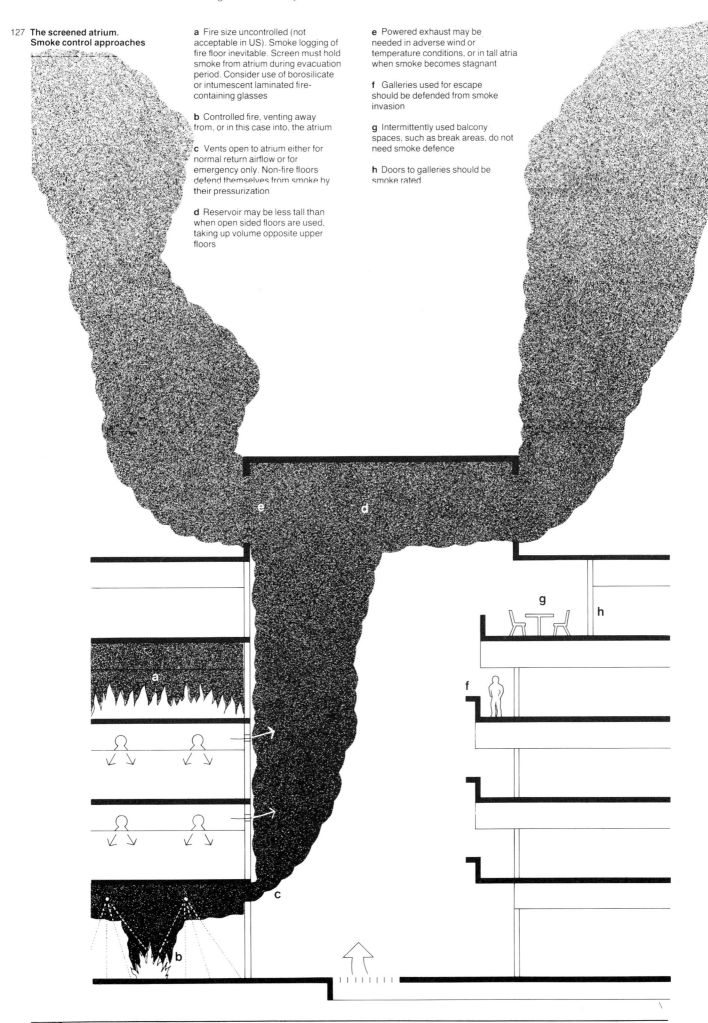

127 The screened atrium. Smoke control approaches

a Fire size uncontrolled (not acceptable in US). Smoke logging of fire floor inevitable. Screen must hold smoke from atrium during evacuation period. Consider use of borosilicate or intumescent laminated fire-containing glasses

b Controlled fire, venting away from, or in this case into, the atrium

c Vents open to atrium either for normal return airflow or for emergency only. Non-fire floors defend themselves from smoke by their pressurization

d Reservoir may be less tall than when open sided floors are used, taking up volume opposite upper floors

e Powered exhaust may be needed in adverse wind or temperature conditions, or in tall atria when smoke becomes stagnant

f Galleries used for escape should be defended from smoke invasion

g Intermittently used balcony spaces, such as break areas, do not need smoke defence

h Doors to galleries should be smoke rated

Constructing the atrium

A reservoir will be needed in the atrium roof. For natural venting the area of vent needed will reduce as the height of the reservoir increases: the 'head' of smoke pushes it out. The width of the reservoir need only be sufficient to capture the rising smoke. The reservoir depth may include upper floor levels if these are screened off (see **129**).

Difficulties arise in taller atria. Cool smoke may not lift itself out of the atrium, and powered extraction will then be necessary. Power will also be needed where outside temperatures are higher than smoke temperatures, or where the atrium roof suffers down-draughts from taller building elements surrounding it.

Smoke-removal fans should not be idle, awaiting an emergency. Ideally they should form part of the normal air-handling equipment, capable of being switched to special duty in emergencies. In this way they will be serviced regularly.

Make-up air for flushing the atrium of smoke needs to be introduced at the base of the space, at a rate matching the smoke-extract

rate after spillage of air from occupied floors is counted. That spillage helps to keep smoke out of open-sided floors where combined with suitable edge profiles.

Screened space overlooking an atrium is well defended against smoke-entry. Not all accommodation need be behind the screen, however. Areas for circulation and break areas can be on galleries and balconies within the open atrium even if smoke is extracted through it. They must not be continuously occupied spaces unless adequately defended, and should be separated from working or living spaces by smoke-stop doors. A considerable feeling of openness can be obtained by this approach.

Any smoke-control system will be complimented by pressurization of protected escape routes (see p. 96). Where conventionally arranged accommodation is above a podium atrium through which smoke is extracted, it is especially important to defend it against smoke-spread. Pressurization of all connecting shafts is the best policy, pushing air down into the atrium (see **130**).

128 **Times Square Hotel, New York,**
John Portman and Associates
Powered ventilation pattern in
emergency caused by fire on the
hotel (upper) atrium floor. The
diagram shows the high air volumes
introduced to and extracted from the
upper atrium, in cubic feet per minute

*from Paul de Cicco and Robert J
Cressi, Polytechnic Institute of New
York*

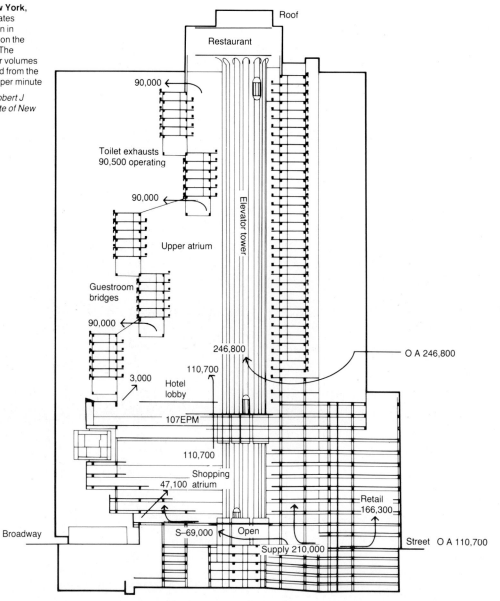

129 Case study: smoke removal calculations for an office building

This case, based on an actual building design, has twelve storeys of offices arranged around a working atrium. The lowest three levels are open-sided, the rest behind glass screens. All floorspace is sprinklered, the atrium floor having a suspended pergola carrying sprinklers above it at third-floor level.

A fire area 3m × 3m is assumed, on the atrium floor, the worst possible case with sprinklers. Its heat output is 5 megawatts. Smoke rises, expanding up the atrium space. By the time it reaches the fourth or fifth floor the smoke temperature is down to ambient, and the cloud moves up only in response to hotter smoke below.

Extraction is via the glazed roof, and can in theory be by natural or mechanical ventilation. Natural ventilation is subject to weather and wind effects and needs high vent areas to avoid smoke logging the entire atrium. Mechanical ventilation rates are shown to achieve equivalent extraction. Note that the upper levels of this tall, relatively narrow atrium become involved as part of the smoke reservoir. Open sides or gallery access only could not be considered for these upper floors.

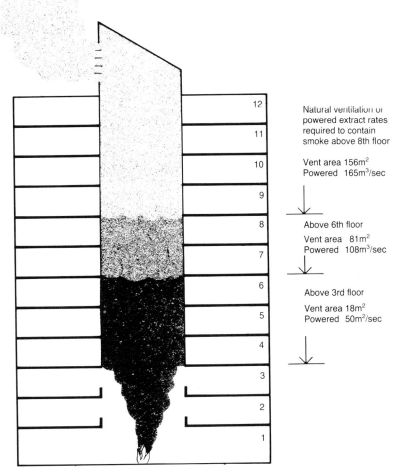

Natural ventilation or powered extract rates required to contain smoke above 8th floor

Vent area 156m²
Powered 165m³/sec

Above 6th floor
Vent area 81m²
Powered 108m³/sec

Above 3rd floor
Vent area 18m²
Powered 50m²/sec

130 Case study: smoke removal from a podium atrium

It is common in podium atrium buildings for the base of the circulation core of the tower to be open to the atrium space. This allows clear view to and from the elevator area of the multi-level space. In this example, based on an existing hotel, the guestroom floors do not open off the atrium, but sit above it. Meeting and function rooms and kitchens open off the four-level atrium, which contains dining areas.

The risk is that smoke entering the atrium from any of these normal- to high-risk areas will be drawn up elevator and stair shafts into the guestroom floors by stack pressure effects. The answer was to provide emergency ventilation, pressurizing guestroom corridors and stairs. Air flows down elevator shafts and stairways, entering the atrium and excluding smoke. Smoke in the atrium is vented through large openings in its sidewall glazing.

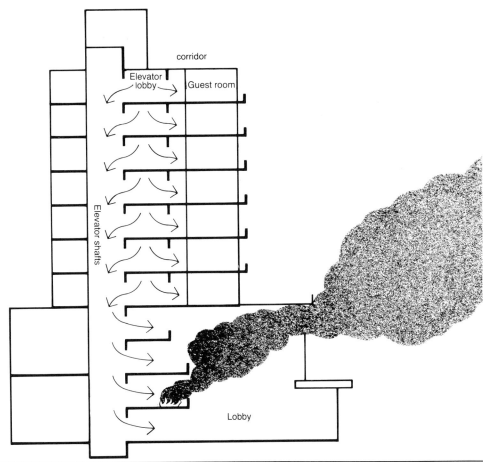

131 **Sprinkler location** for atrium spaces

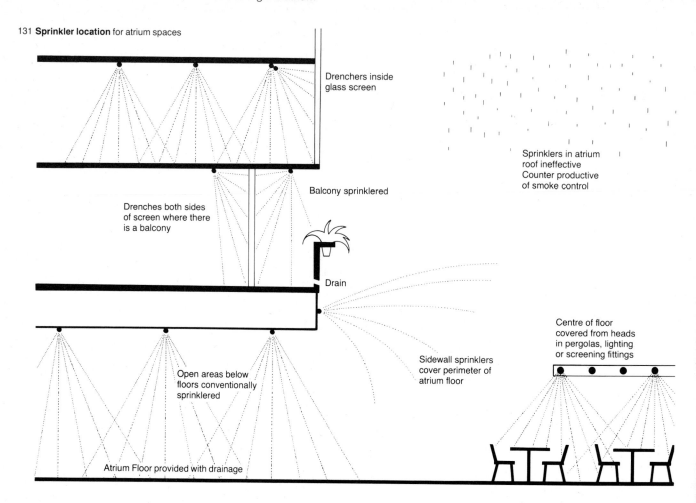

Drenchers inside glass screen

Sprinklers in atrium roof ineffective
Counter productive of smoke control

Drenches both sides of screen where there is a balcony

Balcony sprinklered

Drain

Open areas below floors conventionally sprinklered

Sidewall sprinklers cover perimeter of atrium floor

Centre of floor covered from heads in pergolas, lighting or screening fittings

Atrium Floor provided with drainage

132 **Flame trajectories** from fire floor edges

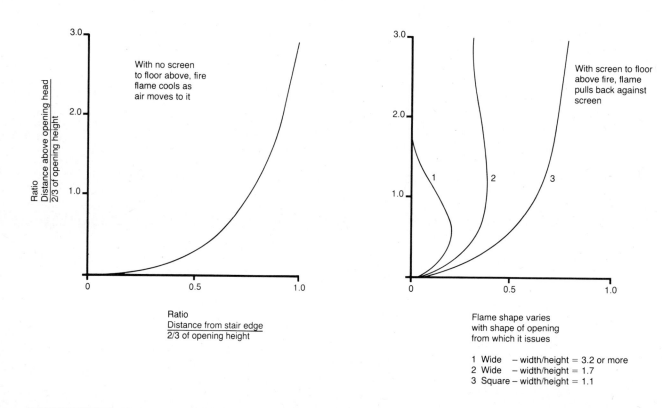

With no screen to floor above, fire flame cools as air moves to it

Ratio $\dfrac{\text{Distance above opening head}}{\text{2/3 of opening height}}$

Ratio $\dfrac{\text{Distance from stair edge}}{\text{2/3 of opening height}}$

With screen to floor above fire, flame pulls back against screen

Flame shape varies with shape of opening from which it issues

1 Wide – width/height = 3.2 or more
2 Wide – width/height = 1.7
3 Square – width/height = 1.1

Fire-control

Fire-size limitation

Smoke-control is the first necessity for life-safety in buildings. But in order to control smoke the size of any fire which breaks out must be strictly and rapidly limited. Once life-safety requirements have been met, and all endangered occupants have escaped, then fire-control measures are more concerned to limit the spread of the fire within the building, or to the adjoining structures.

Limiting of fire-size can be attempted by separating groups of inflammable building contents, and isolating identifiable ignition hazards from potential fuels. This is not likely to be an adequate policy: control of the disposition of building contents is hard to achieve in any event, by designer, fire authority or building management; the protection offered is of limited duration also. Once a group of combustibles is alight, heat will be intense enough before long to ignite more remote combustibles in the same space.

Statutory compartmentation divisions within any building are of such large size as to be irrelevant to this discussion. They serve mainly to limit the size of conflagrations and help to prevent public danger and the involvement of other buildings. Sub-divisions of the occupied space are not usually capable of being fire-tight whilst still allowing the building to function as required. Space division by glazed screens will only contain smoke; radiation through glass can cause fires to break out. Active fire-controlling methods are therefore usually necessary to limit fire-size sufficiently for smoke-control to be feasible. They are essential if an open-sided atrium is sought.

Detection

The first requirement is for early detection of fire. Response can then be manual or automatic. Where automatic detection is necessary it is better to rely on smoke-detection rather than heat-detection to alert emergency systems. Heat-detection is only useful once a real fire has started, to open sprinkler valves and close shutters. Considerable quantities of smoke will already have been released before detectable heat is produced.

Smoke-detection is sensitive to the early stages of fire. Its weakness is that it can be over-sensitive, leading to false alarms. This can be combated by reducing sensitivity settings and by having double circuits so that confirming signals from a second detector are needed to trigger a response. Detector technology is an area of rapid advance, and though not satisfactory today, is bound to become more reliable and discriminating.

Detection in the atrium space itself is difficult. Smoke- or heat-detectors at the top of the atrium will not pick up the presence of fire on the floor of the space until it has grown large. It is advisable to incorporate detectors near the main floor level. This can be done by including detectors in any lighting, ventilation, landscape or interior features which hang down over or stand up from the atrium floor.

The smoke-detection system should be used to inform the building control centre, and possibly the fire service direct, to display the location of the fire and to switch the ventilation system to emergency mode.

Fire-defence systems

Different techniques will suit different occupancy types. In a hospital, where 24-hour human surveillance is available, manual response with portable or fixed extinguishers will be most sensitive and effective, just as the human nose will be the most accurate detector.

Where high-value electronics or other water damageable contents are present, gas-protection systems are worth considering. CO_2 systems are safe for automatic use after hours, but all personnel must be evacuated before the system is triggered in working hours, thus creating a dangerous delay. Life-safe gases are more expensive but will be justified if the value of the equipment is sufficient.

For the great majority of space uses a water sprinkler system will be the most effective, knocking down most fires, or at least containing the fire-size, before the arrival of the fire department. Sprinklers are expensive, with some authorities requiring massive water storage rather than use of the mains. Insurance premiums are not usually diminished by their use, except in warehouses and department stores where contents are of great value. Nevertheless, their effectiveness in limiting fire-spread and making escape necessary for the fewest number of people is increasingly causing their adoption in high-density buildings of all types. Sprinklers will not be an 'extra' for an open-sided atrium building in cities such as New York where all buildings must be equipped.

Sprinklering the atrium floor is not straightforward. Side-wall sprinklers are effective up to certain width limits. Wider spaces will need sprinklers incorporated in the same features of the atrium which can hold the detectors. It is not advisable to try to sprinkler the atrium from high up on the side walls or roof. First, the sprinklers will not discharge until the fire is too large for them: their spray will evaporate before arriving. Secondly, they will cool and mix the smoke in the atrium, causing it to stop rising and to fill the atrium more quickly.

There will be a role for gas fire-fighting systems in relation to any electrical equipment on the atrium floor: serveries are a common example where sprinklers could do more harm than good.

Flame-spread

Even if fire-size is controlled by sprinklers there is a risk of fire spreading to other levels of the building. This is especially true if the fire starts near the external or internal edges of the floors. It is assumed that all weaknesses in floors or walls represented by ductways or construction cavities have been checked and fire-stopped. The remaining risk of fire-spread is thus from flames breaking out of the fire floor and reaching the next floor above, over the edge of the floor-plate.

The external wall condition is the same for atrium and conventional buildings. It is salutary to note that once flames do break through an external wall they tend to hug the face of the building and are often actually sucked into the window of the floor above. Even if the windows of the floor under attack remain sound, radiation from flames can cause ignition of combustible material close to the glass. Upstand walls or projecting fins make little difference to the problem until they are of impractical proportions. The shape of the flame and its tendency to hug the wall are affected considerably by the shape of the window out of which the flames come. Square windows project the flame furthest away from the wall, whilst wide windows suck it quickly back in.

The intriguing behaviour of flames where there are no walls, as in open-sided atrium interiors, is that those breaking out of a floor-edge do not curve back to attack the floor above, but keep the distance of the flame-tip from the floor-edge roughly equal to the height of the opening out of which the flame is issuing. The air supply cools and shortens the flame also. Flames projecting out and cooling quickly in this context allow the consideration of unprotected structure at the floor-edge to the atrium. The condition is the same as that when the structure is a metre or more outside the external wall. This policy has been followed in Murphy/Jahn's State of Illinois Center atrium (1983) to use unprotected steel for perimeter galleries.

It is thus paradoxical that an enclosed atrium, possibly the simplest for smoke-control, is more vulnerable to fire-spread floor-to-floor than is an open-sided atrium. Where the enclosure policy includes omitting sprinklers, this danger is greatly increased. The risk is, it must be noted, no different to that at the outer edge of this or any conventional building.

The idea of water-drenching glass screens to atria or shopping malls in order to contain fire is of limited merit. Keeping the glass cool does not affect heat-radiation through the glass. Furthermore, imperfect drenching is likely and this leads to rapid fracture of the glass where cooled glass meets uncooled, and thence earlier breakout of flames. Laminated intumescent glazing is effective but expensive. So too are metal shutters, designed to fall across the edge openings of floors in the event of fire. The best policy remains early detection and fire-fighting to limit fire-size, and the use of toughened glass to reduce breakage danger.[2]

Fire-fighting

The building's own defences are a prelude to the arrival of the fire department. Final victory over any fire will depend on the department gaining quick and safe access to the seat of the fire. To facilitate this provisions must be built in at the initial planning stage, during discussions on the concept with the fire department. Atrium buildings need no special facilities compared to conventional ones, but several points should be noted.

Space outside the building is likely to be less, due to the site-filling nature of the building form. Areas must be allowed for fire engine arrival, adjacent to the service access-point. This area should be away from smoke-release points, and not used as an evacuee marshalling area. It is also suggested that this point be the focus of building and fire-systems control, and with a dedicated stair and elevator alongside rising services, to give unobstructed access to all levels.

It is always worth considering the provision of an extra stair for fire-fighting access. All other stairs might be in use as escapes when the brigade arrives. In multi-use buildings, a protected shaft for common services, with communications facilities, will help maintenance and security and give a splendid fire-fighting route through the building. The inclusion of a service elevator in this shaft, available as the fireman's elevator, will complete a valuable facility. The elevators within an atrium are not likely to be acceptable to firemen, especially if glass-sided.

In extensive covered developments it may be essential to provide vehicles to carry personnel and equipment through the pedestrian spaces. Modified vehicles may be needed, and should be stored where the department can get at them directly on arrival.

With sufficient forethought, an atrium building can be a model of fire-safe design, and, due to the economy of the built form, at a cost which does not overwhelm savings.

1 See opposite

2 Rapid progress is being made in the development of fire-resisting glazing, and it is impossible to be up-to-date in a book of this type. Discussion with glass suppliers is recommended for each project, to ascertain the state of the art

133

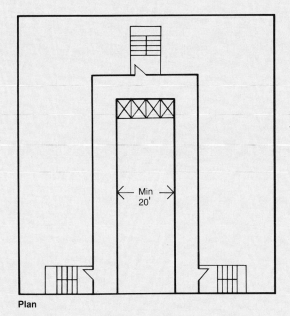

Plan

Min 20'

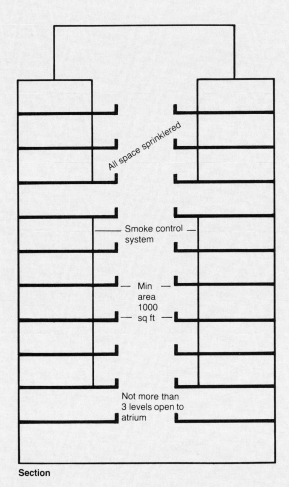

All space sprinklered

Smoke control system

Min area 1000 sq ft

Not more than 3 levels open to atrium

Section

1 American National Fire Protection Association Code, 1981

Until mid-1981 the NFPA Life Safety Code, the basis of discussion for United States designers and fire departments, required enclosure of all horizontal openings in buildings. Atrium proposals achieved approval only by proving that the measures included in the designs gave safety equivalent to that achieved by full enclosure. Successive fire disasters have reinforced awareness of the importance of horizontal openings as fire- and smoke-spread routes if not effectively handled.

After 17 years of atrium building by code relaxation, recognition that large atrium spaces can be safely handled has arrived in the 1981 edition. The code now allows atria provided that

1 They are at least 20 feet wide and 1,000 square feet in area per level, to give adequate volume to cool flame and handle smoke.
2 All space in the building is sprinklered, including the atrium if less than 55 feet high.
3 Engineered smoke-control or smoke-removal systems are provided.
4 Control and alarm systems are activated by smoke-detectors and sprinkler heads.
5 Only three floor levels (at any level) are open to the atrium.
6 Other floors are behind one-hour resistance partitions, or glass screens with drenchers.
7 Space use in the building is of low to normal hazard type.

Access to fire stairs can be via atrium galleries, and escape from the base of the stair towers can be across the atrium floor.

This package of measures sets a new standard for debate about 'equivalency' of safety in proposals which differ from the code and will influence world-wide discussions.

**After John F Behrens
Fire Journal, July 1981**

134

11 Structures and skins

134 **The space frame roof** of the atrium at the National Gallery of Art, East Building, Washington DC

Selection criteria

Atria are, by definition, spaces between occupied blocks of building. Their enclosures, usually predominantly transparent or translucent, are technologies in themselves, but interact strongly with the structure and treatment of the buildings surrounding them. The main building frame will probably derive economies from the use of an atrium, being lower and wider than it would otherwise have been. This chapter surveys the variety of ways in which designers have crossed the gap between these occupied elements, to create vertical, horizontal, sloping, flat or curved envelopes enclosing their atrium spaces.

Atrium envelopes present all the challenges of normal window and roof-light design, which are well covered in the standard texts. Beyond that they have problems of construction and maintenance created by their sheer size. The two basic, interacting considerations are the way in which light and/or view are to be admitted, and the architectural character sought.

Techniques for admitting and distributing light in the atrium (discussed in Chapter 10, p. 92 ff.) will suggest the form of openings, and whether there is scope for the structure to act as a climate-modifier. Structural depth needs to be provided if possible, as long-span window-walls or light-roofs are very costly if the designer is forced to use shallow structure. The envelope structure can offer support for shades, diffusers and reflectors. The classic nineteenth-century treatment was the laylight: outer glazing shaped to handle rain or avoid solar penetration, then an iron or wooden structure, then an inner, often stained glass, soffit to diffuse light.

Depth of structure in light-roofs is easy to accommodate as there will usually be the need for considerable hot air and smoke-reservoir capacity above all occupied levels. Catwalks in the lower chord of deep structure can give access for cleaning, replacement of artificial light sources, attention to ventilation gear and any shading, and for hanging decorative features from the roof.

The problems of slopes
Many atria have sloping or curved envelopes, and these can be stimulating visual experiences in a townscape of verticals and horizontals. Before incorporating these, however, consider the extra difficulties they present. Sloping surfaces, once they become too steep to be walked across, are neither roof nor wall. They may handle weather worse than either. Cleaning rigs usually have to be devised specially to deal with slopes and curves, both internal and external; overhung return slopes are particularly hard to handle. The resultant gear can be unsightly and mar the effect sought. The large sloping canopies at the Eaton Center, Toronto, lose a great deal of their attraction through not being sufficiently clean. Think about the cleaning concept when devising shapes. It may be a valuable simplifying discipline.

In cool climates condensation will often occur overnight on the inside of glass walls as a result of cold-radiation. It will drain quickly off vertical walls, but more slowly off slopes. Condensate drainage needs to be incorporated in designs for these climates.

Slopes present hazards where they are above doorways: whereas rain tends to bounce off vertical glazing, only small amounts running down the surface and attacking doorways, a slope can collect substantial water-flows. Intercepting guttering will be needed. Snow-collection must be watched in those climates where falls are high. If melting coils are not built in, then accumulated snow will have to be stabilized to prevent avalanches.

Movement
Large, metal-framed structures carrying light-roofs or window-walls can be thermally very active. They are subject to solar-gain and night-cooling, and, with little thermal capacity to slow reaction, they will move about much more than the conventional structures to which they are attached. All components of glazed structures will need attention in order to cope with such movement, but the joints between glazed structures and conventional buildings are especially demanding. Here, large daily movements occur. This is avoided in those buildings which structure their atrium envelopes as extensions of their conventional frames, thereby reducing the discontinuity of thermal behaviour considerably.

Sealing the envelope

Atrium glazing will almost certainly be sealed entirely. Natural ventilation is possible in appropriate climates and design concepts, but the glazing system will not usually be able to handle the stress and degree of control required. Openings at the head of the atrium may use greenhouse-roof technology to give summer cross-ventilation and smoke-release. Openings at the base need to be used with considerable care since the strong stack effect induces powerful draughts. Doorways need special attention: draught lobbies are usually provided, as a single-leaf door might be difficult to keep closed; revolving doors or automatic sliding doors are an alternative. In cold climates both draught lobby and revolving door are used to give double draught-protection. The rest of the glazing should be tightly sealed.

Concepts for framed structures

Vertical side-wall glazing

Two broad types of treatment are commonly used. The first extends the frame of the occupied building across the atrium wall, whilst the second changes the look significantly between the occupied building and the atrium, switching to a light curtain structure.

Skidmore, Owings and Merrill have used the extended-building-frame approach in several recent projects including the Pan American Life Building, New Orleans (1980). There is no apparent difference in the external appearance of the occupied building and the atrium walls but at night interior lighting reveals the internal change. An advantage of this approach is that where the space inside the total building envelope has been freely arranged and an irregular atrium volume lies behind a regular massing, the continuing regular façade co-ordinates the result. Indeed, one can imagine floor-arrangements being altered during design in the safe knowledge that the external consistency of the building remains. The result is a strongly framed view of the world from within the atrium, with quite a high shade-factor and insulation area built in.

The Bank of Canada building in Ottawa, by Arthur Erickson and Marani, Rownthwaite and Dick (1979), continues the frame proportions of two 12-storey office towers across a huge bridging atrium. This atrium, almost a building in its own right, envelopes part of an old banking building on the site. The Garden Link, as it is called, has a most sophisticated frame to achieve climate-control. The columns are hollow ducts, feeding air to spandrel beams set at each floor level. These distribute the air between the two glass skins provided, thus eliminating condensation and down-draughts, and keeping interior comfort conditions right through the Ottawa winter.

135 **Hennepin County Courthouse,** Minneapolis; windbracing used to carry the atrium wall

136a **Pan American Life Building,** New Orleans, exterior concealing atria

136b **Interior of lower atrium**

Between extending the normal frame and omitting it comes the idea of using part of the frame. A multi-storey south-facing glass wall is broken into single-storey height steps by concrete play-decks at the Children's Hospital of Philadelphia. The decks also form a massive sun-breaker (see **77**). Matched 10-inch horizontal structural steel tubes at each floor level carry the eight-storey frameless glass wall at the McOG Associates Spectrum Building, Denver. Silicone jointed glazing is here used to give enhanced transparency without the veiling mass of members associated with truss structures.

The building frame which carries the atrium wall need not be a simple continuation of the rectilinear frame each side. At the Hennepin County Courthouse building in Minneapolis (1976), John Carl Warnecke has imaginatively placed wind and seismic bracing-frames across the atrium walls. The X-braced pattern, less acceptable across the fenestration of occupied floors, emphasizes that the atrium is a void with no floor levels, and provides a dramatic and economical frame solution.

Once a separate curtain-wall approach is adopted, trussed metal framing is inevitable if suspended glass cannot be used (see p. 119). This trussing can take many forms. Individual members can be developed into rigid trusses or can be tension-braced. Pairs of mullions or transoms can be trussed together into triangular space girders, an exceedingly successful approach. The space girder can be prefabricated and transported simply, then braced to its neighbours to form a partial space-truss. It has advantages over a full space-truss in that it is easy to prefabricate and erect, and leaves open routeways for inserting glazing or ducts in long lengths. The Washington Air and Space Museum atria are framed in this way, as is the great wall at Welton Beckett and Associates' Hyatt Regency Hotel, Dallas (1979).

If diagonal members are not wanted, it is possible to create a rigid Veirendeel truss wall in welded steel tube. However, the massive glazed walls at Toronto's Royal Bank (Webb, Zerafa, Menkes, Housden) suggest that it is hard to do elegantly: the 'void' has become more substantial than the solids each side.

Sloping surfaces

Some of the same approaches can be used as for vertical glazing. Slopes introduce the complexities outlined above but also the advantage of natural water-shedding and the possible use of lapped patent glazing systems. With these economical glazing systems, spans of three metres can be achieved with normal-sized glazing bars, and primary structure can be simplified to transoms picking up the lines of support required.

Many designers avoid the 'buzz' of structural members involved in trusses, and use rolled steel to considerable spans. The Charles Englehard Court at the Metropolitan Museum, New York, by Roche and Dinkeloo (see **55**) breaks the roof-span with internal columns, but uses large members. The same architects used less steel in the arched gambrel-roof forms at Deere West, Moline, Illinois (see **36**).

137 **Hyatt Hotel, Dallas,** structure of great glazed wall to the atrium

Arch forms are attractive shapes for atria and galleria roofs as they recall vaulting and are similarly efficient. Trussed arches form the marvellous barrel-vaulted roof and side-wall slopes of the Eaton Center, Toronto (see **69**). The two chords follow different shapes, allowing the inner one to be a continuous curve whilst the outer one rises to a point, supporting the glass at a more practical angle. The longitudinal connector members form unobtrusive tracks for a large travelling maintenance rig.

Space-frames are favoured by designers who want a perfectly even effect, with the busy but regular pattern of shadows and silhouettes rather than a clear view through. The atrium of Arthur Erickson's stupendous Law Courts in Vancouver (1979) is roofed by a shimmering shallow space-truss, supported off the concrete 'knees' of the stepping structure below. Space-trusses at Columbia Mall in Maryland (Cope, Linder and Walmsey, 1972) fold into pyramids and prisms as they cover the irregular galleria spaces.

Dome shapes for glazed roofs were common in the Victorian period. Today ready-made framed plastic domes can be obtained.[1] Larger domes can use lamella or geodesic support-principles as well as the intersecting arch form suitable for the smaller proprietary domes. A 'free-form dome' is the best description of the glazing of the atrium at Portman's Peachtree Plaza Hotel, Atlanta (see **2**). The rectangular roof of the lobby is interrupted by the base of the circular guest-room tower. Steel mullions radiating from the base ring-beam of the tower travel inevitably at different angles to cover the varied distance to the edges of the atrium. Plastic panels, domed for stiffness, form the continuously warping surface which results.

Also hard to categorize, but typical of the imaginative structures which atria can use, is the roof of Johnson and Burgee's Crystal Court,

the IDS Centre, Minneapolis (see **3, 65**). The irregular overall slope of the roof is built up of hundreds of cubic welded steel cells, each topped by a plastic pyramidal light. The cells are fixed together into a rigid 'egg crate' with considerable stiffness as it crosses the 20,000 square foot space. The upper-level public walkway is suspended from it.

Structures for horizontal glazing

Horizontal surfaces can be glazed with sloping glass. The principles of 'ridge-and-furrow' glazing pre-date the Crystal Palace and are still used on the newest atria. Horizontal beams support small secondary structures, either symmetrical or asymmetrical. The asymmetrical arrangement, with monopitched and vertical glazing in a saw-tooth pattern, can be useful both to admit light selectively (see p. 78) and to allow for weather-tight louvres for ventilation.

A more common current approach to the design of flat glazed roofs is the use of proprietary plastic roof-lights in multiple arrays. Pyramidal or domed, square, round or strip-form roof-lights can be supported on the chords of trusses or on grillages of beams. Waterproofing must be scrupulous, so that run-off follows the channels between rows of roof-lights. Steel space-frames with pyramidal roof-light modules are common. Roof-lights to fit proprietary space-frame systems are available, enabling a pre-engineered roof to be specified.[1]

Continuous plastic barrel-vault roof-light strips are compatible with any one-way structural system, and provide simple weathering and drainage details if used with a cross-fall in the direction of the channels formed. An unusual application of this technique is Portman's Atlanta Apparel Mart (1980). A fan-shaped atrium forms a presentation theatre, and roof-lights radiate from the stage. A standard width roof-light is

138 **Sloped space frame roof,**
Law Courts, Vancouver, BC

used, giving tapering strips of solid between the lights, and delivering more light towards the focus of the space. The radiating roof beams are of V-form precast, prestressed concrete, the angle of the 'V' changing continuously to accommodate the increasing separation of the roof-lights. Though horizontal (with a slight drainage fall), the combination of angles and varying light levels produces the illusion that the roof slopes upwards towards the focus.

Custom-built space-frame roofs and glazing can produce striking results. At the complex end of the spectrum is the roof of the atrium at I M Pei's National Gallery of Art, East Building, Washington DC. The triangular atrium is 150 feet on base and 225 feet on side. Twenty-five giant-scaled modules form the space-frame, with glazing infilling in triangular pyramids leaving the top chord outside. Very fine geometric detail was required, with perfect alignment of surfaces. The nodes of the roof and the massive top chords are in cast steel, machined to final form. Other members are built up from flat steel, finely welded. The node castings alone weigh five imperial tons. The result, paradoxically, appears almost weightless. Pei's attention to detail shows in the complete integration of shading louvres, roof-drainage, interior lighting and air-handling shown in the edge detail.

Horizontal roofs can of course be structured very simply and inexpensively in the kind of steel roof used for factories. Also apparently obvious is the use of metal-decking where the amount of glazing is limited to avoid excessive solar gain. Whilst the structure produced may be sound, it can be visually unsatisfactory. The eye is drawn naturally upwards in atria, to play over the roof structure. A metal deck on light joisting can look too insubstantial, too 'cheap' for the grand space it covers. This is the case at the Plaza of the Americas in Dallas (1981). The bridging atrium is topped by a solid flat roof, slashed dramatically with slots which stripe the atrium with sun. The roof, however, is too visually flimsy.

The laylight principle, using a lower glazed layer to diffuse light, allows a purely practical structure and roof-light solution to be used, perhaps with economies. The result is a weightless, luminous plane above the space. The Brown Palace Hotel uses stained glass. Portman's first Hyatt uses opalescent acrylic below an array of plastic roof-lights, supported on simple steel lattice joists. Norman Foster's 1978 Sainsbury Centre for the Visual Arts, Norwich (England), uses louvre blades, motorized to respond to changes in outside brightness and to conceal structure, maintenance ways, and artificial lighting in the depth of the roof.

Heavier translucent roofs can be built if thermal or acoustic mass is required. The technology called glass-concrete, in use since the earliest days of twentieth-century concrete design, allows glass blocks to be set like void-formers in a slab, producing a waterproof but translucent deck. It can be flat, sloped or vaulted. Owen Williams used it to roof his remarkable atrium-style Boots factory of 1932.

139 **Fan shaped roof** in tapered precast concrete with strip rooflights. Apparel Mart, Atlanta, Georgia

140 **Hipped, barrel-vaulted roof.** Brunel Plaza, Swindon, England, by Douglas Stephen and Partners

141 **National Gallery of Art,
Washington, DC**
Architects: I M Pei and Partners
Structural Engineers: Wiescopf and
Pickworth
Services Engineers: Syska and
Hennessy

*details from Engineering for
Architecture, McGraw Hill*

a . Plan of the building showing
the atrium rooflight spaceframe
linking the gallery building and study
centre and locating details shown
below

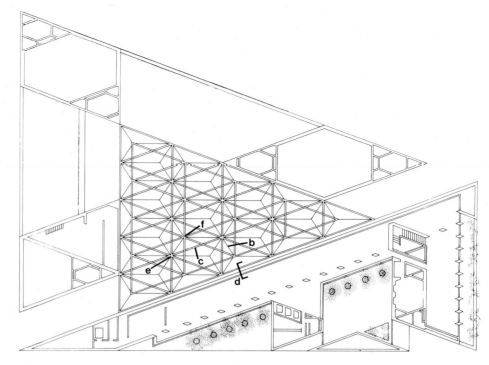

d Section through bottom chord
at perimeter showing integration of
structure, lighting, air input and
cladding details

b Typical bottom chord with
to produce a light appearance

c Typical sloping chord built up
drainage and cable duct space

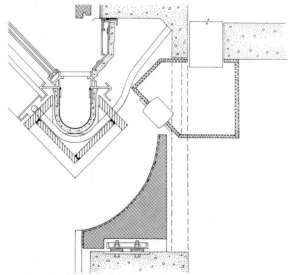

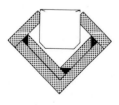

e Cast steel bottom nodes have
six channeled fingers to which the
lower chords are welded and three
diagonal fingers to receive major
sloping chords

f Cast steel top node and chords.
Conventional box section top
chords are welded to cast, tapered
ends, and pinned to the horizontal
fingers of the top node

The whole roof rests on the concrete
towers and beams of the surrounding

structure. Sliding bearings allow
thermal movement. Lugs carrying the
roof are at bottom node points but
often offset to preserve clear sight-
lines where major windows meet
the roof

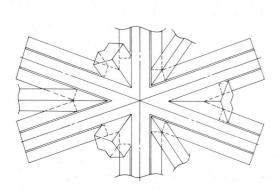

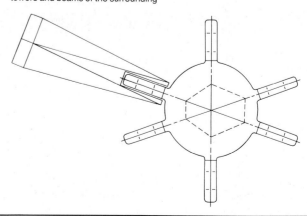

Glazing

The market for light transmitting materials is developing rapidly. This section sets down the broad choices available, and the directions of development which seem promising. The three basic types of skin material on offer—some translucent (light transmitting), some transparent (view transmitting)—are glass, plastic sheeting, and composite materials. Glass and some plastics offer transparency, the composites offer only translucence, but with high insulation-values. The tendency in recent practice is to use glass for vertical vision areas, but to use plastics or composites in roof-glazing where light weight, safety and insulation-value become more important.

Glass

Some security against the effects of breakage is necessary for overhead glass. Toughened glass is far less likely to break, but is not without hazard. Wired glass prevents the fall of loose pieces after a break, and lasts well in fire. Roughcast glass is massively thick and strong. Laminated glass interleaving a plastic sheet between glass layers is expensive but safe.

Wired and roughcast glass are not vision glasses like laminated or toughened glass. Diffused light may be desirable however since it gives a better distribution for working illumination, and reduces solar-radiation discomfort. Most diffusion can be gained from double-glazing with a glass-fibre layer interleaved.

All these roof-glazings are quite heavy and in practice limited thermally to the performance of double-glazing (U = 3.84W/m²/°C). For walls, vision is likely to be the most important criterion, and glass will score due to its excellent optical properties. For the wide, high view-walls which open-sided atria require, the most impressive technique available is the suspended glass assembly. This obviates the need for secondary structure, reducing weight and increasing clarity of view. The basic technology is shown in **142**.

Available until recently only in clear or tinted glasses, toughened glass can now be given surface coatings to perform as selective solar-rejecting glass. Insulation can be enhanced by low emissivity coatings. Double-glazing performance is barely attainable however. Condensation is rarely a problem, even in cold climates. Air movement against the glass surface seems to dispel it.

Suspended glazing is sealed with silicone compounds. These are chemically close to glass and form a strong bond whilst retaining flexibility. Further developments in structural glass techniques exploiting the silicone bond can be anticipated. The absence of projecting glazing beads produces a flush, sealed but flexible surface with superior weathering and thermal properties.

142 Suspended glass assemblies
(Pilkington)

a Typical assembly features

b Alternative stabilizer assembly configurations

1 is a propped cantilever for wind load transfer

2 is a pin jointed version

c Assemblies are top hung and more accurately made than building frames. Adjustable hangers are used, with 'floating' channel restraints to all edges

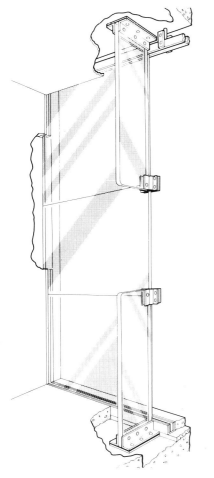

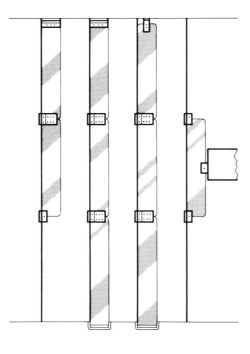

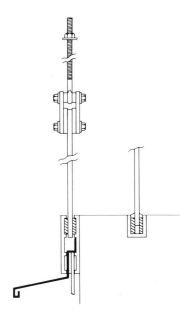

d Typical base details; glass floats in channel

143 Three double wall plastic claddings; span potential increases with thickness

10mm Thermoclear twinwall polycarbonate

16mm Exolite, acrylic or polycarbonate, by CyRo

61mm Everlite, interlocking extruded box sections in PVC or polycarbonate

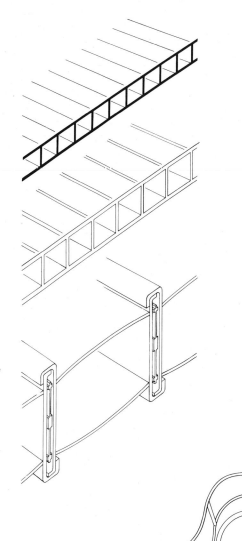

Plastics
The established glazing plastics are Polyvinyl Chloride (PVC), Acrylic, Polycarbonate and Glass Reinforced Polyester resin (GRP). All but GRP can be produced in transparent sheets. Acrylic can be shaped, tinted and coloured freely, to give diffuse or clear light. It is highly combustible, however, and needs sprinklering if used in atria. None of the plastics is completely fire-resistant, creating difficulties where roof-light is sought hard up to the edge of adjacent accommodation: adjacent building enclosures will need to be resistant to fire-spread for an appropriate distance. Polycarbonate is by far the most rigid and strong of the plastics, and though expensive, it is usually preferred where danger of breakage is feared.

In single-sheet form, curved into vaults, moulded into roof-light pyramids or used flat, plastic sheets are thermally similar to single-glazing. Double-glazing is achievable by separately fixing a second layer. An economical alternative where translucency only is sufficient is the use of double-skin extruded plastic. Polycarbonate is used principally for these materials, which are either in wide sheets (1200 millimetres to two metres) or in interlocking strip elements.

Cell-depths vary from 10 to 60 millimetres. The slimmer double-skin sheets can be cold-curved to span two metres. Deeper sections need to be pre-curved and achieve frameless spans of six metres.

144 Clifton Nurseries building, London, 1980 Terry Farrell

Typical structural bay

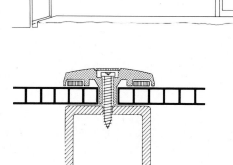

Tubular steel structural 'ladders' carrying twinwall sheeting

Arcade frames

145 Twin wall polycarbonate: fixings designed to allow for considerable thermal movement and to let condensate in internal cells drain to the base (as used in Clifton Nurseries)

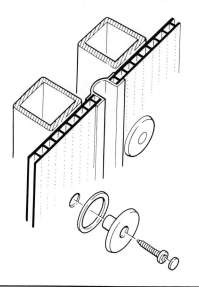

146 **Composite glazing,** Doulton
Thermascreen insulated diffusing
panels

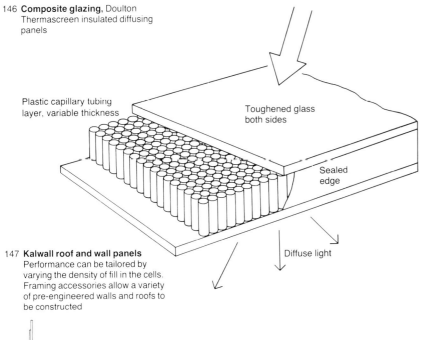

Plastic capillary tubing
layer, variable thickness

Toughened glass
both sides

Sealed
edge

Diffuse light

147 **Kalwall roof and wall panels**
Performance can be tailored by
varying the density of fill in the cells.
Framing accessories allow a variety
of pre-engineered walls and roofs to
be constructed

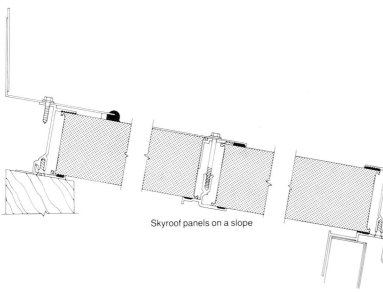

Skyroof panels on a slope

Composites

Combining glass, plastic and even metal can produce higher-performance skin materials than would any of the components alone. These are patent rather than generic products, and must be described as such. A British product, Doulton Thermascreen, separates two sheets of toughened glass with a layer of capillary plastic tubing stacked perpendicular to the glass. Air is trapped to give U values from 3.4W/m²/°C to 1.6W/m²/°C as the interlayer thickness increases from eight to 24 millimetres. About half the solar heat is transmitted, but widely diffused so that radiation is not more than 10 to 15 per cent to the floor of the space. About 60 per cent of daylight, evenly diffused, is transmitted. Normal glazing support structure is required.

The longest established composite is Kalwall, which has been developed in the United States over 25 years: GRP skins are bonded to both sides of aluminium framing, normally 2¾ inches thick. The cells are then filled with a varying density of glass fibre insulant, depending on the balance of light transmission, insulation and shading selected. U values range from 0.4–0.1 (BTU), with corresponding diffused light transmission ranging from 60 per cent down to five per cent. Shade factors range from 0.85 to 0.09. Kalwall roofs can be carried on purlins at eight-foot centres, and pre-engineered wide spans and shapes are available. Walls have varied integral mullion sections attachable to spans up to 30 feet. A variant called Sunwall has enhanced solar transmission for covering collectors or sun-spaces such as atriums.

Highly insulated skins are of interest in warming and convertible atria, especially when high comfort is sought in the atrium itself. The diffused light produced can be distributed deep into the occupied spaces, but quantity of light must not be reduced in the interests of insulation to the point where more artificial light is needed.

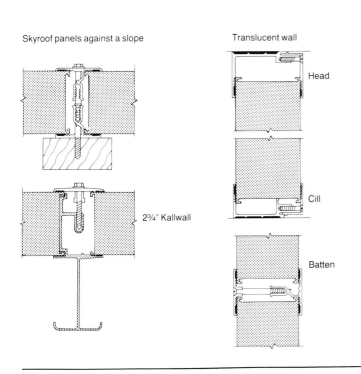

Skyroof panels against a slope

2¾" Kallwall

Translucent wall

Head

Cill

Batten

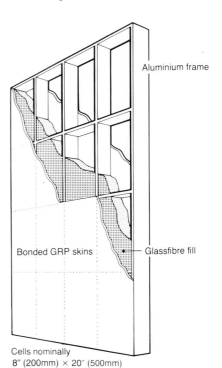

Aluminium frame

Bonded GRP skins — Glassfibre fill

Cells nominally
8″ (200mm) × 20″ (500mm)

148 Bullocks Store, San José, California
Architects, Environmental Planning and Research Engineers, Gieger Berger Associates

The pioneering use of a fabric roof over an atrium in a conventional structure. Laminated timber arches carry the fabric over 18,000 sq ft

Stresses from the roof are resisted by catenary cables between arch roots. An alternative would have been to use the store roof as a diaphragm

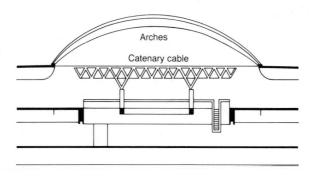

Part cross section showing arches and cables

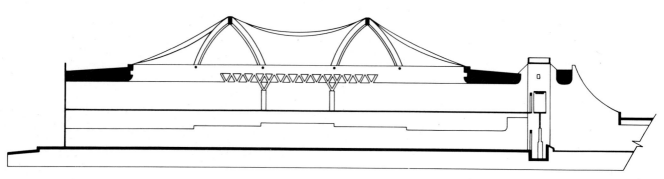

Long section through store

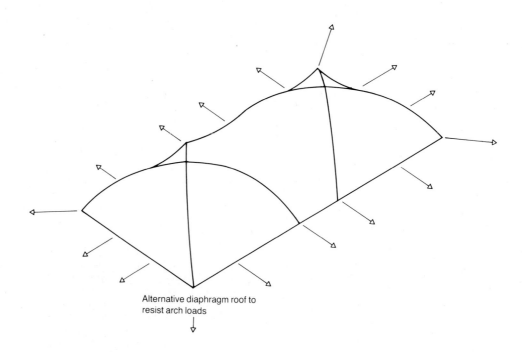

Alternative diaphragm roof to resist arch loads

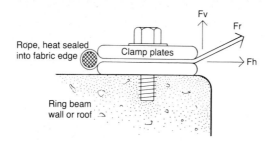

Rope, heat sealed into fabric edge
Clamp plates
F_v F_r F_h
Ring beam wall or roof

Load transfer detail between membrane and conventional structure

Fabric structures

An idea worth considering
Compared to frame and skin structures, fabric structures are cheap, uncluttered, can be spectacularly shaped, are light and quick to erect. Fabrics now exist which have excellent performance for at least 20 years' life. They can withstand any climate, deal with wind, snow or seismic loads, resist fire, and keep themselves clean. Air-supported or tensile structures can be considered. It is quite likely that pre-engineered roof modules will be available on the market before long. The drawbacks are the relatively low light-transmission possible, low insulation, and the shorter life compared to most skin materials.

Fabric properties
Structural fabrics have advanced significantly in the last decade. From the canvas tent, evolution has passed through several

plastics, which suffered in ultraviolet light, to a stable, very strong combination: glass-fibre fabric coated in fluorocarbon resin (Teflon). Both elements have been in use for over 40 years. They have a long track record in combination, in the manufacture of electrical insulation, conveyor belts and space suits. As a building fabric the material emerged in the early 1970s. 'Teflon-Coated Fiberglas Fabric' (TCFF) is supplanting vinyl-coated polyester, the material from which many early structures were made. That was a more flexible material, useful for demountable structures, but it stretched, deteriorated within seven years and burnt easily: TCFF is stiff, unaffected by ultraviolet light and temperature, and does not support combustion. It can really be considered a permanent building material. TCFF is manufactured only in the United States by Owens Corning. It comes in a variety of specifications to suit the application.

Translucency varies with the amount and type of inorganic filler in the fabric, but is very low compared to most glazing materials. Increased filler can be selected to give greater solar heat reflectivity, but at the cost of decreased light transmission. The energy equation for any location will vary considerably and the choice should be made with the whole building energy-design in mind. With a sky-vault brightness of 100,000 lux, obtained in hot, desert conditions, a 10 per cent translucent roof would deliver up to 10,000 lux of diffuse light in the atrium, and 200 lux to overlooking space with a sky-factor of two per cent. However, in a cloudy northern climate with sky brightness at a typical 5,000 lux, hardly 500 lux would enter the atrium, and only 10 lux reach overlooking spaces on the two per cent sky-factor contour. This range of performance suggests that fabric roofs have most to offer on cooling atria in sunny climates, where their shade factor is welcomed and useful daylight can still be achieved. The example of the Bullocks store in San Jose, California, where the atrium is shopping space, uses the daylight available in the atrium itself, but does not expect more than 'psychological lighting' to surrounding spaces. Substantial savings on lighting costs are achieved, however.

The converse of translucence is that the fabrics reflect well: 70 per cent reflectance from a bright, white surface rejects solar heat in the day-time and means that night-illumination of the atrium can be economical. Indirect lighting can be used, and the shadowless character of daylight under a fabric roof thus continued at night.

Fire performance of the fabric is good. It will burn when subjected to flames, but, when not subjected to flames, it does not provide fuel and extinguishes itself. It is acceptable as an interior lining in most building codes.

Acoustics can be unusual in a fabric structure: the curved surfaces needed for structural performance can focus reflections. Suspended banners or partial linings of lightweight fabric break up sound paths and stop the echo effect.

149 **Teflon coated fibreglass fabric, performance tables**

source: Owens Corning Fiberglas Corp

Solar optical properties

	Medium strength fabric	High strength fabric
High translucency % Solar transmission % Reflectance	13 ± 2 73 ± 3	9 ± 2 73 ± 3
Low translucency % Solar transmission % Reflectance	9 ± 2 75 ± 3	7 ± 2 75 ± 3

Translucency/Reflectance

	High translucency outer fabric	Low translucency outer fabric
Combined* solar translucency (%)	5.5	4
Combined** solar reflectance	75	76

*Combined translucency of 2 fabrics $= \dfrac{T_1 T_2}{1 - R_1 R_2}$

**Combined reflectance of 2 fabrics $= R_1 = \dfrac{R_2 T_1{}^2}{1 - R_1 R_2}$

Where T_1 and R_1 are the transmission and reflectance of the outer fabric, and T_2 and R_2 the transmission and reflectance of the inner liner.

Solar heat gain coefficients

Example	1 Medium strength high translucency	2 Medium strength low translucency	3 Medium strength low translucency with liner
Solar transmission (%) Reflectance (%)	13 73	9 75	4 76
Absorption (%)	14	16	20
Solar heat gain (%)			
Radiation alone	20	17	11
7.5 mph wind*	16	12	7

*Standard summer conditions recommended in ASHRAE Handbook of Fundamentals.

Solar transmittance for plant growth

Transmittance	Fabric #1 Medium strength low translucency	Fabric #2 Medium strength high translucency
Total solar transmittance (%)	9	13
Transmittance at 0.44μ (blue)	1	4
Transmittance at 0.66μ (red)	9	13

A detailed point: the warp direction of the fabric is stronger than the weft and stretches less. Fabric panels, which come in widths from three to four and a half metres will need to be aligned lengthwise to follow maximum stresses. This will create a pattern which becomes a design feature.

The choice between tensile and pneumatic structures

Pneumatic structures are cheaper, but tensile structures have fewer restrictions.

Pneumatic structures give very long, clear spans, well beyond what could be expected in atrium conditions, but they call for some skill and constant attendance to operate successfully. Inflated structures, ones where two fabric skins are held apart by air, may be a better idea than air-supported structures, where the whole atrium needs to be pressurized. Only if a climate-control and fire-safety strategy involving a positively pressurized atrium can be adopted will an air-supported roof be viable.

Tensile structures can be applied more freely. They can be added to existing buildings, supported in a variety of ways, and be very varied in shape. Safety problems are insignificant, as there is no collapse-risk similar to that where pneumatic structures are involved. Air-handling decisions are unaffected.

Tensile structures. As few designers are yet familiar with the design of tensile structures, the advice of experienced engineers and specialist contractors is essential from the start. Indeed, just one United States engineering firm, Geiger Berger Associates, has done much of the development work to date.

One of the first challenges to conventional design presented by tensile structures is that they are naturally curved. Mating compound-curved roof structures to a rectangular building calls for imagination. The curves are essential however: fabric can be tensioned successfully only in compound curves, as no bending or shear forces can be carried. Modelling is an essential tool to visualize and analyze the design.

The fabric membrane is anchored at the connection to the conventional building on a compression ring-beam. Support across the atrium can be created in two principle ways: by arches below the skin, or by masts inside or out. Bullocks San Jose store is the pioneer atrium with a tensile roof, and it uses laminated timber arches to carry a low-profile roof in a saddle shape. Catenary cables counter the thrust of the arches. A partial inner lining avoids acoustic and condensation problems and varies the quality of the light. The Bullocks roof does not require cables to reinforce the fabric as the arches provide regular support. The fabric rides freely over them, and their rounded cross section prevents snagging or point stress.

Masts within an atrium may be acceptable in some contexts: a 'big-top' ambience would result, suitable for such leisure structures as the recent Florida Festival complex. The proportion of the cone-shapes which mast-support creates is variable. The higher the cone angle the lower the stress on the surrounding ring-beam. The volume within the roof structure is welcome, providing a heat- and smoke-reservoir protecting the upper occupied floors.

External mast structures can support a cone. The Haj terminal at Jeddah uses multiple 45-metre bays to cover 50 hectares. A single bay forms a good model for an atrium roof structure. The tension ring at the crown can provide controlled ventilation, working with vents under the edges of the roof.

Pneumatic structures. The optimum form for a pneumatic roof is a low pitched dome over a super-elliptical plan. Rounded forms are most appropriate although regular symmetrical polygons can be roofed. The low roof-pitch avoids wind forces by enlisting lift effects from passing air.

For atrium roofs, the low pitch of a pneumatic roof may mean it needs to be set higher in relation to the highest occupied floors to avoid heat- or smoke-collection problems. This could be problematic if the main-structure roof is not then available as a ring-beam. A double-skin inflatable roof would need to be set even higher to ensure reservoir volume beneath it.

Pneumatic fabric roofs have cable nets attached, anchored to the ring-beam. The whole roof is assembled in the 'collapsed' mode, and clearance to allow full collapse is essential in the design. The roof must not hit anything or endanger air- or smoke-handling if it collapses. A central emergency drain detail is needed to release water from the roof in the event of collapse. Pneumatic structures have to have a manned control room with a view of the roof, which must always be accessible in an emergency.

1 A comprehensive catalogue of pre-engineered glazed roof systems is available from IBG International (USA). Many of the examples mentioned are illustrated

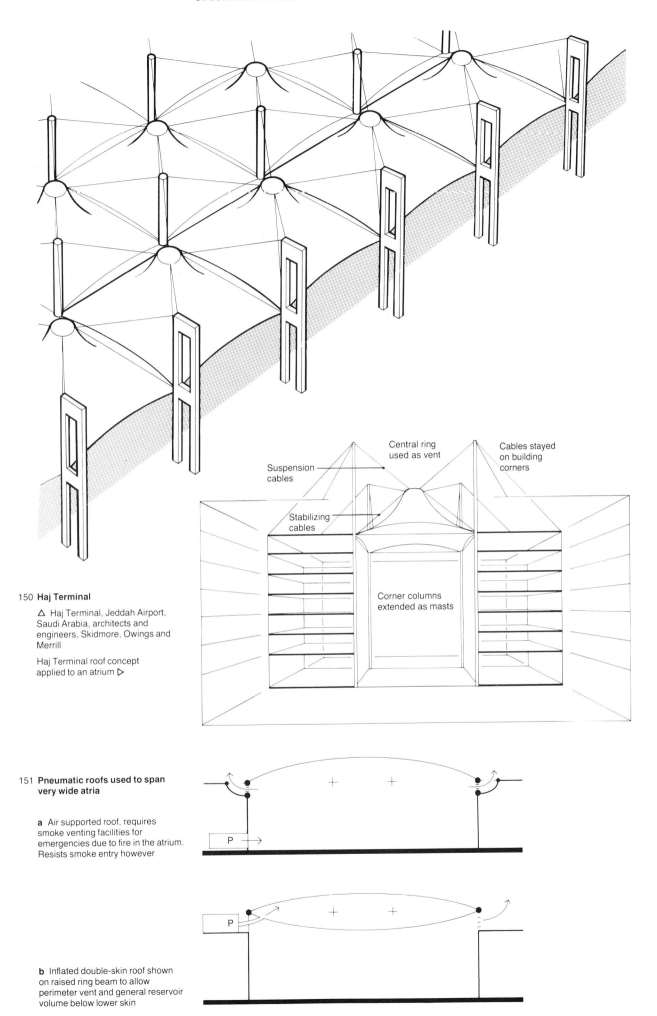

150 **Haj Terminal**

△ Haj Terminal, Jeddah Airport, Saudi Arabia, architects and engineers, Skidmore, Owings and Merrill

Haj Terminal roof concept applied to an atrium ▷

Suspension cables

Stabilizing cables

Central ring used as vent

Cables stayed on building corners

Corner columns extended as masts

151 **Pneumatic roofs used to span very wide atria**

a Air supported roof, requires smoke venting facilities for emergencies due to fire in the atrium. Resists smoke entry however

P

b Inflated double-skin roof shown on raised ring beam to allow perimeter vent and general reservoir volume below lower skin

P

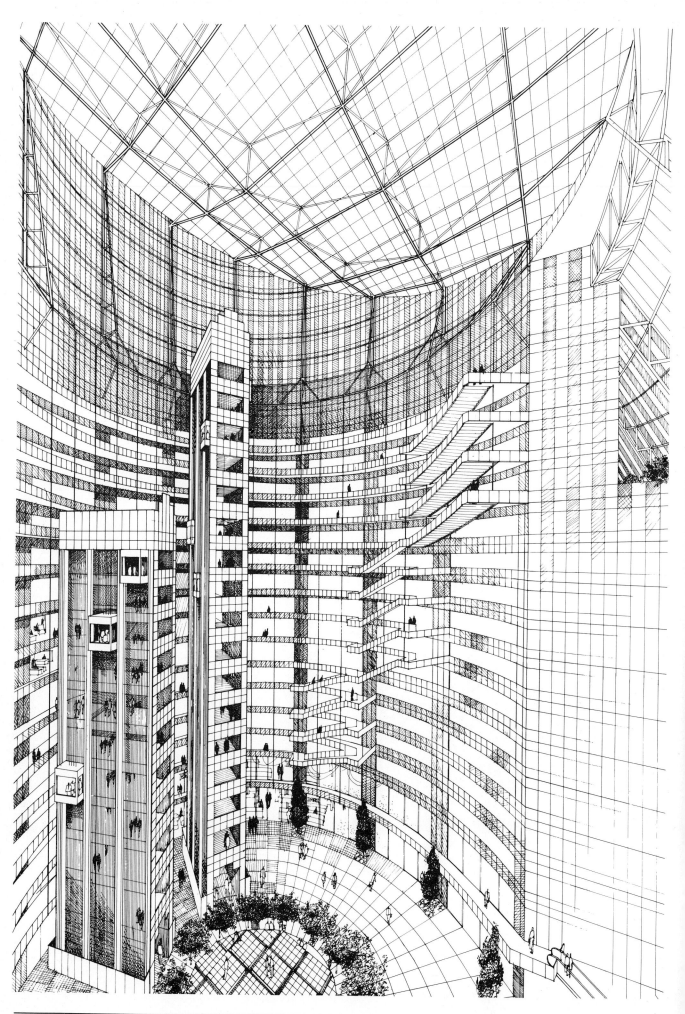

12 Transports of delight

152 **State of Illinois building, Chicago**
Atrium interior with freestanding
elevator towers

Planning the circulation focus

A combination of advantages
An atrium proper is the place of arrival in a building. It is the point of orientation around which the occupied spaces are grouped, and the natural location for pedestrian and mechanical circulation systems. One of the inherent advantages of this kind of planning is that it creates buildings which are much more comprehensible to users and visitors than is the conventional product of modern building. On arrival you can see the various parts of the building, and you can usually see how to get to them. Inside the building you can easily tell where you are if the spaces or secondary circulation routes give views into the atrium.

An atrium building should have economical circulation facilities compared to high-rise development of the same floor-areas. Floors will be fewer and larger, with higher population on each level. If a single point for vertical circulation is provided, the number of elevators needed will be significantly reduced. The number of floors served dictates the scale and cost of installation needed to serve a given population.

These functional and economic advantages can be combined with aesthetic advantages if the opportunity is taken to dramatize the circulation system. An atrium is a theatrical space, with the ability to draw people in to watch each other on its many stages. Exposing elevator, escalator and stair movements to view gives the populace a stimulating experience and a new viewpoint onto the total space. It also displays them and the equipment to those watching on all levels. It can be a kinetic art-form, and is open to elaboration of form and lighting effects.

Consider escalators
Because of the high population likely to be served on each floor of an atrium building, it is worth considering at the start whether an all-elevator solution is appropriate. In retail development escalators are usually preferred because of their continuous, no-waiting service and their high capacity for peak loads. Conditions similar to a department store may exist in low-rise, large-floor buildings, and make an all-escalator solution more sensible.

Foster Associates' office building for Willis, Faber and Dumas (Ipswich, England, 1974) illustrates the potential, its staggered flights providing a 'stairway to the stars'. A three- to four-storey building like this is about the tallest which can be served economically solely by escalators. One escalator unit is the price of one elevator over several storeys, but does the work of three or four elevators.

In taller buildings, or those with diminishing floor sizes on higher levels, the time taken for an escalator ride will compare badly with elevator travel and a mixed installation may be better. Since providing an elevator service to the first and sometimes also the second level above the lobby is comparatively uneconomic, escalator service can be given to these lowest levels, perhaps saving one or two elevators. If double-decker elevators are used to reduce shaftway area, escalators will be teamed with them to provide the two lobby levels required at the base of the atrium. Depending on the characteristics of the traffic it may be worth providing the number of elevators sufficient to handle only off-peak traffic loads, and installing a single reversible flight of escalators to cope with peaks.

The use of escalators is often rejected in tall buildings because of the large amount of floor-space they consume. This is less of a problem in atrium buildings if the escalators are positioned in the atrium void. Either crossing the void, or slung along its edges, they consume no useful space and need no fire enclosures.

Foster Associates' Hong Kong and Shanghai Banking Corporation headquarters and Richard Rogers' Lloyd's Insurance building in London both use their atrium spaces to house escalators economically. The Lloyd's Insurance building links several lower floors together into the one giant 'room' so that insurance trading can grow yet still remain compact. The 'room' can expand by engaging further floors upwards, and adding escalators in the atrium. The Hong Kong Bank uses escalators in an exciting and original manner to let its visitors float diagonally through the void.

Water Tower Place Shopping Center, Chicago, exhibits creative use of escalators and elevators in tandem (see **46** and **168**). A flight of escalators in a landscaped setting of great skill and wit takes shoppers from street level up to the main level of this high-rise shopping development. Proceeding along a short mall, one then reaches a seven-storey atrium dominated by three hexagonal glass elevators in crystal shafts—glazed enclosures of brilliant construction. These provide spectacular express journeys to upper levels, but only carry a fraction of the traffic. Across the atrium is a bank of escalators providing inter-floor travel. An elevator ride to the top followed by a gentle progress around each floor and then descent by escalator, one level at a time, is a common way to use the building.

Atria as sky lobbies

A building, even with atrium planning, may be tall enough to justify several separate zones of elevators. Here atria have proved to be useful in providing space for interchange levels or 'sky lobbies'. In such buildings there may be several stacked atria. Where all elevators start from street level there will need to be a level for interchange between low- and high-rise banks at the top of the low-rise section of the building. If all cars open on the one level, the best service is offered. Where this cannot be achieved an escalator link is needed. An expanded floor at interchange level, either projected into the main atrium, or forming the base of a second stacked atrium, takes advantage of the break to give a second lobby level. This can give a welcome 'front door' to a major tenant.

Increasingly a pattern of elevator service is being used where shuttle elevators travel from street level to one or more sky lobbies. Passengers transfer at these levels to local elevators which only run through their own zone. With careful design, banks of local elevators can share the same shafts, one zone above another. At least six metres of headroom is needed between the highest and lowest floors served in this way, and a tall sky lobby is needed, with escalator links between local elevator banks.

The Pan American Life building in New Orleans, by Skidmore, Owings and Merrill (see **136**) is a simple solution with two sky-lobby atria. Each atrium serves as an interchange floor and shuttle stop. One notable new building teams shuttle elevators with banks of escalators instead of local elevators. The Hong Kong and Shanghai Banking Corporation headquarters is divided into five elevator zones. At each of four sky lobbies, three-level atria open the whole cross section of the building to the outside. The first sky lobby forms the light scoop for the building's major atrium, a 10-storey central well down to street level.

153 Hong Kong and Shanghai Banking Corporation Headquarters

a Section of building, lowest ten levels of centre bay form an atrium

b Open sides to the street, and a fan of escalators draw people in

c The soaring central space

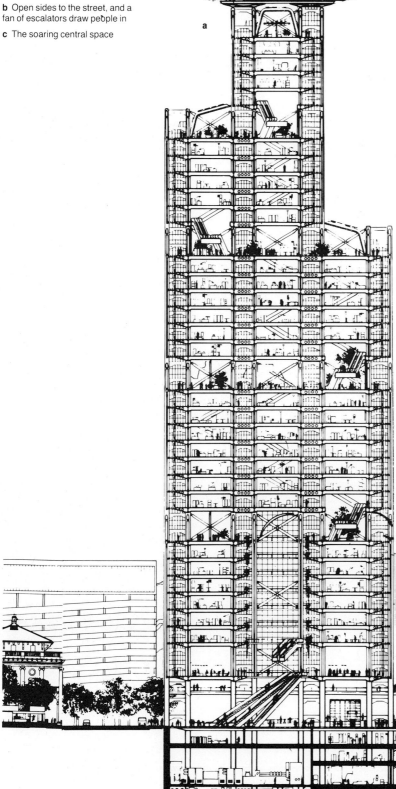

a

Elevator location and design

Locating the elevators within the plan is an integral part of planning the circulation pattern of the building, and the means of fire-escape. A single elevator point will offer superior service and economy, compared to distributed single or grouped elevators. The walking distance penalty in extensive buildings is counterbalanced by reduced waiting times. The diagrams in **155** show established ways in which elevators have been located. It is notable that the use of observation elevators is far from universal.

Some schemes use a mixture of conventional and observation elevators. Such a mixture is often purely for economy or ease of planning, but it caters for the proportion of the population who are slightly agoraphobic and cannot tolerate riding in observation cars. The problems of these people should not be underestimated or ignored. It is easy to design atrium buildings which induce vertigo in the most balanced person, on overexposed circulation galleries, in elevators or on escalators. The space must be stimulating without being frightening.

The passenger elevators may not meet all the building's needs, especially if only observation cars are provided. Goods must be moved, and fire-fighters must have a protected elevator for their use. These may be combined with advantage and located over the service entry to the building.

With the greater plasticity of building form which often accompanies atrium design one question occasionally recurs. Designers, trying to be yet more original ask the elevator manufacturers: 'Must elevators be vertical?'. The answer, for all practical purposes, is: 'Yes'. An 'inclined elevator' actually becomes a cable car, carrying part of its weight onto a track. The movement of an inclined car is very confusing to the human body, having horizontal and vertical movement components. Seating is, therefore, probably essential or at least bars and straps for horizontal restraint of passengers. A custom-built cable-car system is feasible, overcoming problems of levelling at stops, synchronous door-opening, and passenger comfort. However, its cost is not likely to be in the same league as that of elevators, but closer to that of personal rapid-transit systems.

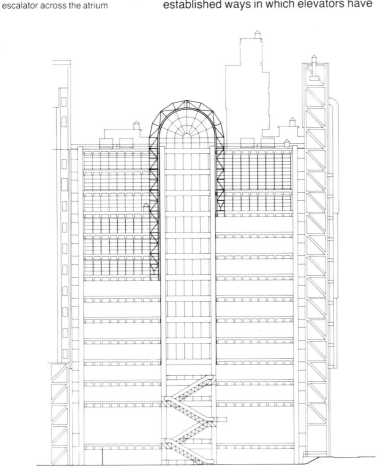

154 **Lloyds building, London,** cross section showing the three initial levels of the trading room linked by escalator across the atrium

b

c
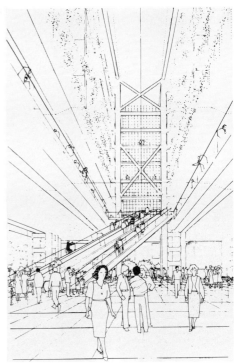

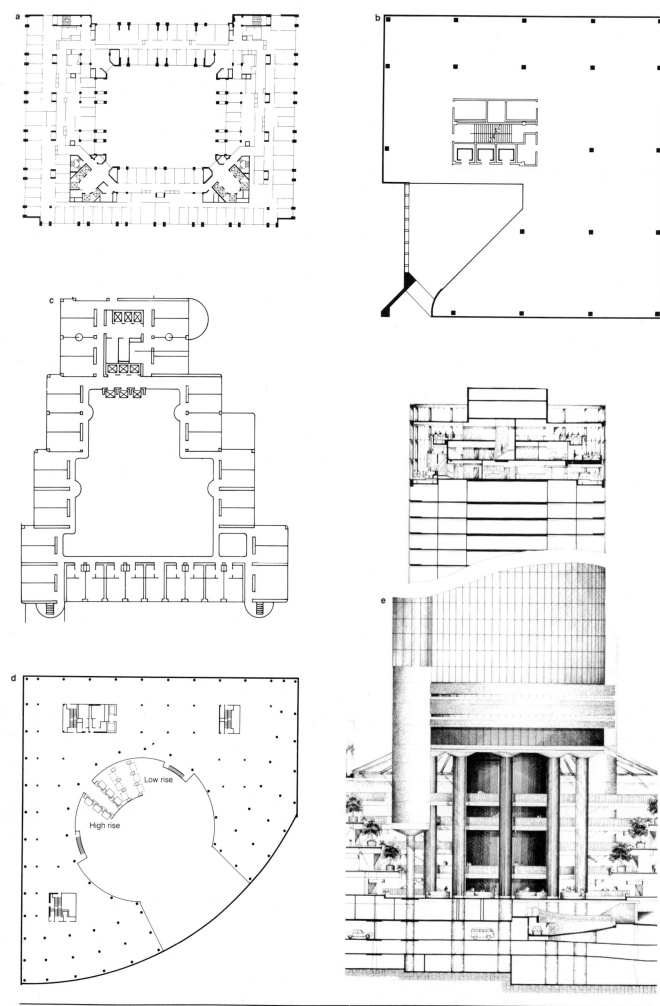

155 Elevator location and planning options

a Elevator lobbies away from atrium but with view into it. IMF HQ, Washington DC, Vincent Kling and Partners

b Elevator doors facing atrium across circulation. Spectrum building, Denver, McOG architects

c Elevators in atrium (wallclimbers) attached to balcony edge. Conventional elevators inboard

Hyatt Hotel, Dallas. Welton Beckett and Associates

d Free standing elevator towers in atrium. Separate low and high rise towers. State of Illinois Center, Chicago, Murphy/Jahn

e External tower elevator rising' from within podium atrium. Peachtree Plaza Hotel, Atlanta. John Portman and Associates

f Staged elevator system using atria as sky lobbies. Pan American Life Centre, New Orleans, Skidmore, Owings and Merrill

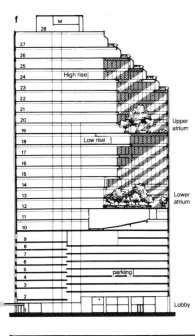

Observation elevators

The observation elevator is an integral part of the atrium concept in the minds of many designers and of the public. The hotels which re-introduced the atrium made such dramatic play with their glass elevators and drew such popular response that the idea continued into more sober office and trade-centre buildings, as well as in shopping centres where the crowd-drawing concept is understandable.

Observation elevators, also known as wall-climbers, vista elevators, or, in Britain, glass lifts, are not essential to the exploitation of an atrium as circulation and orientation focus, but they are also not difficult to provide. Compared to conventional high-quality elevators they cost between five and 80 per cent more, depending on the degree of custom-building required. Considering that atrium buildings can save substantially on the number of elevators needed, a higher unit cost may be bearable (see Chapter 14). Another off-setting cost factor is the potential of elevators to use floorspace in the atrium which would not have otherwise been useful.

Guideways
As an atrium elevator does not need to be in a fire-protected shaft there is a choice of how the guideway gear is supported. A C-shaped concrete slipform can be used, concealing the guide rails and counterweight within, or the gear can be fully exposed in steel framing.

At the Tandy Center, Fort Worth, by Growald Architects (1978), glass traction elevators are carried in openwork trussed steel frames reminiscent of the towers of the George Washington bridge. At the Eaton Center, Toronto, the elevators between parking, office and shopping levels are carried on apparently insubstantial frames off the main concrete structure. Motor gear is carried on the main concrete roof, and all stresses on the guideway rails are transferred back to the building frame, leaving only a light visible structure. Where elevators discontinue at an upper level the 'pit' usually required is merely a steel basket bolted onto the side of the building (see **160**).

Four cost levels
There are four cost levels to choose from in the design of gear and car. The cost comparisons are made for a conventional but high-quality traction-elevator installation: so much attention is focused on atrium elevators that ride and finish must be good.
Level 1 Use of a standard car and shaft arrangement but with one or two sides of car and shaft glazed. This need cost only five per cent above datum.
Level 2 Use of a cantilevered wall-climber, to a manufacturer's model design: 20 per cent above datum.
Level 3 Use of a custom-designed car on model wall-climber gear: up to 50 per cent above datum.
Level 4 Use of custom-designed gear and car standard-hung or cantilevered: from 65 to 80 per cent above datum.
Layout guidance on the use of model and custom-designed elevators is given in **156–161**.

Traction of hydraulic?
There are two basic kinds of elevator drive: traction and hydraulic. Traction elevators use motors to wind a counterbalanced cable-carried car up and down a shaftway. Logically, the motor room should be at the top though, with penalties in energy, structural stress and maintenance, it can be at the base or away from the shafthead. Hydraulic elevators rise on a ram, usually from below, with a useful maximum rise of five storeys. They have no counterweights and the motor room can be remote at no cost penalty.

For buildings of five storeys or less, hydraulic elevators are an attractive option. They are economical, uncluttered and smooth-riding, giving a high-quality feel without sophisticated gear. They are not suited to very intensive traffic. Prolonged, continuous use can heat the hydraulic fluid and reduce the accuracy of travel until the lift has rested. For most low-rise applications however, they can be considered fully equivalent to traction elevators. In high-rise buildings they are often found linking parking and subway levels to lobbies, or substituting for escalators to service shopping levels at the base of taller developments.

Car design
Detailed car design is illustrated by one of John Portman's now classic designs (see **158d**). The extended mullions forming ogee-curved crowns above and below the car interior serve to hide the structure and gear. Lighting for the car interior is in a cove moulding which also throws light up onto the opalescent infill panels of the crown. The ceiling of the car lifts down easily to enable a maintenance worker to service the head gear from a safe enclosure behind the crown. Safety enclosures are highly advisable for maintenance work. They are visible as simple railings on the Eaton Center car roofs

Riding in a wall-climber elevator can give the impression that the car is all glass and hanging outside the shaft. In reality nearly half the car area and more than half the weight are within the shaft. This minimizes the cantilever, and gives plenty of interior surface for mounting controls, indicators, ventilation, telephones and other features.

Safety enclosures
At atrium floor level a hazard is presented by open shaftways and cantilevered cars, and this is also the case if the elevator passes through other floor levels. People must be kept from approaching the moving cars or gear. An up-stand wall at a safe distance is the minimum protection needed. A landscape feature is often used, providing a depth of planting around a screen wall. Water is an alternative, used to great effect by Portman. In the Regency Hyatt, Atlanta, a shallow pool is held back from the car outline by a metal blade dam, with minimal clearance. The car then seems to be entering the water, and ripples caused by air pressure spread over the pool as the car passes. If floor-space is limited, a doorway-height glass or solid screen around the floor-opening should be provided.

156 **Model wallclimber traction elevators**
Otis Elevator Company

Section–shaft and motor room

Plan–motor room

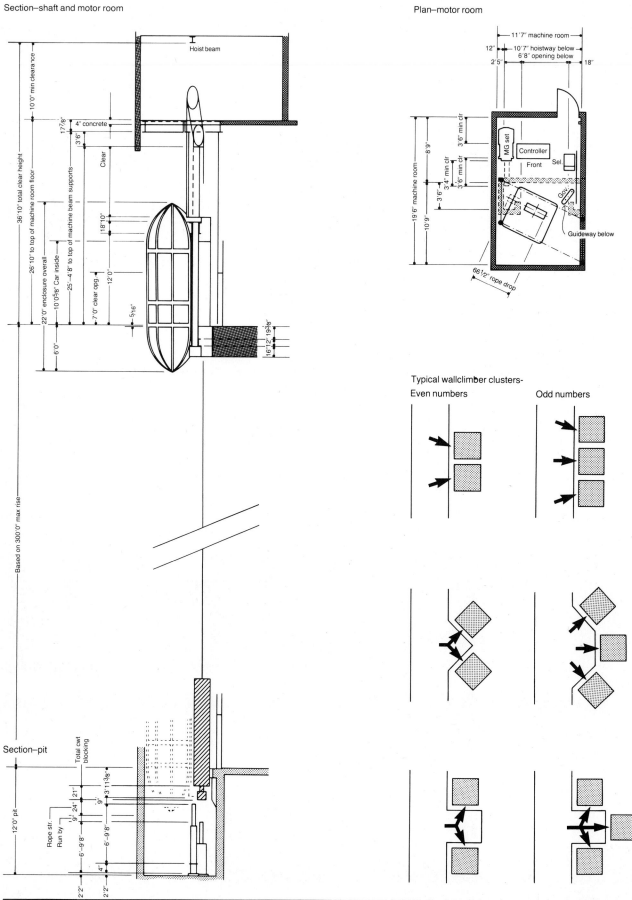

Typical wallclimber clusters-
Even numbers   Odd numbers

Section–pit

Model wallclimber traction elevators

Typical plan, dimensioned

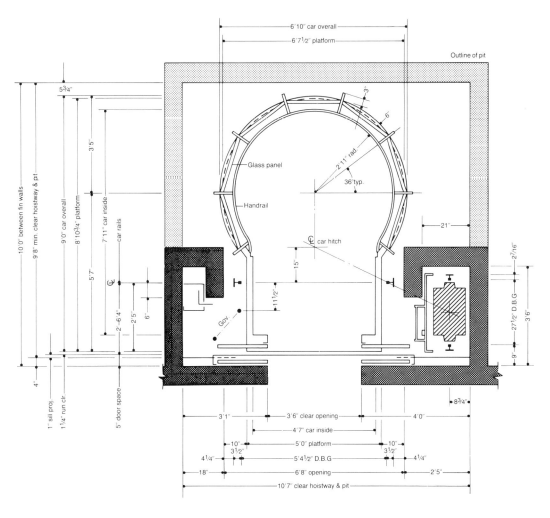

Alternative car forms on the same gear

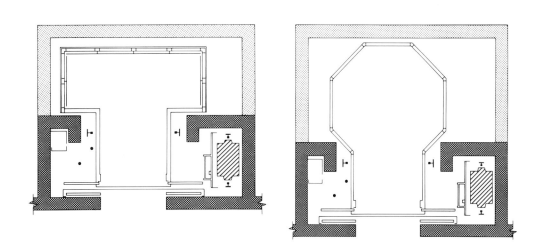

Glass enclosed shaft variant on the same gear

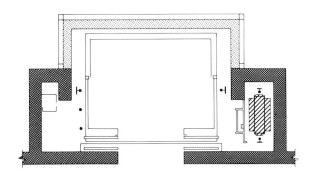

157 Hydraulic elevators

a Typical hydraulic elevator. San Antonio Hyatt Hotel, Texas

b Special hydraulic elevator in centre of grand staircase. Caesar's Palace Casino, Las Vegas, Nevada

Motor rooms remote and at low level *both elevators by Dover Corporation*

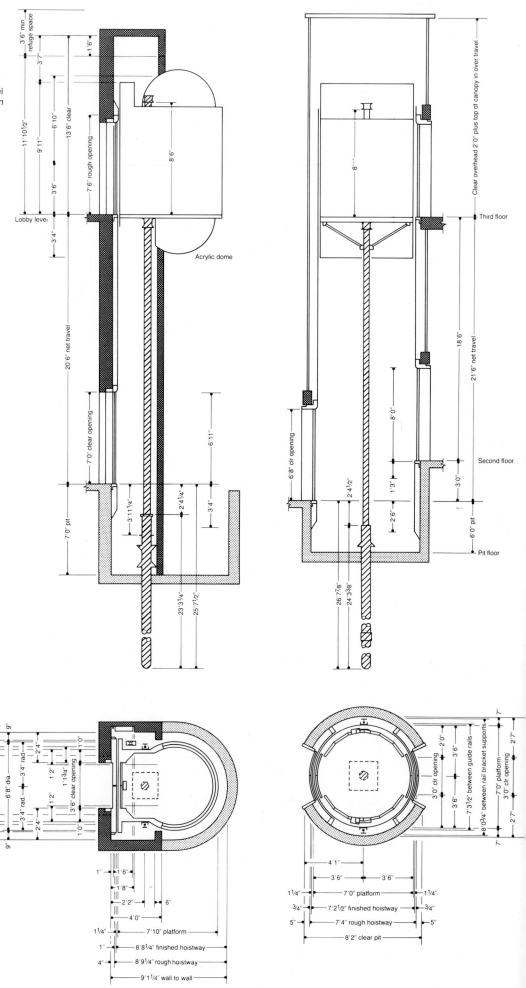

158 Custom built elevator cabs. Cabs can be made in any form imaginable

a Gilded cage–Huntzlers Store, Baltimore

b Bubble–Sofitel hotel, Paris

c Antique lantern--Lincoln Life, Louisville

d The most famous shape–that used by John Portman in his hotels. This section and plan are of the 1983 versions, in the Marriot Hotel, Peachtree Centre, Atlanta

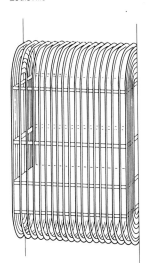

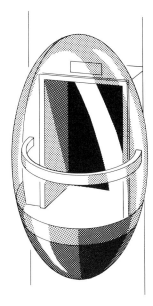

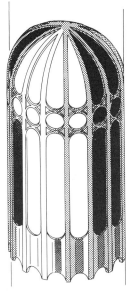

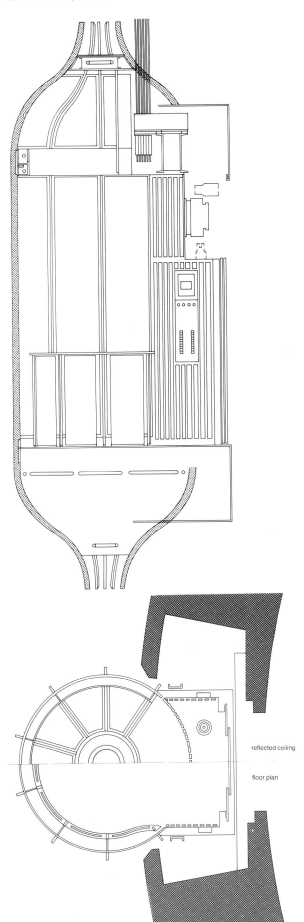

reflected ceiling

floor plan

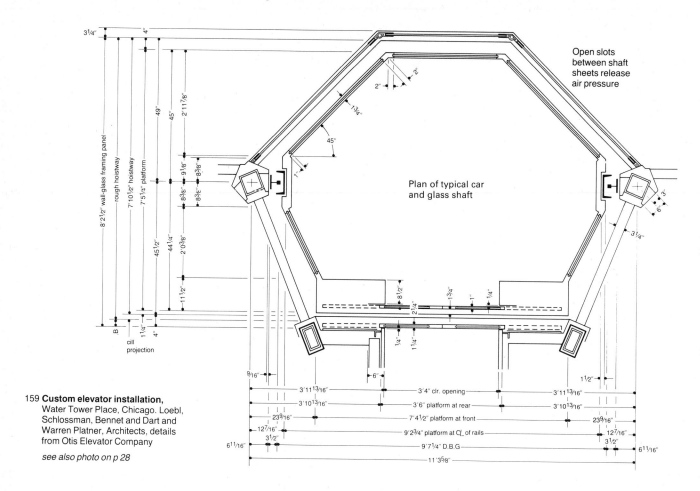

Open slots between shaft sheets release air pressure

Plan of typical car and glass shaft

159 **Custom elevator installation,**
Water Tower Place, Chicago. Loebl, Schlossman, Bennet and Dart and Warren Platner, Architects, details from Otis Elevator Company

see also photo on p 28

Section through upper shaft

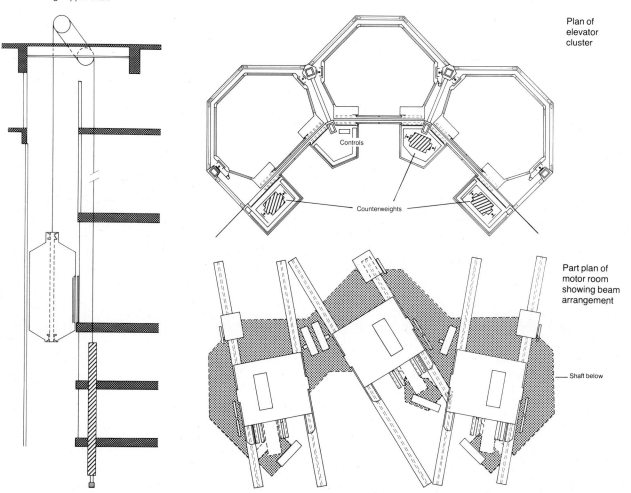

Plan of elevator cluster

Controls

Counterweights

Part plan of motor room showing beam arrangement

Shaft below

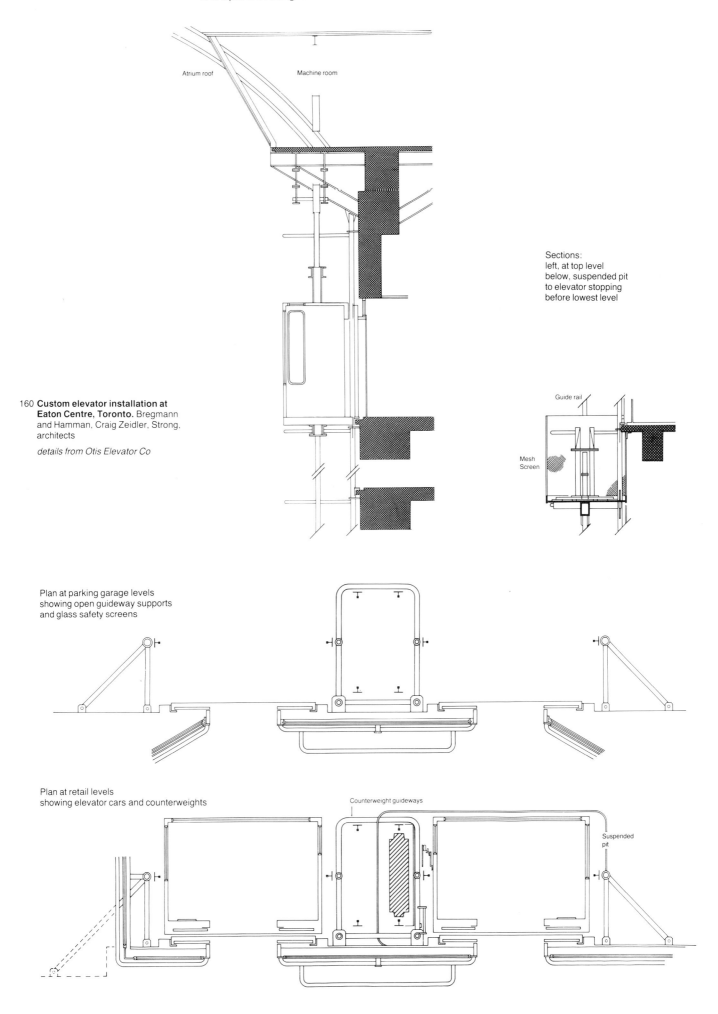

Atrium roof

Machine room

Sections:
left, at top level
below, suspended pit
to elevator stopping
before lowest level

160 **Custom elevator installation at
Eaton Centre, Toronto.** Bregmann
and Hamman, Craig Zeidler, Strong,
architects

details from Otis Elevator Co

Guide rail

Mesh
Screen

Plan at parking garage levels
showing open guideway supports
and glass safety screens

Plan at retail levels
showing elevator cars and counterweights

Counterweight guideways

Suspended
pit

Connecting with the city

Public and private interests

An atrium is or can be an urban room, one of the suite of memorable spaces which make up a city's character. How the public gets into it and passes through it has to relate not only to the facilities and spaces connecting to it, but also to what the building itself does and the way it works.

The key issue, which emerges from study of the existing stock of urban atrium buildings, is the relationship between public movement and the private purpose of the building. The more successful designs use judicious separation of public and private circulation patterns to avoid conflicts of interest. Only in a single-purpose development is there no need to think about the issue: all comers are welcome because they have come for the one purpose. In shopping or leisure developments this singleness of purpose can mean that all circulation can be continuous and open. The occasional problems of undesirable elements using the space as a loitering area will need to be overcome. After all, the 'Street Theatre' attractions and comfort of atria appeal power-fully to street people. A discreet security presence will be required. At Chicago's Water Tower Place a manned desk inside the entrance gives the impression that the space is private, discouraging its casual use. Staff can intervene if anyone behaves unacceptably. In addition, as this is not a through-route in the city, it can contain itself effectively.

Most city-centre atrium developments are multi-use. The upper-level activities may be offices or hotels, whilst near and at street level shopping, banking and leisure facilities will often be provided. The public transport system may connect into it, and public parking facilities may be provided.

Early experience with a completely open-planning approach revealed the problems. At the Omni International in Atlanta the shopping levels are on a through-route to a sports arena. The crowds generated have been of a size and type to prejudice the success of the up-market shopping complex which was originally created, and the centre has gone substantially down-market in the affected areas. Inclusion of an ice-rink has had a similar effect in the Omni and at the Galleria, Houston (Helmuth, Obata, Kassabaum, 1972, 1977). Whilst giving pleasure to many, it creates a noisy, teenage environment which will not lead to the prosperity of, for example, adjacent antique shops.

Grade separation

Where a public walkway system has to be incorporated in the development, as in many rapidly developing cities, selectivity of circulation is a necessary ingredient in planning. It can help both to provide clear orientation for users and to make facilities commercially successful. Level separation between public through-routes and the private or selectively public activities of the building is the most promising technique to adopt. And perhaps the most successful relationships are achieved where the public levels are below the private ones.

The Royal Bank Center, in central Toronto, is a spectacular complex of two triangular office towers with a bridging atrium between them. At street level and above are the banking halls, whilst at two levels below the street are shops, restaurants, the metro station, and connections to all adjacent blocks in the central Toronto walkway system. Physical connection between the banking and shopping levels does exist, but is discrete and can be closed after hours. Visual connection, however, is total. Wells in the banking levels open down to a water-garden at the centre of the shopping levels. Passage through the public walkway system is a low, tunnelling experience for the most part, but at the Royal Bank the view explodes upwards to daylight and to the enormous volume of the bank atrium. The space is shared, but separate, with mutual benefit.

The same strategy is being tried at the new Hyatt Hotel in San Antonio, Texas (1982). Thompson, Ventulett, Stainback, and Ford, Powell and Carson have used a site on the marvellous Paseo (river walk) which runs one storey below the street level of the town. The opportunity has been taken to continue the public Paseo through the atrium at low level, and connect it to the town's other great attraction, the Alamo.

It is noticeable that these examples of developments with public levels below private ones do not allow continuous vertical circulation between the upper and lower levels. Elevators from parking, transit or shopping levels run up to the lobby level of the private space and then begin again, after a control-point, up to the private levels. Escalator banks are similarly split.

161 Integrating public and private levels: shopping, metro station and bank at Royal Bank of Canada, Toronto

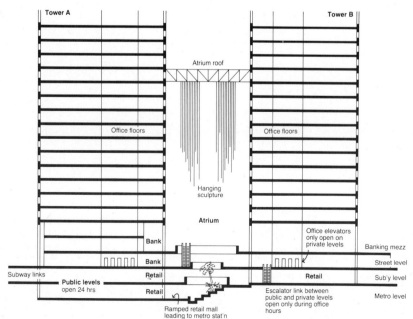

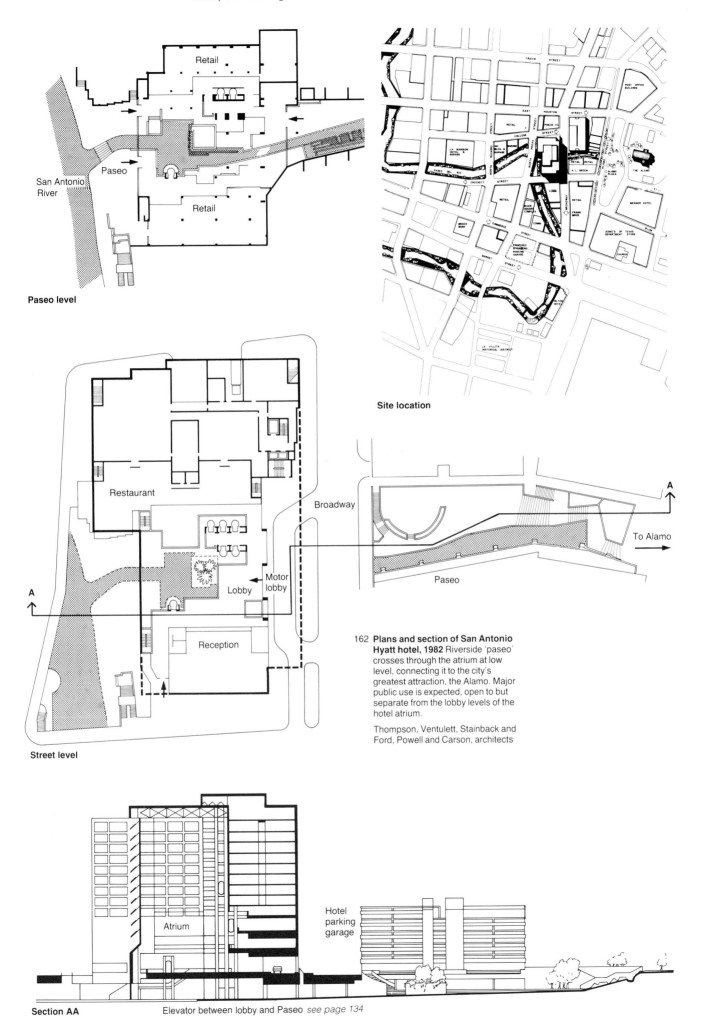

Paseo level

Site location

Street level

Restaurant

Broadway

Lobby

Motor lobby

Reception

Paseo

A

A

To Alamo

San Antonio River

Paseo

Retail

Retail

162 **Plans and section of San Antonio Hyatt hotel, 1982** Riverside 'paseo' crosses through the atrium at low level, connecting it to the city's greatest attraction, the Alamo. Major public use is expected, open to but separate from the lobby levels of the hotel atrium.

Thompson, Ventulett, Stainback and Ford, Powell and Carson, architects

Atrium

Hotel parking garage

Section AA   Elevator between lobby and Paseo *see page 134*

163 Fort Worth National Bank, Fort Worth, Texas
John Portman and Associates 1974

The podium atrium is created by spreading the bearing wall mullions into a conical form. Three floor levels are then cantilevered from the core within the atrium. Public circulation is at street level, with semi-public uses above, a restaurant, and below, a banking hall

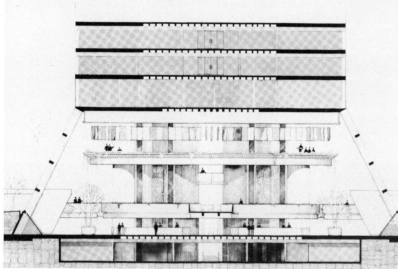

Section looking west

Street level plan

Where there is no grade-separated walkway policy it is possible to achieve separation by skilful planning. John Portman's bank tower at the First National Bank, Fort Worth, mixes a banking hall and restaurant with public through-traffic by level separation within a podium atrium.

Public circulation at a level above the street is well developed in Minneapolis and Calgary. As distinct from the perimeter routes taken by open-air walkway systems in Europe when they were popular in the 1960s, these cities fight long winters and run indoor routes from centre to centre of each block. There is no doubt that it is harder to arrange private circulation around an elevated system than it is around a below-grade network. The routeways tend to cut through private levels. Private spaces in this situation usually have separate street-level lobbies, and controlled access into them off the upper level.

There is a great potential for relating urban transit-system terminals to atrium development. Whilst the systems themselves can rarely be as magnificent or welcoming as those of Moscow or Washington DC, they can potentially connect directly to these great sheltered public spaces. This has already happened in Canada. In Toronto the underground train stops at Royal Bank and Eaton Center. In Montreal the metro emerges in the vast Complexe Desjardins (Societé La Haye & Quellet, 1979), a shopping atrium which forms a podium for three office towers and an hotel. London could have had such a system at Hammersmith in the Foster Associates Scheme (see **84/87**) and on the Strand at Coutts Bank (see **50**) where the underground station emerges beneath the building.

Chicago is acquiring two interesting examples of what can be done, both by Murphy/Jahn. The State of Illinois Center (see **97/152**) has connections into its atrium from two transit lines, elevated and subway, on Lake Street. At Northwestern Station a development is planned which shows the enormous potential for combining major public transport facilities with buildings, using the atrium principle. A space reminiscent of Grand Central Station will result.

If the next generation of rapid transit is the lightweight, overhead type, there could be more direct integration of transit and atrium. So far seen only in the fairground architecture of Expo '67 or Disneyworld, this could be the shape of things to come, in central, resort or airport development. John Portman has done a preliminary study for central Miami, integrating transit proposals into an atrium (see **90**).

All of these examples show what can, or in some cases cannot, be done successfully to integrate atrium buildings with urban movement. In most cases the wish to connect has been fundamental to the form of the building. Atrium building and urban design are inextricably involved with one another.

164 **North Western Station, Chicago**
Project by Murphy/Jahn for an office
building above the concourse, 1981

Section between Madison
Street and the tracks

View of concourse passing through
office core. Elevator banks are
suspended at the sky lobby level
above main pedestrian flows to
trains

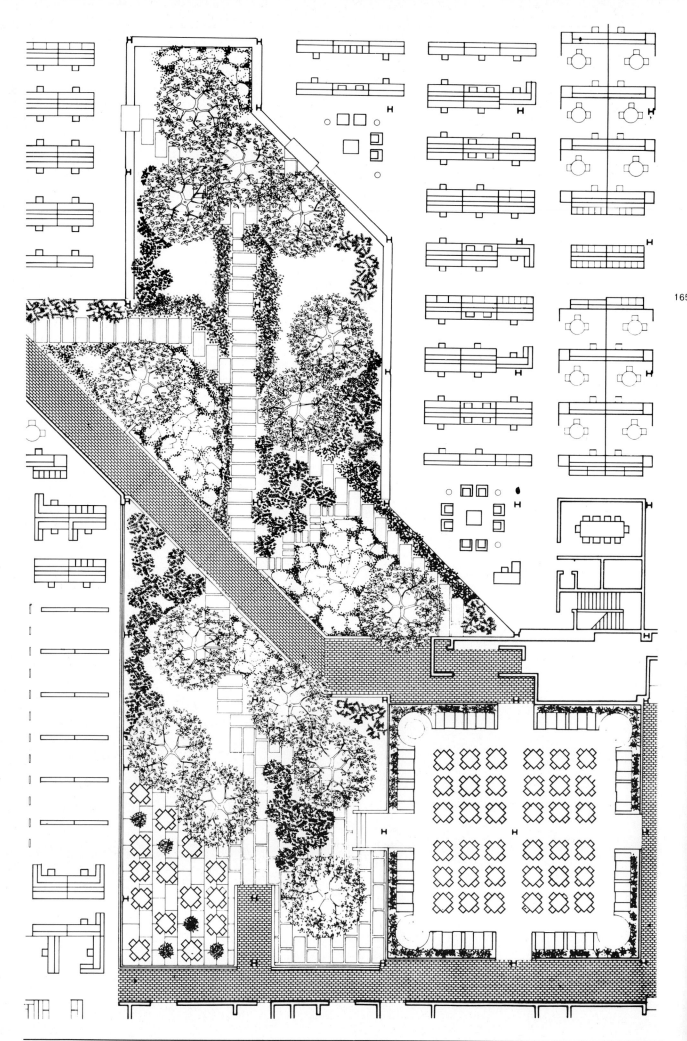

13 The living atrium

Landscape concepts for atria

It is natural that planting and atria go together in the designer's mind. After all, one of the formative influences on atrium building was the glasshouse. Nevertheless, atria are not greenhouses and it cannot be assumed that anything will grow in any atrium. Plants are not as tractable as other design elements: if the artificial climate, growing medium, plant choice or maintenance are wrong, the required ambience will not be achieved. Plants do not generally survive as well indoors as in their native habitat. Successful indoor-landscaping has been cynically described as the situation in which the plants die slowly. It must be accepted that a planted interior will require continued care, but if the environment provided for them is considered from the start, the chances of long-term success are good. Specialist advice from a suitably experienced landscape designer will be needed, and this section aims to brief the architect for creative interaction with a consultant.

A modern atrium is a metaphor for the outdoors. Viewers into the atrium from surrounding spaces are satisfied with it as a substitute exterior space if it gives relaxing, long vistas, and is quite different in feel from the working spaces around it. Planting is a major element in the creation of this illusion of the outdoors. It can be used in several ways, to create either a formal streetscape or an informal garden. The floor of the atrium is the obvious location for planting, which emphasizes it as 'ground', but planting on upper levels can also be very effective.

Two grand informal garden atria are the Ford Foundation, New York (1967) (with Dan Kiley as landscape architect) and Deere West, Moline, Illinois (1978) both by Roche Dinkeloo. The first pioneered the concept, and the second is its finest example. The Ford Foundation attempted initially to have large-scale planting of temperate species. Space was provided for eucalyptus to grow over 100 feet tall. It proved impractical to achieve the sustained low temperatures needed for a winter rest by temperate species, and some of the original trees were replaced by the tropical ones which are now almost universally used in atria. A dense, complex, jungle effect has been created and the garden is now an extraordinary sight. The full storey change of level makes it feel very natural and almost wild. Side- and top-light are available, though predominantly the former. This has led to some shape problems of trees, which will not be overcome until they have grown closer to the roof-light.

Deere West has a more airy, spacious garden. Again, a level change is used, acting as a pathway down to the restaurant, but it is through shaped banks of ground cover, beds of flowers and individual trees. It is by far the most ambitious atrium garden yet attempted, and uses a wide range of plant material to give contrast of texture, colour and scale. Climbing plants are used to cover columns and rocks, and bamboo as a screen. This sort of garden requires substantial and continuous attention. Seasonal variations are made in bedding-out plants and flowering species. Only in very high natural light levels such as are achieved here can the range of species and colour be supported and look their best.

Atria North, a Toronto office development by architect Ron Thom, exhibits a much less sophisticated but very successful informal landscape. A spiral change of level from garage up to entrance has been planted in stepped beds with a water feature cascading down them. Plenty of natural and supplementary light produces bright 'growth colour' from ficus benjamina trees with ground planting of fern and ivys, all set in brown paviour tiles, with blue enamel handrails. Concrete pylons in the garden carry roof-top services, but also provide discreet mounting for artificial lighting (see **34** and **167**).

Formal landscape concepts evoke a different response, one of serenity. Citicorp, the bank headquarters in New York built by Hugh Stubbins and Emery Roth, has its small (70 feet) court ringed by a raised planter bed. Ficus benjamina trees rise past the over - looking gallery, where philodendron trailing plants form a soft edge to the balcony. Ground cover in the raised planter helps to absorb conversation noise and gives some degree of privacy to those dining in the court from the scrutiny of shoppers in the ring of speciality food retailers around it. The planting in Citicorp is not fully successful: it is short of light, robbing the plants of new growth and colour (see **67**).

166 **Notable landscaped atria**

a Ford Foundation, New York City, Roche and Dinkeloo. A grand, picturesque garden of lush planting containing the main approach to the accommodation, but enveloping the whole building

b 'Citicourt', the gallery at the Citicorp Centre, New York, by Hugh Stubbins and Emery Roth, architects.

A semi-formal design based on a paved dining terrace with over-looking galleries

c Hyatt Hotel, O'Hare, Chicago, John Portman and Associates.

A formal garden, largely paved at its main level, but with hanging gardens of vines extending to the roof

A three-dimensional formality is used at John Portman's Hyatt O'Hare Hotel. The great court is paved in radial-patterned white glazed tiles with ficus trees in raised tubs arranged around three sides of the central 'access tree' of glass elevators. Colourful plants in table-height beds divide activities on the atrium floor. The eight levels of galleries and bridges surrounding and dividing the atrium are a solid mass of greenery, as if the space were carved from a hedge. Thousands of philodendron plants are ranged along each balustrade, trailing down to cover all structure. Suspended lights provide top-up and accent light for the trees. They are switched on during the day and off at dusk, to be replaced by up-lighters from the tub bases.

Other similar hotel lobbies use tiny christmas lights to create night-time sparkle effects in their trees.

The most successful indoor formal landscaping design to date does not use daylight at all. The escalator flight at Water Tower Place, Chicago, entices shoppers up a pathway reminiscent of the Baroque garden effects of Tivoli. Architect Warren Platner set rows of ficus trees in travertine crags stepping up the slope, with water cascading down planters between the escalator flights.

Seasonal flowering plants and trailing philodendron fill the planter surfaces. The escalator flights diverge towards the top of the

a
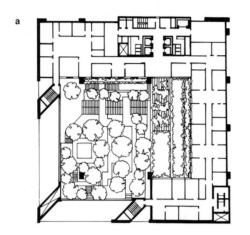

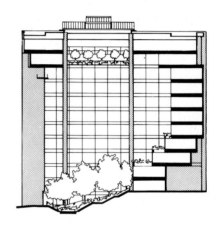

b
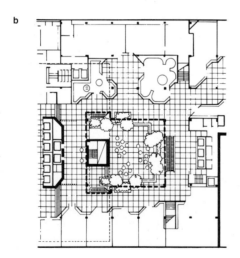

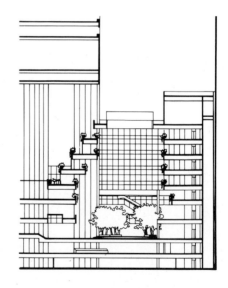

c
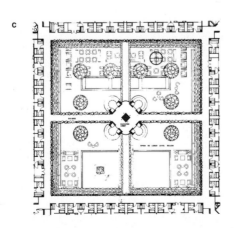

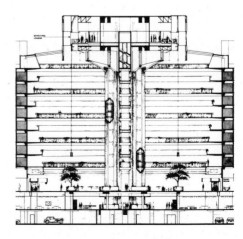

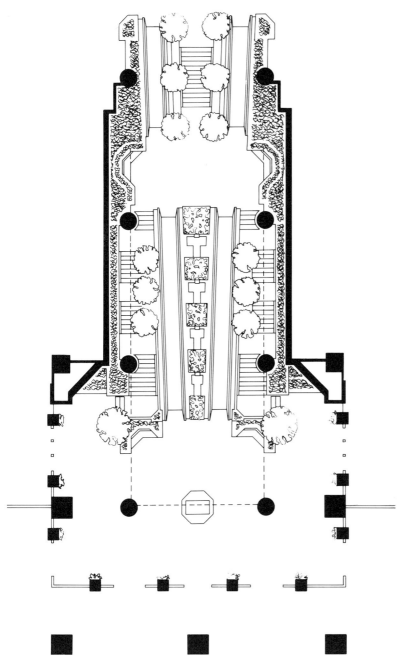

flight, shortening the apparent distance to be travelled. Alternative staircases wind around columns and crags and provide sitting areas. The success of the whole is dependent on the artificial light. It is of superb quality and power, delivering at least 2,000 lux with excellent colour-rendering. The result is year-round buoyant growth, glossy leaves, and sparkling water (see **168c**).

A unique example of this type of landscaping design is the headquarters of Centraal Beheer, Apeldoorn, designed by Herman Hertzberger. Here the building is organized around many small atria, and the greenery is provided in the overlooking work-spaces by plants which are tended by the employees (see **5**). Staff work on nine metres square trays of floor-space, stacked four or five high beneath a glass roof and linked at the centre of each side by bridges three metres wide. All staff have a day-lit balcony edge to their work-station. The policy is to allow any form of decoration and planting to be done, so that the work areas are personalized. The result has been varied and successful, with, amongst other effects, ivy crossing the void on strings and enveloping spiral stairs.

Where atria have side-wall glazing there is a temptation to try to run the landscape treatment continuously from outside to inside the building. This is only possible in sub-tropical and tropical climates where the same species thrive outside and in.

In all these schemes, the most important factor in determining success is the level of light available. High light levels in the atrium are essential if any working illumination is to be delivered to overlooking spaces. It is also the key to bringing the atrium to life. When plants are healthy there is a tangible feeling of hope, expectancy and springtime.

The choice of species for atrium planting is not very great. Most of the examples use a limited number of proven, tropical species, though more daring selections are possible, and new species are being introduced. Examples of plant selection and arrangement are shown in **168**.

167 **Landscaped stair and escalator flights**

△ Water Tower Place, Chicago, Warren Platner, architect

▽ Section, Atria North, Toronto, Ron Thom, architect

168 **Typical plant usage in atria**

a John Deere West
Moline, Illinois

Architect: Roche and Dinkeloo

The planting design at John Deere West is a sublime composition of interior plant material. Forms and textures are juxtaposed harmoniously with unusual restraint and skill, the value of each species being clearly recognisable. Into this composition bands of seasonal plants which last only a few weeks are introduced throughout the year to give a colourful emphasis.

b Household Finance Corporation International Headquarters
Prospect Heights, Illinois

Architects   : Loebl, Schlossman and Hackl Inc
Landscape Architects: Lipp, Wehler and Associates

In this design the major trees used are Schefflera actinophylla 7m to 10m high which create a canopy with a bold umbrella-like scale of foliage. These emerge from islands of simulated rock surrounded by rippling water planted with dramatically contrasting foliage plants. The planting forms a rich and romantic focal point in the building.

Species illustrated

1	Ficus benjamina	Weeping fig
2	Nephrolepsis exaltata bostoniensis	Boston fern
3	Asplenium nidus	Bird's-nest fern
4	Hedera helix	English ivy
5	Seasonal planting	Chrysanthemum, Poinsettia, Zinnia etc
6	Seasonal planting	Chrysanthemum
7	Spathiphyllum Mauna Loa	Peace lily
8	Pittosporum tobira	
9	Schefflera actinophylla	Umbrella tree
10	Philodendron selloum	
11	Dracaena marginata	
12	Aglaonema 'Silver Queen'	
13	Phoenix roebelenii	Palm
14	Ficus pumila	Creeping fig
15	Philodendron cordatum	Sweetheart plant
16	Fatsia japonica	
17	Cissus rhombifolia	Kangaroo vine

c Water Tower Place
Chicago, Illinois

Architect: Loebl, Schlossman and Hackl Inc with Warren Platner
Landscape Architect: Dan Kiley and Partners

The planting consists predominantly of large Weeping Fig trees and Philodendron cordatum which cascades down the huge rusticated travertine planters. It transforms a steep narrow space into a dramatic escalating garden enticing the shoppers upwards.
Despite the relatively sparse amount of greenery, the thriving plants give the effect of an abundance of planting constantly bathed in welcoming sunshine.

d Bradford Exchange
Niles, Indiana

Architects: Weese, Seegers, Hickey, Weese
Landscape Architect: Joe Karr Associates

Simulating a woodland stream running through a planted valley in an entirely artificial environment the plants Joe Karr uses are the dense ground hugging form of Ficus pumila, the clump forming Boston Fern, the climber Cissus antartica rambling over rocks and the accent plant with bold palmate foliage, Fatsia japonica.

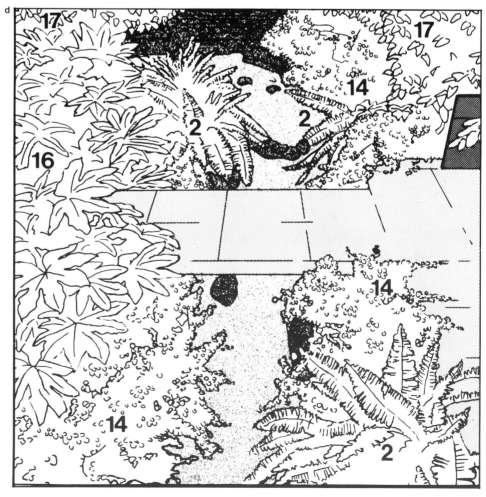

169 The anatomy of a plant

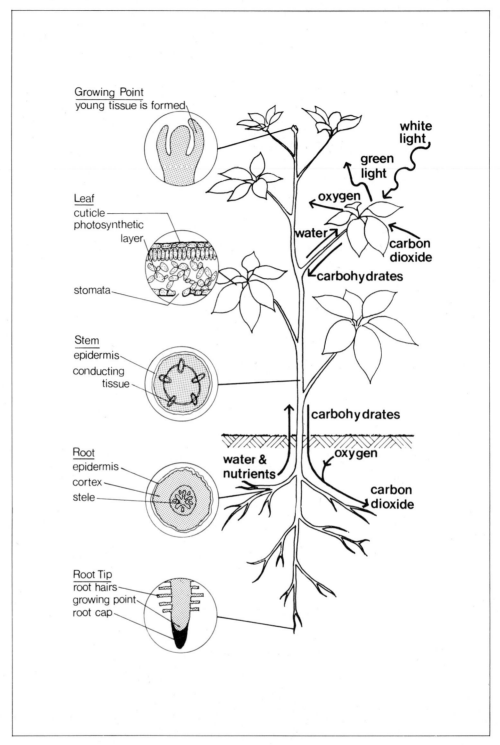

170 The response of plants to light

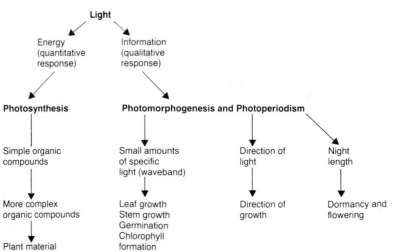

Plant environment

The physiology of plants

Plants are alive and their physiological needs must be met by their environment. That environment has two distinct parts, one in the growing medium, and the other above it. The former conditions what can be done with the plant container, the latter with the atrium space itself, its light and temperature conditions.

The parts of a plant above 'ground', the stems, leaves and flowers, are all active cell-producers, controlled by hormones affecting the rate and location of growth to keep the shape of the plant. Hormones enable the plant to note the length of days and thus fulfil its seasonal pattern. They also produce different growth patterns with varying light levels or colours. Thick, dense growth occurs in high light levels; more slender etiolated growth in lower levels, or in 'far red' light.

The basic energy-converting process is done by the leaves. Carbohydrate fuel for growth and metabolic processes is produced by a reaction within the leaf between carbon dioxide and water in the presence of light and a catalyst, chlorophyll. This is photosynthesis. Pores in the leaf breath carbon dioxide in and allow oxygen and water vapour out. The chlorophyll catalyst is located in the heart of the leaf, in 'chloroplast' structures. These are arranged to cope with the light levels to which the plant is habituated. Slow adjustment is possible within the range of a species, but the basic configuration varies between high-light-level types and shade plants. Chlorophyll absorbs light selectively in the red and blue wavebands, reflecting green. Two essential reactions occur in the leaves, one in the light and one in the dark.
The dark reaction actually constructs the carbohydrates and allows them to disperse to growth points and fuel stores. Continuous light by artificial means is therefore damaging.

Metabolic energy is created by respiration, oxidizing the fuel produced by photo-synthesis. Oxygen is taken in and burned, and carbon dioxide released. Thus a proportion of the products of photosynthesis are recycled. The rate of respiration is usually sensitive to temperature, doubling for every 10 degrees C rise. There is a compensation point for any plant at which light level and temperature combine to allow fuel production equal to the needs of respiration alone. Growth can only occur above the compensation point.

Flowering only occurs indoors in very high light levels. Flowers strain the metabolism, consuming carbohydrates and water rapidly.

Below ground is a different physiology, the root system. It provides anchorage, and takes up water and nutrients through its surfaces. It depends, however, on the energy created by the leaves in order to function and grow. The exchange process between the two is called translocation: chains of water molecules are pulled up the minute capillaries of stems by evaporation at the leaf and nutrients ride up with the water. Carbohydrate solutions return downwards to power root-growth and to be stored.

There is a natural balance between root-spread and the size of the visible plant, the so-called root: shoot ratio. It only occurs in ideal natural circumstances and can be hard to achieve indoors. If nutrient is fed to the roots this can reduce their need to spread for food and thus threaten the plant's anchorage. Root-spread is also inhibited by dry soil, lack of oxygen and nutrients, or, of course, by lack of spare carbohydrates from the metabolic process.

The physiology of the plant thus balances on flows of light, gases, heat, water, nutrients and adequate drainage, all of which the designer must assure.

Temperature and air movement

Plants have permissible air temperature regimes based on their natural habitats and these temperature regimes cannot be exceeded if they are to survive. The rules have been learnt by experience: the use of temperate plants in a tempered atrium at the Ford Foundation was unsuccessful. Sub-tropical planting is found in most atria because the year-round temperature regime for people is similar to subtropical conditions. Some diurnal variation is actually welcomed by plants. A range of 21 to 24 degrees C in daytime is ideally contrasted with 15 to 18 degrees C at night. Radiation from atria at night can lead to lower temperatures. With subtropical planting they should not be allowed to fall below 10 to 13 degrees C. In normal building use there should not be a problem, but in winter, during weekends and holidays systems should maintain the minimum temperatures and light inputs, or plants may die.

It is the air temperature which is critical, affecting leaf health: soil temperature changes very slowly and cannot compensate for too low an air temperature. Minimum soil temperature should, however, be 15° C. Radiant heat is not acceptable, and, if used, should be aimed away from planting.

Within an acceptable overall atrium climate there are areas where plants will not thrive. Cold radiation close to glass will kill. Focused solar radiation caused by flaws in glass may burn leaves near to the glass. Doorways will be cold and draughty, and plants will die back from openings, unless revolving doors are used. Service outlets pose a problem. Lamps should not be allowed within a metre of leaves, and air inputs will chill or scorch leaves with air movement above 1.5 metres per second. Humidity is not a great issue in design. Plants like higher humidity than is normally available indoors, and they help to create it. They do not suffer unduly from reduced humidity, however, and as it is difficult to raise atrium humidity levels artificially, the subject is better left alone.

171 Preserving good tree shape

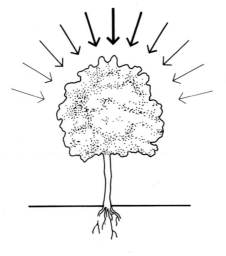

A tree's shape is based on natural sky brightness distribution

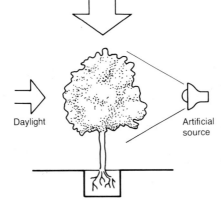

Where atrium light is not even, supplementary artificial light can maintain shape, here where skylight and one side light are available

Daylight

Artificial source

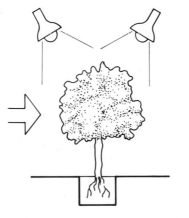

Where supplementary top light is required. Several off-centre lights are better than one vertical

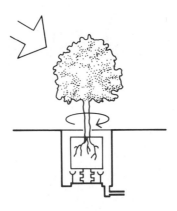

Rotating tree pit to allow tree to keep shape in one-sided natural light (Coutts Bank, London, by Sir Frederick Gibberd and Partners)

Light

Light works on plants in three ways: to provide energy for their life, but also to give them seasonal guidance and regulate their shape. These latter two are subsidiary effects in nature, but anomalies can arise in indoor environments.

Sheer quantity of light is the strongest determinant of success in atrium planting. Sufficient light to promote growth must reach not only the trees, but also the ground-cover planting below them. The energy needs of most suitable plants are equivalent to at least the supply of 700 to 1,000 lux for 12 hours per day, with 500 lux over a similar period as the absolute minimum for survival. In daylighting terms, a factor of 14 to 20 per cent will be needed under the 5,000 lux standard sky. Since this supply may not be available all year, supplementary sources must also be provided. These sources should preferably be off at night, keeping the daily rhythm normal.

The way daylight enters the atrium will affect its level and the growth pattern of plants. Much higher sky brightness exists at the crown of the sky than near the horizon, and roof-lights will deliver two or three times as much light per unit area as side-glazing. Roof-light is more desirable for plants as a direction-giver: the photomorphogenesis effect makes plants grow towards light, and top-light preserves a natural shape. Some side-light helps to give balanced shape, but if the atrium is predominantly side-lit it may be necessary to position artificial light sources to provide compensating illumination. Another strategy is to rotate plants to give growth signals to all sides.

Where artificial light forms part or most of the plants' diet, light levels should also be between 700 and 1,000 lux, depending on the plant species used. A wide-frequency spectrum is desirable, from 400 to 700 nm, to activate all the plants' functions. Ultraviolet and infra-red light are not good for plants, and some artificial sources do deliver wavelengths below 350 nm and above 700 nm. Most of the generally used light sources do not, however, give enough of these damaging emissions to cause problems for indoor landscape. There is no advantage in using special horticultural light sources in atria. Benefits are too marginal and colour rendering is poor.

Colour rendition can be a problem with some light sources: a limited spectral output may be selectively absorbed by leaves. Fluorescent lighting can be very well colour-balanced, whilst mercury and sodium light are harder to modify for colour. Mercury lights tend towards the blue end of the spectrum and sodium emits either a single wavelength yellow (SOX) or a broader, but still orange-y, colour (SON). Under SON light leaves may appear grey or black. Despite this, these latter types of sources, the high-intensity discharge lamps, are favoured for atrium lighting because they are efficient in high spaces. Mixing the two of them can produce good colour rendition on plants and this has been done at Citicorp in

New York. The light fittings look strange, however, since the two source colours are very obvious where either one alone would be read as 'white'. In the rare atrium situations where discharge lighting is used as the predominant plant energy source it will have an effect on growth. Blue light tends to stunt and compress growth, whilst red light causes extended but slender, weak, growth. Tungsten light is not an option in atria; it is too inefficient for large-space lighting, and the red-end colour is not desirable.

The most attractive light source for planting available at present is the metal halide lamp. It delivers a strong full-spectrum light which, when falling on folliage, looks like sunshine. It is used most effectively at Water Tower Place in Chicago.

Switching of atrium lights is best done automatically. Solar-corrected timeswitch-operation may be tolerable, as the atrium is not a working area. Photocell- activated switching will keep overall light levels closer to a norm in varying weather conditions, but must not be too sensitive if discharge

sources are used: once extinguished they do not switch on again for a period. Similarly they cannot readily be dimmed. Timeswitches should allow a rest period for the plants: from four to six hours of darkness each day is needed for the 'dark reaction' of the plants' chemistry. Security lighting during this period should be as dim as possible.

Once plants have received their daily daylight requirement, a lower level of 'effect lighting' should be sufficient, simply for people to move safely about or to dine beneath the trees. Assessing when that requirement has been satisfied is a job for a microprocessor, and has yet to be done.

172 Lighting needs of plants

Spectrum of sunlight at noon

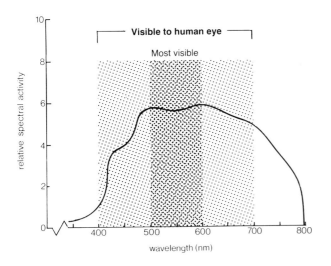

Rate of photosynthesis relative to spectrum

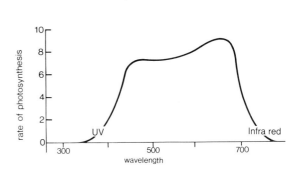

Relative 'whiteness' of artificial sources. The CIE chromaticity diagram shows pure white at the centre of the triangle, pure colour at the edges

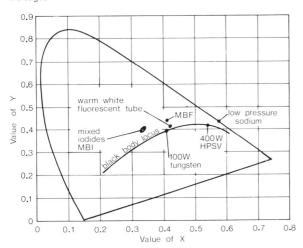

173 Automatic feeding and watering

Compost culture–a typical
self-watering free standing planter

A possible large scale
hydroculture circulation system for
built in planters

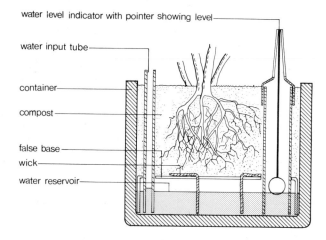

water level indicator with pointer showing level
water input tube
container
compost
false base
wick
water reservoir

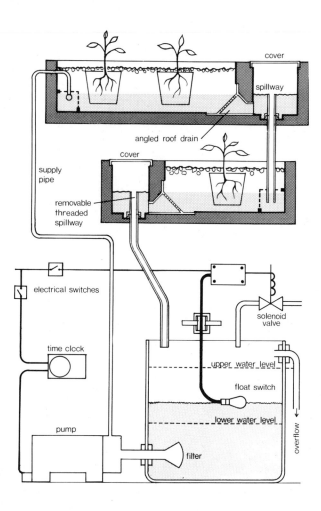

cover
spillway
angled roof drain
cover
supply
pipe
removable
threaded
spillway
electrical switches
time clock
pump
solenoid
valve
upper water level
float switch
lower water level
overflow
filter

Hydroculture–a typical free
standing planter

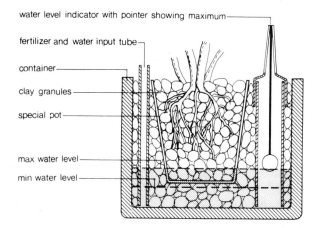

water level indicator with pointer showing maximum
fertilizer and water input tube
container
clay granules
special pot
max water level
min water level

A possible automatic irrigation
system for compost culture in built in
planters

diagrams after Scrivens

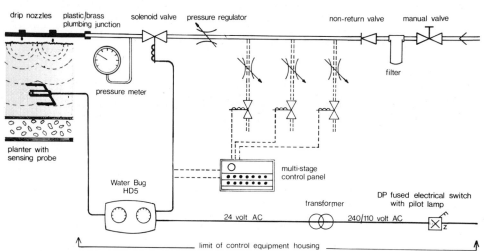

drip nozzles
plastic/brass
plumbing junction
solenoid valve
pressure regulator
non-return valve
manual valve
filter
pressure meter
planter with
sensing probe
Water Bug
HD5
multi-stage
control panel
transformer
DP fused electrical switch
with pilot lamp
24 volt AC
240/110 volt AC
limit of control equipment housing

Accommodating plants

Growing media

With the supply of physical support, water, nutrients and oxygen, the media used to provide indoor planting have a complex task. They are required to be simultaneously solid, liquid and gaseous. They are asked to perform far better than natural media as the volume of medium available to the plant will be restricted compared to natural conditions. Suitable media will therefore be of low density compared to natural soils, with large pore spaces to improve the flow of air and water.

The choice of medium will be important for the atrium design. Large-volume planters are very heavy, and some media are much lighter than others. The approach to irrigation will also vary, with implications for installation design.

The two fundamentally different approaches to growing plants indoors are compost culture and hydroculture. A hybrid form, half-hydroculture, combines the two. Hydroculture is especially useful for small, distributed plants. Compost-growing is for the larger trees and plants most frequently found in atria, where structural support requires a firm medium.

Compost. Essentially the use of composts involves the creation by selection of natural and artificial materials, of a low-density substrate of the right drainage and air-entrainment qualities. Peats (sphagnum or sedge) and barks can be mixed with inorganic materials like sand, clay and loams, or with synthetic materials like perlite, foamed plastic, expanded vermiculite and leca (light expanded clay aggregate).

Watering and feeding can be manual or by automatic systems. Watering systems can either be through reservoirs in the base of planters, feeding the compost above by capillary action, or by piped irrigation. Reservoir systems are ideal for free-standing planters. Several proven patent systems are available. All use the principle that the compost is held in an inner container, with water and fertilizer in solution in an outer one. Wicks of capillary fibres, porous ceramic or columns of compost link the reservoir to the main compost bed. The rate of supply depends solely on the rate of evaporation from the soil and of transpiration from the leaves, where capillary action draws the water up. Thus the varied needs of plants in shade and sunlight will be matched precisely.

Topping up of the reservoir may be needed only once a month, but indicator floats from the reservoirs enable a quick check on water levels at any time.

Above a modest scale the reservoir is hard to construct economically, and piped irrigation is then necessary. System design and installation is a specialist task. Water is introduced to the planter by either drip or spray-emitters set along pipelines. The type of emitter and its arrangement depends on the compost and plant selection. Unobtrusive arrangements are possible, with only the small emitters themselves visible, though these do not wash the leaves.

Nutrient-bearing water is fed into the compost by pumped supply, activated by detectors in the planter. Di-electric detectors exist which measure water content in the soil by noting the variation in its electrical conductivity. These buried, solid-state 'water-bugs' can activate solenoid valves to operate the irrigation whenever moisture falls below a set level.

Hydroculture is the term applied to a form of hydroponics developed for interior planting because of its simplicity from the plant-production point of view. However, it also offers simple maintenance and comparative freedom from disease and pests.

Plants are grown in a continuously moving, nutrient-bearing solution. Physical support is provided by an inert granular medium which also allows air to the roots. The most popular medium used is leca (light expanded clay aggregate). This is a closed-cell brown bead-like material made by heating clay particles so that their water-content turns to steam and inflates them. In use the roots bind around the granules, with water moving over the granules by surface tension. The voids between granules supply plenty of air to the roots.

A continuous irrigation system is needed for hydroculture, rather than the intermittent approach for compost culture. Pumped circulation of nutrient solution flows through each planter. Planters need a spillway and reservoir alongside, with a submersible pump and level-detecting device. In an atrium installation there may be several planters at different levels. These can be linked into a cascade system, allowing the liquid to descend by gravity from pumped input to the highest planter level. Careful pipework design and float-valves are needed to regulate the flow from one planter to the next. Suitable hardware has been developed and is available.

Half-hydroculture. The hybrid of compost and hydroculture, half-hydroculture, is an expedient to convert plants produced in compost to a hydroculture regime in the building. It is also useful if hydroculture is chosen for large specimen plants, where, nonetheless the physical support provided by compost is better than that afforded by leca.

The compost sits above a layer of leca through which the nutrient solution flows. The reservoir approach may also be used, with still water held in leca: capillary matting separates the compost from the leca, and prevents roots penetrating. Water is drawn up by capillary action into the compost.

It is salutory to note that the successful atrium landscapes to date are almost all compost-grown, with manual feeding and watering. Pressure for labour-cost saving is, however, increasing interest in automation.

Planters. Planting in atria may appear permanent when it is in fact entirely 'potted'. Some designers and maintenance experts prefer to keep all plants in production containers so that they can change seasonal plants and quickly replace unhealthy ones. Planters in this context are simply features for enclosing containers. Wire mesh fitted over the container and dressed with bark-chips produces the 'permanent' look around a tree base. Manual feeding and watering goes with this approach, and it is used with great success in, for example, Water Tower Place. Even planter locations do not have to be fixed. Where small plants are in 'hard' settings, such as balcony-edges or space-dividers, this is probably the ideal approach.

Where a 'permanent' approach is required, and large-scale planting is contemplated, the use of built-in planters has considerable advantages in atria. They can handle the large-scale plants required, and can contain plumbed-in irrigation. They can, depending on their scale and treatment, be a substantial feature of atrium floor-layout and appearance

Planters need to have sufficient depth to provide for the natural root-spread of the plants intended. This can vary from 300 millimetres to one metre of compost. The planter surface can be countersunk into the atrium floor, or stand on it, rising to the required height. This decision may well depend on whether use is to be made of a floor below the atrium level. Another important structural consideration—where the atrium floor is suspended—is the weight of trees. It may well be necessary to place them over columns, or place columns under them, depending on the freedom of layout possible.

Raised planter-beds can be very effective. They provide side walls for seating and define pedestrian routes. This avoids any tendency to use the planter area as a short-cut circulation route and reduces damage to plants. If planters are to be countersunk to atrium floor level, a 300 millimetre strip of impervious material should be left around the edge of the compost surface. This will give a tough surface for maintenance work and avoid damage to any of the more vulnerable floor finishes used in the rest of the space.

Plants will generally be delivered in their production containers and it is common practice to leave them in the containers to avoid risk of damage. Trees, for example, can come in baskets of 1,200 litres. Their roots will spread into the planter compost in due course. The planter is required to provide additional support, irrigation and drainage systems to the production container. A proven approach is to build drainage into the planter base by sloping it at 1 in 40. A drainage layer of 150 to 100 millimetres of leca is then laid to give a horizontal base on which to place the production container. Compost is packed around the container and over its edges to blend it into the whole. A capillary matting must be inserted to stop roots and compost spreading into the drainage system.

The drainage hardware used can be straightforward roof- or balcony-drainage outlets. These can be linked to the building drainage system through a silt-trap.

Planters have to be watertight. Waterproofing is not straightforward because of the chemical condition created by soil. A one-piece reinforced concrete container can be waterproofed with an applied coat of GRP or pitch. For larger planters the full range of basement-tanking and roof-waterproofing technologies need to be considered. Internal liners of butyl, GRP or lead are alternatives to membranes. Pipework and wiring entering and leaving the planter must be allowed for. Far simpler waterproofing is possible if the planters contain potted plants, rather than compost; the membrane can then act as on a roof.

Many atria now have water features in their landscaping. The construction of water-containing pools and cascades is very similar to that of planters, and common detailing can be used.

Where the atrium floor is on natural ground it may be assumed that planting can be done directly into the available soil. This is not the case. Building sitework usually compacts soil until it is too solid to allow good drainage or root penetration. A depth of new compost and suitable drainage facilities need to be provided, and a full artificial planter is usually the best way to do this.

The choice of materials for planters in atria is restricted to minimize fire-load and risk. Some plastics and synthetic rubbers, and indeed some compost-topping materials like sphagnum, are not suitable in public circulation areas.

A final detail: large trees will probably need guy wires for stability after transplanting. Anchorage points in planter-edges should be considered.

174 Planter design

Planter acting as decorative enclosure for 'potted' plants in their production containers. Such plants can be interchanged readily. Manual care is assumed, with no plumbed services

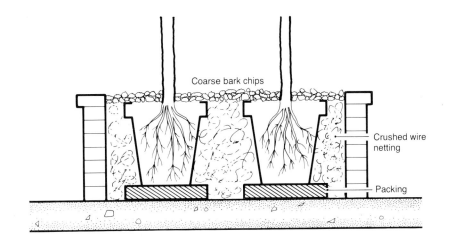

Coarse bark chips

Crushed wire netting

Packing

Built-in compost planter for a major tree. On a suspended floor it is best to place trees over columns due to the great weight of tree and planter. Raised planter protects tree from soil compaction or other damage by pedestrians

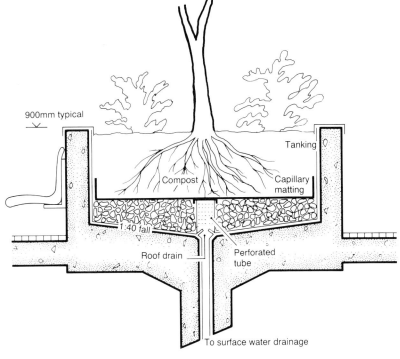

900mm typical

Tanking

Compost

Capillary matting

1:40 fall

Roof drain

Perforated tube

To surface water drainage

Countersunk linear planter shown in suspended floor as a structural channel

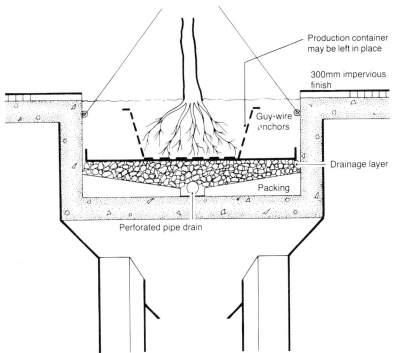

Production container may be left in place

300mm impervious finish

Guy-wire anchors

Drainage layer

Packing

Perforated pipe drain

Care and maintenance

Care in design, by itself, is no guarantee of success in indoor landscaping. The scheme will be made or broken by the quality of after-care, and this will depend on the commitment of the building owners. Be realistic about this before deciding on the level of sophistication of the design.

Maintenance of plants grown in compost is similar to that of outdoor gardens. Regular watering and feeding are necessary, and this can be very labour-intensive if left to manual methods. It can also be risky since sufficient skill-levels are not always available to avoid plant damage through over- or under-watering and feeding, or from compaction of the soil.

On the other hand, there are difficulties with automatic-feeding and -watering systems above the small scale. Though effective and economical, they are prone to human problems. Labour-demarcation issues may mean that garden supervision is being carried out by plumbers. Alternatively, lack of mechanical knowledge amongst the landscape staff may lead to system-breakdowns and flooding. Both manual and mechanical approaches must be adopted with care and with management commitment to succeed. At least the large landscapes in atria atttract more ambitious and skilled maintenance staff than do lesser challenges.

The planting installation should be one of the last elements in completing the building. Dust raised by cleaning, moving or stone-polishing can coat plants and entail very expensive washing of each leaf.

Initial planting density should bear in mind that good growing conditions will have been provided. Leave space for growth, or plants will become entangled. It is ideal to acclimatize the plants in glasshouses for a period before moving them into the atrium. This reduces shock and losses after installation. There will inevitably be some losses, mainly amongst smaller plants where a 10 to 20 per cent annual replacement should be planned for. Dying plants should be removed quickly to keep up good overall appearance.

Skilled attention to plant health will be needed at intervals, whether manual or automatic basic maintenance is provided. Correctness of feeding and watering must be checked, and the presence of disease or pests spotted and stopped. Leaf-cleaning may be required occasionally in the atrium, since there will be no rain to remove dust. Plant or human litter in planters must be regularly removed for both fire-safety and appearance. Water and power supply, and drainage, in addition to that provided for irrigation, will be convenient and time-saving for maintenance staff, and avoid the trailing of hoses and cables across public spaces.

Accessibility to planters is obviously important. Routes should be planned to allow access for the equipment needed for installation, maintenance and replacement. The whole atrium will need appropriate gear to give access for the cleaning of glazing, the changing of lamps, and other work at high levels. An hydraulic 'cherry-picker' type platform may combine these duties with landscape maintenance. It allows atttention to large trees without damage to them or the compaction of soil.

175 Balcony edge planters

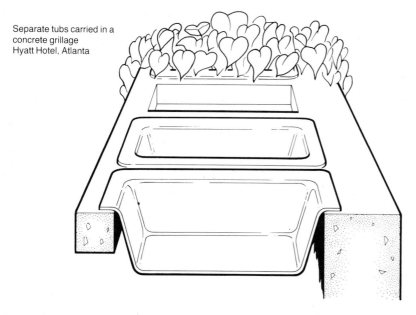

Separate tubs carried in a
concrete grillage
Hyatt Hotel, Atlanta

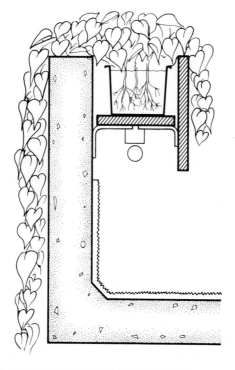

Continuous trough behind
parapet
Hyatt Hotel, O'Hare, Chicago
both by John Portman and
Associates

176 Tree care in an atrium
With large scale planters and trees,
access for attention is difficult. As
atria also need maintenance gear to
change light fixtures and clean upper
walls it is worth considering a
hydraulic mobile platform for
combined use. A 'cherry picker' can
do all these jobs quickly and without
damage to planting

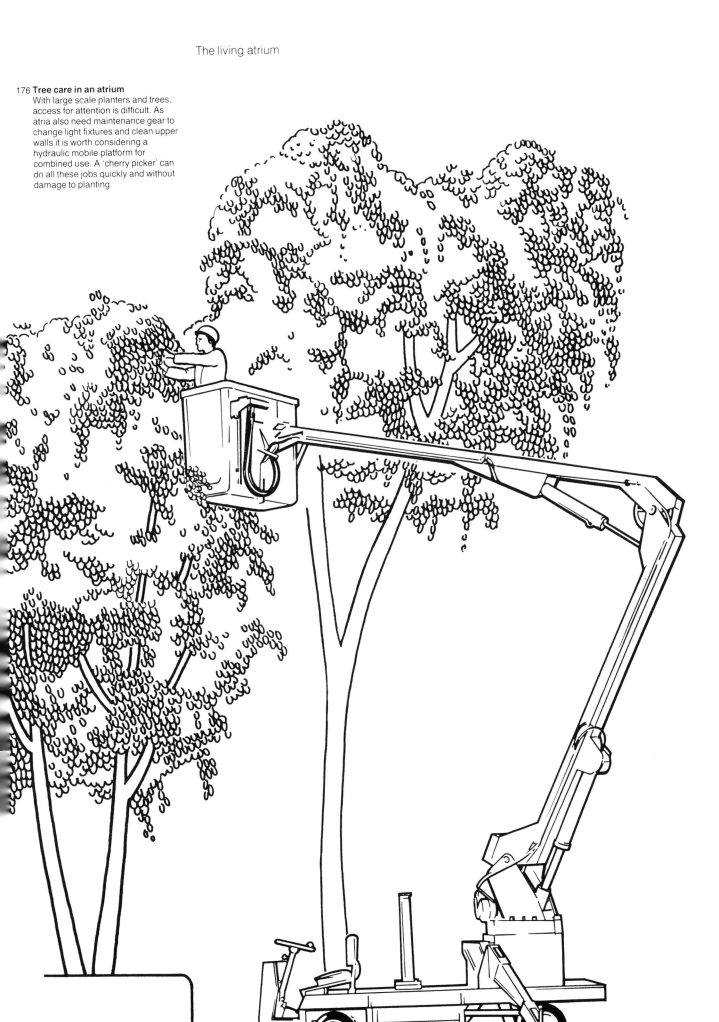

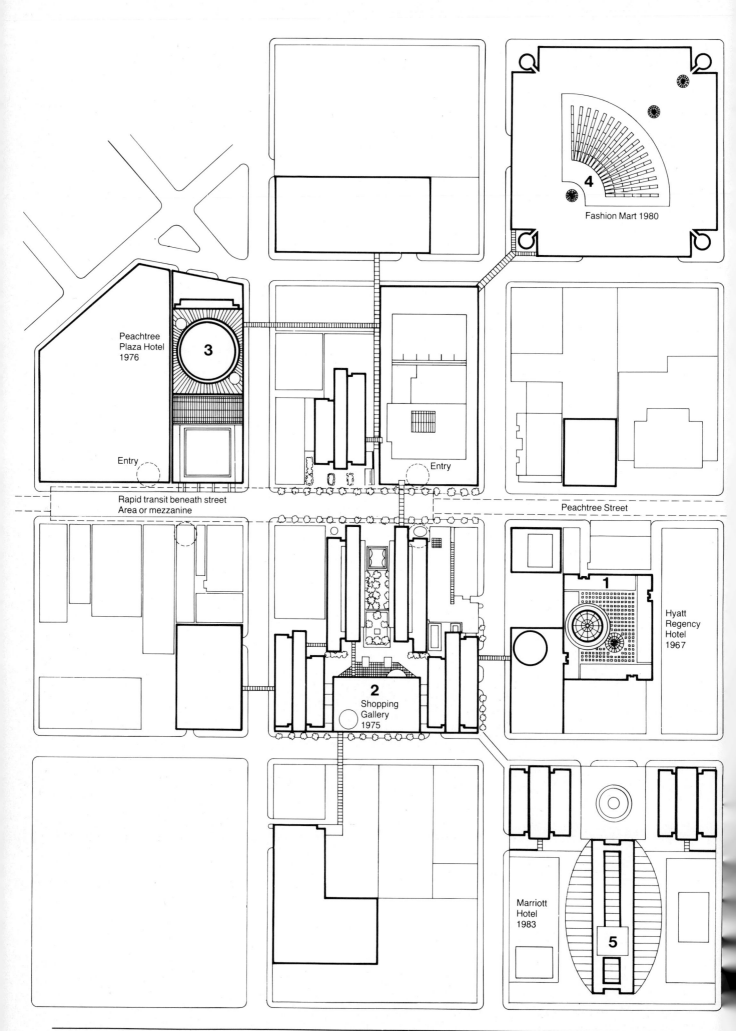

Fashion Mart 1980

4

Peachtree
Plaza Hotel
1976

3

Entry

Rapid transit beneath street
Area or mezzanine

Entry

Peachtree Street

1

Hyatt
Regency
Hotel
1967

2

Shopping
Gallery
1975

Marriott
Hotel
1983

5

14 The economics of atria

177 Peachtree center
The economic case for atria as effective investments can be studied in the history of Peachtree Center, Atlanta. John Portman's twenty-year programme of development has added five atria in a spiral outwards from the hub

The economics of atrium buildings are very competitive with those of conventional building forms. In typical circumstances an atrium building can out-perform a conventional design in capital-cost and operating-cost comparisons and in return on investment. This generalized claim may surprise, given the established and often repeated subjective assessment that atrium buildings are 'extravagant', that they 'waste space', and are 'luxurious'. Compared to conventional ways of arranging buildings, there are indeed many atrium buildings which are formed and fitted out in a very opulent manner: the opportunities for grandiosity afforded by the atrium concept have been lavishly developed. Nevertheless, the underlying concept is not the cause of the high cost; it should also be noted that lavish projects have still proved very profitable where sound economic judgments were made.

The purpose of this chapter is not to provide a definitive statement on the relative costs of atrium and conventional building, but to provide a framework for economic evaluation. Each site and client will require their own solutions and comparisons. We propose to evaluate the economics in three stages.

1 Capital costs of constructing atrium as against conventional buildings.

2 Revenue costs: the costs of operating buildings over their economic lives.

3 Investment return, which expresses any difference in earning power between different approaches.

Capital costs

Atrium buildings can cost less to build than conventional buildings of the same size: they usually have simpler frames, less external wall, fewer elevators and stairs–and these savings more than offset any higher servicing costs. They are also constructed more easily and rapidly, reducing the effects of inflation and interest charges.

As a broad generalization, capital costs tend to rise with building height, and decrease with increasing plan-depth. Of all the ways of arranging a given amount of space, the likely lowest cost version will be the deep-plan, low-rise solution; the most expensive will be a slim tower. Plan-depth has a strong effect on operating cost, however, and often on commercial value. Taking lifetime costs into account, the operating economy of daylightable plan-depth is likely to outweigh the constructional simplicity of deep planning. If plan-depth is limited for these reasons, then the courtyard form will deliver larger and thus fewer floors than the slab or tower equivalent. This is its basic capital-cost advantage.

Elemental comparisons
The pattern of capital costs in a building can best be seen by dividing the total into functional elements. A building houses its activities by supporting them on foundations, frames and floors; it protects them from the elements by walls, windows and roof; it compartments activities for safety and privacy; it conditions the occupied space to achieve year-round comfort; and it looks after the needs of its inhabitants to move about, keep clean and carry out their tasks.

As a basis for evaluation we have devised test buildings on a standard site, an atrium form and a tower form, and have set down their element-costs. Percentages have been used, to avoid figures dating or being in unfamiliar currency or measurement. To give international usefulness we have developed our test site to two density levels: a typical 'old world' density of 3:1–three times as much gross floor-space as the site area–and a typical 'new world' development density of 12:1. At above 12:1 density tower development is more or less inevitable on the site, and an atrium alternative would be as a podium atrium to a shorter tower. An office building has been used as the basis for comparison, with the plot ratio (floor-area ratio) applied to the gross space rather than to the rentable or useful space. Comparisons on other bases can be derived easily.

178 Cost comparison, tower and atrium forms

Our model site is 60 m square, 3600 m² (40,000 sq ft)

It is developed at two densities:
For Europe 3:1–10,800 m² (120,000 sq ft) gross
For N. America 12:1–43,200m² (480,000 sq ft) gross

For Europe the building is assumed to be single occupancy, 500 population, 30 car spaces

Tower option

12 storeys at 9000 m²
Upper floors 3.300 m high
Ground floor 4.95 m high

Artificial vent (no cooling), air plant on each floor, curtain wall, metal panel and tinted glass

75% of typical floor usable (10 levels)

40% of ground and 12th usable (rest of 12th is plant)
4 lifts

All usable floorspace naturally lightable

Single loaded ring circulation on each floor

Maximum space depth 25 ft (7.5 m)

No sprinklers or smoke handling. Fire detection and pressurized stairs

Atrium option

3:1 plot ratio
4 storeys
Ground floor 3000 m² (+ cars)
1st, 2nd, 3rd 2475
Rooftop plant 375

Usable:
Upper 3 floor 86.5%
Ground floor 60%

All naturally lightable

Usable space up to 15 m wide

Double loaded circulation

External wall and finish as tower, for comparison

Party wall

Concrete frame. Possibly 15 m span or 7.5 m grid

Atrium roof 30×37.5 m

1.5 m grid space truss

Plastic pyramid rooflights on each cell

Stands 3 m above roof, with glass (clear) wall around

Vents in glazing for heat release

Air system supplies offices from corner rooftop plants

Exhaust returns via atrium

Pressurized stairs

Sprinklers to 3 upper floors

Solar blinds to upper floor edges– venetian type, hand operated

Extensive landscape work in atrium. Floor planters and tree pots, balcony planters

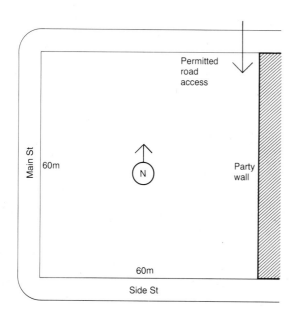

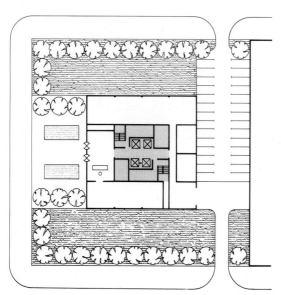

European density/ Tower option

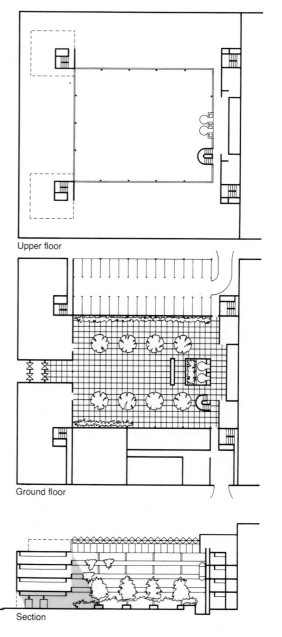

Upper floor

Ground floor

Section

Atrium option

179 Comparison of cost of atrium or tower solution— plot ratio (3:1)

Atrium

Area gross

Ground Floor	3000m²
Upper Floor 3 × 2475	7425m²
Roof Plant	375m²
	10800m²
+ Car Park	570m²
	11370m²

Nett area

60% × 3000m²	1800m²
3 × 2475 × 86.5%	6423m²
	8223m²

Tower

Area gross

30m × 30m × 12 floors	10800m²
+ Car Parking 38m × 15m	570m²
	11370m²

Nett area

75% × 10 × 30m × 30m	6750m²
40% × 2 × 30m × 30m	720m²
	7470m²

Atrium

Element	Specification	Quantity	% of total cost
Foundations	RC column bases and ground slab	3570m²	5%
Frame	Structural concrete on 15m × 7.5m grid	7800m²	7%
Upper floors	RC flat slab spanning 7.5m	7800m²	10%
Roof	RC flat slab with asphalt waterproof membrane 1.5m space truss with plastic pyramid rooflights to atrium	3475m²	6%
Stairs	RC staircases	16 flights	1%
External walls and windows	Metal panel curtain wall with double glazed solar control window panels with solar blinds	3060m²	7%
Internal walls and partitions	Spandrel open sided walls to atrium Fire compartment walls to lower atrium walls RC internal structural walls to staircases and lift shafts Internal partitions to floor by tenant	2600m²	3%
Internal doors	Included in internal walls	—	—
Wall finishes	Plaster & decorative finish to internal walls and internal face of ext. column	—	0.5%
Floor finish	Carpet to main floors. Ceramic tiles and paviors to core and atria floor	11370m²	3%
Ceiling finishes	Metal tile acoustic suspended ceilings	—	4%
Services	Disposal installation from roof and toilets water supply to storage tanks Hot and cold water supply to toilets, kitchen and atria Rooftop boiler plant and calorifiers Ventilation supply to offices with return air via atria Core and staircases with pressurized air supply Sprinkler installation to three upper floors Lighting and power including fire alarms	—	32%
Elevator installation	Two wallclimber elevators rising four floors from atria	—	4%
Site works	Internal planting to atria comprising floor and balcony planters External perimeter pavings	—	1%
Drainage	Soil and surface water drainage connections	—	1%
External services	Electricity, water and gas connections	—	1%
			85.5%
Preliminaries	Contractors overheads, lifting plant, scaffolding and construction management	—	14.5%
			100 %

Tower

Element	Specification	Quantity	Factor adjusted for quantity quality and cost	% of total cost of atrium solution
Foundations	Piled foundations and RC pile caps and ground beams RC ground slab	1470m²	0.5	2.5%
Frame	Structural concrete on 7.5m × 7.5m grid	9900m²	1.5	10.5%
Upper floors	RC flat slab spanning 7.5m	9900m²	1.5	15.0%
Roof	RC flat slab with asphalt waterproof membrane	1470m²	0.3	1.8%
Stairs	RC staircases	24 flights	1.5	1.0%
External walls and windows	As atrium	5175m²	1.5	10.5%
Internal walls and partitions	RC internal structural walls to staircases and liftshaft	5360m²	2.0	6.0%
Internal doors	Included in internal walls	—	—	—
Wall finish	As atrium	—	1.4	0.7%
Floor finish	Carpet to main floor Ceramic tiles to core areas	11370m²	0.9	2.7%
Ceiling finishes	As atria	—	1.0	4.0%
Services	Disposal installation from roof and toilets water supply to storage tanks. Hot and cold water supply to toilets and kitchen Rooftop boiler plant and calorifiers Ventilation supply and return from local air handling plant at each floor Cone and staircases with pressurized air supply Lighting and power including alarms and fire detection system	—	0.9	28.8%
Elevator installation	Four elevators rising twelve floors from centre core	—	1.75	7.0%
Site works	External pavings and landscape	—	1.5	1.5%
Drainage	Soil and surface water drainage connections	—	1.0	1.0%
External services	Electricity, water and gas connections	—	1.0	1.0%
				94.0%
Preliminaries	Contractors overheads, lifting plant, scaffolding and construction management	—	1.2	17.4%
				111.4%

180 **Comparison at a density of 12:1, tower scheme**

27 floors

26 at 1575 m² gross

1 at 900 m² (ground)

1 at 1550 m² (basement)

24 usable office floors

Floors 2–12 75% usable

Floors 14–26 80% usable

Usable area 70% daylight
(in perimeter bay)

Plant at basement 13 & 27. Full air conditioning, 50% of usable space in interior zone

Two lift zones 1–12; 14–26

Two sets of 6 high speed lifts

Two hydraulic lifts from parking to lobby (611 capacity)

Steel or concrete frame 7.5 m bay

Windbracing in core and party wall. 3.3 m floor to floor

Lobby and plaza finished to high specification (marble)

Exterior cladding:

Aluminium panel curtain wall, reflecting glass.
1.5 m module

Usable interior unfitted

Sprinklered throughout, with pressurized stairs. No smoke drainage system but smoke detection

2 parking basements for 300 cars

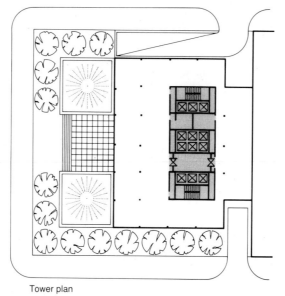

Tower plan

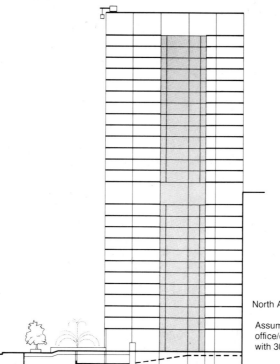

Tower section

North American Density 12:1

Assumed to be rental office/commercial with 300 car spaces

The economics of atria

181 Comparison at a density of 12:1, atrium scheme

43,200 m² gross

basement 1350 (+parking)

ground 3600

mezzanine 900

2nd to 8th 2250 each

9th to 16th 2600 average

rooftop 900

Usable percentable

ground   55%

mezzanine 80%

2nd to 8th 80% Part

9th   65% (Plant

10th–16th 83% level)

All usable floors in perimeter bays daylightable

Structure:
Steel or RC frame

7.5 m bay up to 10th

7.5 m × 15 m bay above, except bridging storeys, carried on trusses in 9th floor plant room

Inclined storeys edge frames become portals, completed at rooflight. Little wind bracing required

Exterior skin as tower option

Atrium walls in partitioning quality glass and white laminate infill

Atrium floor and lift lobbies marble as tower option. Tree pits, fountain pool

Glass screen over entrance suspended glass assemblies

Rooflight: assymetrical steep north slope in insulating diffing plastic shallow south slope in clear laminated glass in aluminium framing. Exterior motorized louvres reflect or shade sun to maximize diffuse light into atrium. Vents for hot air release

Elevators : 3 sets
low rise; 4 conventional

high rise, 4 two conventional two special glass sided in open shaftway

parking: two hydraulic between lobby and basements

Escalators to low rise lobby on mezzanine

Full air conditioning. Tempered air supply to atrium from 9th floor bridging plant room. 4 local plants on each level intake make-up air from atrium. Exhaust toilets and external wall. Heat recovery from hot pocket under roof for winter and DHW use. Blow through in summer

All usable space divided from atrium by glazed walls except atrium floor retail/dining

Fire concept:
Pressurized atrium and stairs, sprinklered throughout, smoke vented to outside wall from affected floor

Minimum fire load in atrium. All floor intakes close if smoke does enter atrium

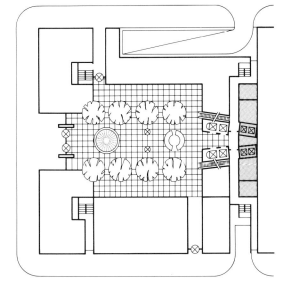

Plan, street level

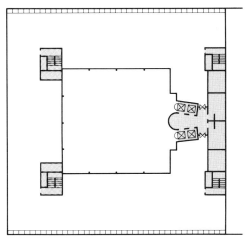

Plan 12th floor

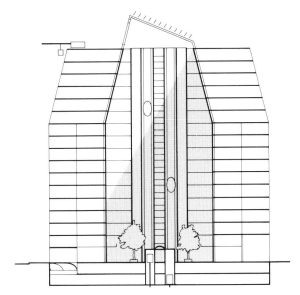

Section north/south

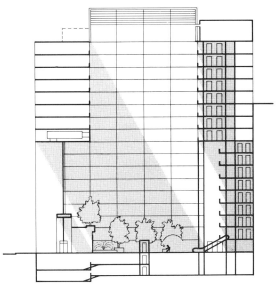

Section east/west

Low-density comparisons

The test designs and elemental costs for the European density development are shown on pp. **160** and **161**. It will be noted that the tower alternative costs 11.4 per cent more than the atrium scheme, whilst delivering only 90 per cent as much useful floor-space within the same gross area. The plan efficiency of the lower building derives simply from its need for fewer elevators and toilets, and the ability to serve more space per floor from a single core. Compounded, the cost per usable unit of space is 23 per cent higher in the tower form.

The differences are as follows:

Foundations. The tower has less foundation area, but more heavily loaded bases.

Frame and upper floors. The suspended floor area of the tower is higher, and the frame must resist more wind force.

Roof. The atrium solution has more roof, and the roof has a higher unit cost than that of the tower.

Stairs. The atrium has more stair-shafts, but only two-thirds the stair-flights.

External walls. The atrium form has a better surface to floor-area ratio.

Internal walls. The atrium needs more, but not at great cost.

Services. The atrium building will have a higher servicing cost, even if equal energy performance is sought. The fire-defence systems account for an extra, whilst the climate-control system is on a par for this example, even though the atrium is serviced to full-comfort standards.

Elevators. The saving in numbers of elevators is not overtaken by the increased specification of those provided. (For costs of observation elevators see p. 131).

Landscape. The internal landscaped area of the atrium solution is less than the external area in the tower form. Specification will differ, but costs are likely to favour the atrium in this case.

Preliminaries. The contractor's costs rise with the number of storeys built. Equipment and time needed increase, and energy costs of construction are higher in tall buildings.

To show the comparison between deep- and shallow-planning, Goran Lundquist's recent Swedish study (Camera Solaris, 1980, p 64) compared a low-rise linear atrium office building with a deep-plan form of the same number of floors. The atrium building was 6.5 per cent more expensive in capital terms, but overtook the deep-plan building on lifetime costing.

High-density comparisons

The comparisons on the high-density development schemes differ slightly with the balance tilting more firmly towards the atrium solution (see pp. **162** and **163**). Foundation costs will be near parity, as both buildings have basements over the whole site. On some sites the atrium building might have cheaper foundations if a different technology were needed to carry the tower.

Servicing installation costs should favour the atrium solution if equal energy performance standards are being met. Lower cooling loads in summer will reduce the scale of the installation. Heating loads will be similar. Smoke-extract fans will be needed, but are here part of the return-air system for atrium air. Both buildings are assumed to need sprinklering to comply with codes. Toilet costs are lower for the atrium, due to higher-density provision.

Elevator costs are much lower in the atrium form in high-density development—less than half in this case. Only two custom-built elevators are specified. This is the largest single saving on an element.

Landscaping costs will compare more favourably in the atrium here, assuming that similar high specification would have been used on external plaza areas. Internal construction of paving is simpler, whilst planters are of similar complexity.

The tower form would cost about 15 per cent more than the atrium design, for similar gross area, whilst the better space-efficiency of the lower building raises the cost of the tower's useful area to 20 per cent above that of the atrium building floor-space. The deeper-plan tower is more space-efficient than the shallow 3:1 ratio tower, although it will pay the price in operating costs.

The comparison is borne out by an unpublished researched study conducted by Atlanta architects, Thompson, Ventulett, Stainback and Associates, with engineers Brady and Anglin. In 1978 they compared an atrium solution to a client brief (program) for which they had completed a tower building in Charlotte, North Carolina, in 1973. The alternative 12-storey atrium design was shown to be 85 per cent of the cost of the tower when put in terms of constant dollars. An earlier Canadian study of 1976 by Robert Tamblyn of Engineering Interface Ltd, Willowdale, Ontario, produced very similar results.

Hotel comparisons

Office buildings are the type most likely to make use of the atrium idea and to benefit from it in capital-cost terms. It was hotel-building which revived the idea, however, and here the economic picture is rather different. In hotel-development the most important factor is the potential earning-power of the building. The scope for increased earning-performance is considerably greater in hotels than in offices, and dependent to a great extent on the building design and how the operator exploits it. Capital cost is never, however, irrelevant.

The most economical atrium hotel configurations are those retaining conventional double-loaded guest-room planning, with guest-rooms overlooking the atrium. But the classic atrium hotels do not do this: they use open gallery circulation to outward-facing guest-rooms, and suffer the extra circulation area due to this single-loading of corridors. A recent cost-exercise demonstrates that this need not lead to an overall loss of economy. Studies for a new hotel in Exeter (England), by Stevenson Associates for Granada Motorway Services, compared a slab-type guest-room building and adjacent public rooms with an atrium plan. The atrium plan put dining, bar and reception facilities into a 'baronial hall', overlooked from guest-room access galleries.

Savings in the circulation area to the public facilities offset the losses in extra guest-room corridor area, and the whole atrium solution was shown to be 0.6 per cent less costly than the conventional alternative. Significant in the capital savings were the thermal efficiency of the form, saving installation costs to warm circulation spaces, and the speed of construction: a 20 per cent reduction in construction time was achievable within the lower but compact atrium form.

In the early John Portman atrium hotels it is interesting to note what economies were made to finance the increased volume, before there was any certainty of their enhanced performance. Portman adopted a very basic construction approach, with minimal finishes to public areas. This was more than offset, in the guests' eyes, by the use of eye-catching artwork, landscaping, and good furniture, all at far less cost than the up-market finishes used by typical competitors. The end-product is opulence of effect with minimal means.

Interaction and trade-offs
All the technical aspects of atrium design interact. Sometimes consideration of two aspects leads to complimentary solutions; sometimes an advantage in one is gained at the expense of a disadvantage in another. These interactions all have capital- and operating-cost implications. To highlight some of them

1 If useful daylighting is sought via an atrium to surrounding floor-space, the kind of light levels needed in the atrium will easily support plant-growth. If, however, plant-growth is encouraged on surfaces which can act as daylight reflectors, the level of illumination to surrounding spaces will drop.

2 The raising of a glazed atrium roof to form a hot-air and smoke reservoir also enables it to collect more daylight. The payoff is therefore in cooling savings, artificial light savings and reduction in venting-area or fan-power.

3 Greatest energy savings come from atria which are unserviced buffers. Raising the comfort-level of an atrium, either for planting or for people, raises operating costs. This may of course be justified by the usefulness of the space. The more comfortable the atrium the more the emphasis on insulation and shading shifts to the outer atrium envelope.

4 Daylightable plan-depths do bring the possibility of general savings on environmental servicing costs, always provided that the building has adequate summer shading, and sufficient exposed thermal mass. Boosting daylight delivery by means of devices or by increased building volume, in order to get deeper floor-space, can easily become economically impractical.

5 If the building can be kept at, or below, four to five storeys, several options are available: escalators can be considered rather than elevators; hydraulic rather than traction elevators can be used; smoke-extraction from an atrium can probably be by natural convection alone.

Revenue costs

We here consider the differences in the costs of running the two contrasting forms of building. Operating costs will comprise cleaning, maintenance, security and energy costs. Of these, only energy costs will vary materially between the two forms. There are two ways of looking at energy costs. Where building energy performance standards (BEPS) or equivalent do not exist, both building types will tend to invest a similar amount in servicing for climate-control. Their operating performance will then differ, and so will costs. Alternatively, where BEPS are in force, and both schemes aim to do no better than keep within the legal limit, then the higher-performance design will have lower capital costs to achieve the standard. The operating cost in the former case can be converted to a capital-cost equivalent by discounting, thus enabling both approaches to be seen on the same basis.

Significantly lower energy costs (or more economical achievement of the BEPS) are found in well-designed atrium buildings. The reasons vary with design and climate: in the 3:1 plot ratio example a warming atrium is provided and passive solar gain will probably halve the building heat-load over the year. Summer-time comfort is aided by effective shading of accommodation in the atrium, and the induced cross-ventilation provided. In the tower building, windows cannot be comfortably used for high ventilation rates in summer, and external shading is not provided. Mechanical ventilation and internal shading will probably not achieve the comfort of the atrium building, and some cooling capacity may be needed. Other small savings come from domestic hot water supply—the fewer toilet blocks, closer together, lose less heat—and from the elevator drives. Lighting costs will be similar if both tower and atrium use daylight to full advantage.

In the high-density example a continental climate is assumed, with full air-conditioning. A convertible atrium is provided, with external operable shutter/louvres to collect or exclude sun. The savings pattern is quite different from that in the low-density example. First the

182 The atrium as an investment
Advertisement in the New Yorker
Magazine, April 20, 1981

Located in the heart of the busy Grand Central/Midtown Manhattan area on Prestigious Park Avenue and 46th Street, The Park Avenue Atrium offers retailers a splendid opportunity to take advantage of the most advanced concept in urban marketing. . . an indoor selling environment.

This magnificent retail selling space provides a readily accessible luxury shopping area for the thousands of business people in the immediate vicinity, and the entrances on Park and Lexington Avenues, East 45th and 46th Streets assure a continuous flow of buyer traffic.

Stores of 1000 to 4000 sq. ft. are available for June 1981 occupancy. For leasing information call or write Jack Feder, Sr. Vice President, Olympia and York Properties, 245 Park Avenue, New York, N.Y. 10017. Telephone 850-9600.

OLYMPIA & YORK

tower building is partly deep-planned, with 30 per cent of its floor-space more than 7.5 metres away from the windows. Half its floorspace will need permanent artificial lighting compared to 10 per cent or less of the atrium building plan. If both buildings use modern task-ambient lighting, with photocell control to favour daylight, the atrium building will use only half the power of the tower for lighting. This in turn reduces the release of heat into the usable space, and thus the reduces year-round air-conditioning loads also. The next major saving is in cooling loads derived from solar gain. With so much of its window area shaded the atrium avoids solar impact. In the notional city represented by the model, the external walls will also receive less sun on the site perimeter than they would if set back as in the tower: other buildings shade them. In winter the tower building will heat itself by lighting, whilst the atrium will need fuel plus solar energy. The latter will cost less in primary energy, though we have already counted the lighting cost difference.

Overall the energy need for atrium buildings can be from one-half to two-thirds of the needs of a tower equivalent, if similar capital costs are allowed. A given BEPS will cost substantially less to achieve in the atrium form.

To be specific: it is suggested by survey data that annual revenue costs are in the range of five to six per cent of initial capital cost. This figure is based on averaging all costs, including periodic plant replacement and refurbishing over the 40- to 60-year life of the building. Energy can constitute half the operating costs, and will become more important as the century progresses.

Let us look at the effect of a one per cent difference in revenue or operating costs. If the atrium example had a five per cent annual operating cost (two per cent energy, three per cent the rest), and the tower building a six per cent cost (three per cent and three per cent), we can apply a reasonable discount rate of seven per cent over 60 years to give a capital equivalent. Let us assume that capital costs are the same, in spite of earlier comparisons.

**183
Revenue cost comparison**

Atrium building

Capital cost	100%
5% operating cost at 14 years' purchase (7% discount) gives a present worth of	70%
Total capital equivalent of capital cost	170%

Tower building

Capital cost	100%
6% operating cost at 14 years' purchase (7% discount) gives a present worth of	84%
Total capital equivalent of capital cost	184%

This demonstrates the true saving in having lower operating costs which reflect on the value of the building and the potentially viable capital cost.

Investment value

Atrium buildings were reintroduced as commercial buildings and have proliferated as such. Hotels, trade marts, office buildings, shopping centres and, especially, combined, multi-use developments, have exploited the atrium concept vigorously since the late 1960s. This is because they pay. The developments which have set the pace have not been banking on the capital economies of the building form, or its lower cost-in-use: they have been exploiting its higher earning power and therefore its greater investment value. Lower costs merely enhance the effect.

To some degree, the immediate outstanding returns produced by most early atrium developments must have been the result of their novelty and sensational design. Occupancy rates for the early Regency Hyatt hotels averaged over 95 per cent, compared to the 85 per cent anticipated. Since it is the last few percentage points which determine profits, the effect of this 12 per cent increase in occupancy was electrifying. Even as the novely has worn off and more atrium hotels have been built, many in the same cities as their prototypes, the occupancy rates have not diminished. A stronger hotel market has developed, with convention business and tourism of overseas visitors centring on the resort-like atrium hotels.

Consumer enthusiasm is a very good basis for measuring enhanced investment value, but it is a comparatively subjective part of the equation. There are very solid, objective reasons why an atrium building can earn more for each unit of investment than can a conventional building. First is the higher efficiency of the plan-form, especially in the case of office buildings. Site-development density in most cities of the world is limited by ordinance in order to control traffic congestion and demand for main services. Where this control is in terms of gross floor-space ratios, an atrium building will deliver more rentable space within the limit. Where the limit is on net rentable floor-space, an atrium building will have a lower gross area, and thus a lower capital cost.

Here is a calculation of the gross development value for the two types of office buildings at European density under consideration, with the permitted limit on the gross floor-space. The values are shown in pounds sterling, at 1981 rental levels for prime sites outside London.

In this example the return from the atrium design is enhanced by the potential of using some of the floor-space for retailing. On this very favourable basis the atrium building either produces a far higher return for the same investment (ignoring the capital-cost difference already shown), or can be built at a cost 25 per cent higher than the tower and still show the same return. The extra earning power can be used in the market-place to secure good sites by bidding over the figure calculated by competitors on a conventional development basis. It can also be used to enhance specification and offer premium space with long-term attraction, perhaps in an over-supplied market.

The premium available for retail space is an important factor leading to the addition of such space to most city-centre office developments in North America in the 1970s. The tower form cannot follow the frontage of a shopping street in normal circumstances: light angles and floor-space incentives for providing a plaza combine to set it back, sterilizing it for retailing and damaging the street's shopping continuity. If the atrium form is used, or a podium atrium is grafted onto a tower, the public plaza can be provided inside the development. One or more levels of the building may be able to sustain shopping and restaurants, adding to the attraction of the office space as well as to the resilience of the whole investment. Doing good to the city thus brings fortune, as it should.

184 Investment value comparison	Atrium design		Tower design	
Net lettable space:	8223m^2		7470m^2	
Annual rental value:				
Office space of 6723m^2 at £50	£336,150	Office space of 7470m^2 at £50	£373,500	
Retail space of 1500m^2 at £85	£127,500			
Total annual rental	£463,650		£373,500	

Assuming a yield of 8%, year's purchase (YP) = $\frac{100}{8}$ = 12.5%
Gross development value = annual rental × YP

Gross development value	£5,795,625	£4,668,750

The office space may command a premium rental also. Shallow-plan, daylit office space allows more accommodation to be in private offices, thus catering for top executives and professionals. Even in open-plan, the coveted space is beside a window, and the more there are, the better. The perimeter became reduced in the deep buildings of the past generation, giving windows the status of 'positional goods'. A corner office is particularly sought, and some developers have realized that articulated building profiles, providing more 'corners', more than recover their cost in enhanced rental value. The atrium building form gives more potential for perimeter, articulated or straight, and if the articulation is inside the atrium, allows this to be without thermal penalties.

As office work changes under the impact of electronic technology so the junior roles in offices will become fewer. Smaller work-groups and higher average status will mean a demand for more prestigious and intimate office accommodation, more in the image of a law firm than of an insurance company of the immediate past. The evidence is there in the proliferation of suburban corporate buildings planned around open courts or with highly articulate perimeters.

The occupancy rate is the measure of attraction. If people-pleasing is profitable then there can be no conflict between the aims of designer and developer. Once both accept the 'pleasure principle' in design and in investment, the public will be better served and will favour such developments. Atrium buildings have proved their pulling power, with rapid take-up of space, high hotel occupancy rates, premium rentals on prime sites and prime rentals on secondary sites.

It is common to hear designers urging investors not to be totally obsessed with the 'bottom-line' and to build things to be proud of. Developers have remained unmoved, assuming that designers were seeking their own glory; pension funds look for their pride in performance. John Portman did most to break the deadlock, first by reviving and modern-izing the atrium concept, and secondly by being his own developer and showing what could be done (see **179**). The developers' reluctance to accept new ideas was shown to be largely the product of conventional thinking, of assumptions that space-costs matter more than specification-costs. Portman showed that more volume could cost less and earn more.

It is the hope of this book that the ideas and techniques gathered together will inspire and inform designers and their clients. Much more can be done economically with buildings than has been conventionally attempted. The atrium approach to building is one way to a better future for both the creators and users of buildings and cities.

Appendix 1

Checklist for shaping and servicing
the building

Basic form

Analyse site to guide the overall envelope
form.

Consider planning for daylight; plan-depths
and storey-heights are inter-related.

Consider alternative generic forms to meet
site and client needs.

Orient atrium side walls and roof-forms to
face north or south, depending on thermal
strategy.

Lighting

Use models in 'artificial sky' to test the design.

Admit light in a way compatible with the
thermal strategy.

Convert sunlight to diffuse light for better
distribution.

Provide sufficient diffuse reflective surfaces in
the atrium to transmit light downwards.

Consider collecting light into rooms by means
of light shelves; orient structure suitably.

Integrate artificial and natural light
approaches, by arrangement and control.

Climate control

Determine site climate and thermal nature of
building use: select warming, cooling or
convertible atrium type.

Select level of comfort required in the atrium
itself: canopy, buffer, tempered buffer,
comfort.

Develop appropriate arrangements for
insulation, thermal capacity, shading and
air-handling.

Consider using the atrium as a duct routeway
or plenum.

Appendix 2

Checklist for fire-safe design

Pre-planning	Recognize that all atrium proposals are different: be prepared to work from first principles, to take time and trouble, unless codes cover proposals.
	Assemble all relevant consultants early.
	If not proposing to meet codes: take the fire department into confidence early; visualize problems, make visits; prepare clear presentations for lay committees.
Escape	Try to minimize need to evacuate.
	Get unprotected travel distance right for the building purposes.
	Use familiar routes as escapes, or intercept familiar routes with emergency routes.
	Pressurized stairs, and take them direct to outside if possible.
Smoke-control	Choose between smoke-extraction away from the atrium and via the atrium, or use both in an integrated design, depending on atrium use and ventilation strategy.
	Make venting systems fail-safe.
Fire-control	Remember, no smoke-control is possible without fire-size limitation.
	Use smoke-detection to activate defence systems.
	Select extinguishing systems compatible with building uses.
	Reduce flame-spread risk by design of floor-edges or openings.
	Make provision for fire-fighting access to and through the building.

Consider the form and performances needed climatically.

Take advantage of the atrium to simplify the main building frame.

Provide deep structures, where possible, for walls and roof.

Choose structures in scale with the space enclosed.

Consider the use of vertical curves and slopes carefully before adopting them.

Allow for large thermal movements between the building and atrium if a lightweight envelope is used.

Seal the envelope well.

Consider suspended glass structures for side walls.

Consider plastics and composite high-insulation roof-skins for warming atria.

Consider fabric structures for cooling atria.

Appendix 4

Checklist for circulation-system design

Planning

Remember, substantial transport economies may be achieved in atrium buildings: exploit the atrium to give a memorable focus of movement; use the 'kinetic art' potential of dramatized movement.

Use a single service-point to give best service and economy.

Consider location in relation to escape proposals.

Think about use of escalators, alone or in tandem with elevators.

For high-rise building consider stacked atria corresponding to elevator zones.

Remember the agrophobic: provide a conventional elevator alternative and make all routes feel safe.

Remember service and fire-fighting access: consider a separate core or lobby.

Elevators

Consider hydraulic elevators for buildings of up to five levels.

Consider the use of 'model' observation elevators to reduce costs.

Allow for safe maintenance access to car roofs and to guideways.

Screen around open-car movement-paths at atrium floor level and alongside open galleries.

Urban integration

Integrate the building circulation with the urban movement pattern if appropriate.

Match atrium activity to the type of through-traffic generated.

Consider grade separation of public and private activity areas.

Do not run elevators or stairs continuously through private and public levels.

Concepts

Be sure of the level of management commitment to landscape care before beginning.

Work with a landscape designer experienced in indoor installations.

Choose plant material suitable for the atrium climate, and be prepared to temper that climate to achieve success.

Environment

Respect plant physiology to achieve healthy growth.

Provide as much daylight as possible, or supplement it.

Provide good colour-rendition artificial light, for plant appearance and health.

Allow a daily dark period.

Provide the temperature range necessary for the selected species. Tropical plants which are the usual choice, must not be allowed to get too cold.

Beware of draughts from air inlets and doors and of radiation from lamps, heaters, and glass.

Accommodation

Decide whether to use the potted or planted approach.

Use compost media for large-scale planting.

Consider hydroculture for smaller-scale elements.

For compost choose manual or automatic watering/feeding, depending on the local balance of advantage.

Be aware of structural implications when positioning built-in planters.

Allow for service runs through waterproof planter construction.

Care

Allow space for plant growth in initial layout.

Expect 10 to 20 per cent annual replacement of smaller plants.

Provide power, water and drainage convenience points for maintenance.

Allow for machine access to plants.

Ensure that skilled care is available.

When comparing the economics of atrium and conventional designs, take into account lifetime costs and earning power.

Capital costs

Remember that for any given plan depth the lowest building, on the fewest floors, will probably be the most efficient and the most economically and rapidly constructed.

Plan to maximise nett to gross floor space ratios.

Achieve maximum savings in major cost elements by using a single elevator and service core, even with a dispersed plan.

Major extra costs are in the atrium envelope and in fire safety features. Concentrate on their economic design.

In hotels, single loaded gallery access to guest rooms can be economic if offset by circulation savings on public levels.

Consider the economic implications of the interaction of all technical factors.

Do not forget the value of a shorter construction period.

Revenue costs

Major savings will be in electricity costs, for lighting, refrigeration and elevator drives. Do not seek daylight at excessive capital cost however.

Investment value

Maximise rentable area by the plan efficiency of atrium design.

Maximise retail value by street-following planning and use of the second, atrium frontage.

Remember that shallow plan office space, especially with frequent 'corners' commands a premium. Atrium frontage can be highly desirable.

The high earning power of atrium buildings depends on the people-pleasing space inside. Ensure that the design and management of the space achieves this.

Appendix 7

Measurements quoted in the book are in the units used in the country of origin of the example. Below are approximate factors which can be used to convert the metric measures used into imperial (US) units and vice versa.

To convert between one system and the other, read the equations as set down below.

Metric to imperial

Measure	Imperial unit (US)		Metric unit		Factor
Length	Feet (ft)	=	Metres (m)	×	3.333
Area	Square feet (sq ft)	=	Square metres (m^2)	×	10.76
Volume	Cubic feet (cu ft)	=	Cubic metres (m^3)	×	35.316
Air movement	Cubic feet/minute	=	m^3/second	×	2119
Energy	BTU	=	Kilowatt/hours (kWh)	×	3412
Temperature	°Farenheit (°F)	=	°Centigrade (°C)	×	1.8+32
Insulation (U)	Btu/sq ft/hr/°F	=	W/m^2/hr/°C	÷	5.678
Illumination	Foot candles	=	lux	×	10.76

Imperial to metric

Measure	Metric unit		Imperial unit (US)		Factor
Length	Metres (m)	=	Feet (ft)	÷	3.333
Area	Square metres (m^2)	=	Square feet (sq ft)	÷	10.76
Volume	Cubic metres (m^3)	=	Cubic feet (cu ft)	÷	35.316
Air movement	m^3/second	=	Cu ft/minute	÷	2119
Energy	Kilowatt/hours (kWh)	=	Btu	÷	3412
Temperature	°Centigrade (°C)	=	°Farenheit (°F)	−32	÷1.8
Insulation (U)	W/m^2/hr/°C	=	Btu/sq ft/hr/°F	×	5.678
Illumination	lux	=	Foot candles	÷	10.76

Select bibliography

These books and articles were sources for this book, and expand on aspects of the of the subject.

Greenhouses

Das Glashaus
Georg Kohlmaier and Barna von Sartory, Prestel Verlag, 1981 (German)

Glass
RIBA Journal feature, February 1981

The Glasshouse
John Hix, MIT Press, 1974 and 1981

Urban Rooftop Solar Greenhouse
The Ehrenkrantz Group, Northeast Solar Energy Center, 1981

Futurism and tomorrow's atria

**Architectural Visions
the drawings of Hugh Ferris**
Jean Ferris Leach, Whitney Library of Design, 1980

The Architecture of Sir John Soane
Dorothy Stroud, Studio, 1961

Architecture Without Architects
Bernard Rudofsky, Museum of Modern Art, 1964

Arcology, The City in the Image of Man
Paulo Soleri, MIT Press 1969

The Buckminster Fuller Reader
Jonathan Cape, 1970

The Future Metropolis
ed. Lloyd Rodwin, Braziller, 1968

**Megastructures
Urban Futures of the Recent Past**
Reyner Banham, Thames and Hudson, 1976

Piranese
Nicholas Penney, Oresko Books, 1978

Social Purpose in Architecture
Helen Rosenau, Studio Vista, 1970

Conservation

Buildings Reborn
Barbara Lee Diamondstein, Harper & Row, 1978

Saving Old Buildings
Sherban Cantacuzino and Susan Brant, Architectural Press, 1980

Energy

American Building, the Environmental Forces that Shape It
James Marston Fitch, Houghton Mifflin, 1972

The Architecture of Energy
Dean Hawkes, Construction Press, 1982

Camera Solaris
Goran Lundquist, Spanbergs Tryckener, 1980 (Swedish)

The Energy Within The Space Within
Donald Watson, Progressive Architecture, July 1982

Urban design	**Arcades: The History of a Building Type** Johann Friedrich Geist, MIT Press, 1983
	The Art of Islam Titus Burkhardt, Festival of Islam Publishing Co, 1977
	Death and Life of Great American Cities Jane Jacobs, 1962, Jonathan Cape
	Delirious Manhattan Rem Koolhaas, Oxford University Press, 1978
	Design of Cities ed. Bacon, Thames and Hudson, 1967/1975
	Downtown USA Kenneth Halpern, Architectural Press/Whitney Library of Design, 1978
	The Heart of our Cities Victor Gruen, Thames and Hudson, 1965
	Paris, a Century of Change 1878–1978 Norma Evenson, Yale University Press, 1979
	The Social Life of Small Urban Spaces William H Whyte, The Conservation Foundation, 1980
	Urban Design Manhattan Regional Plan Associates, Studio Vista, 1969
	Urban Space Bob Krier, Academy Editions, 1979
Fire	**Designing for Fire Safety** E G Butcher and A C Parnell, Wiley, 1983
	Smoke Control E G Butcher and A C Parnell, E & F N Spon, 1979
Structure	**Engineering for Architecture** Architectural Record Books, McGraw Hill, 1980
Landscape	**Interior Planting in Large Buildings** Steven Scrivens, Architectural Press/Halstead Press, 1980
	Interior Plantscaping Richard L Gaines, Architectural Record Books, McGraw Hill, 1977
Economics	**The Architect as Developer** John Portman and Jonathan Barnett, McGraw Hill, 1976 (also the best illustration of Portman designs up to 1976)
General	**Architecture, a Performing Art** John Andrews and Jennifer Taylor, Lutterworth Press, 1982 (covers the varied atrium designs of John Andrews)
	Frequent articles on atrium buildings and aspects of their design appear in these magazines: **AIA Journal (US)** **Architectural Record (US)** **Architectural Review (UK)** **Progressive Architecture (US)** **RIBA Journal (UK)**

Index (Atrium buildings are referred to in **bold**)

See IF-1.05 for 1/4" scale dwg. of Central Cocktail Lo

See IF-1.02 for 1/4" scale dwg. of Lobby Bar